# Tudor Inspirations

## ELEMENTAL BEADWORK

Melanie de Miguel
— & —
Heather Kingsley-Heath

Tudor Inspirations
Elemental beadwork
ISBN 978-1-912300-14-3

Published in 2018 by SRA Books
© Heather Kingsley-Heath and Melanie de Miguel

Photography © Michael Wicks
www.michaelwicks.com

The rights of Melanie de Miguel and Heather Kingsley-Heath to be identified as the authors of this work have been asserted by them in accordance with the Copyright, Designs and Patents Act 1988.

A CIP record of this book is available from the British Library.

All rights reserved. No part of this book may be reproduced, stored in a retrieval system, or transmitted in any form or by any means, electronic, mechanical, photocopying, recording or otherwise, without the prior written permission of the copyright holder.

No responsibility for loss occasioned to any person acting or refraining from action as a result of any material in this publication can be accepted by the author or publisher.

If you do find any errors or you have any questions, please contact us as we would be delighted to have the opportunity to make corrections in the next print run. Please note, this book has been written using the UK English spelling of words such as: colour, neighbour, practise (used as a verb only), etc.

Printed in the UK.

## ooo◉ooo FOREWORD BY MARCIA DECOSTER ooo◉ooo

When I first heard there would be a collaboration between Melanie de Miguel and Heather Kingsley-Heath I knew it would be outstanding. These two women have made remarkable contributions to contemporary beadwork, while still making connections to its long history.

*Tudor Inspirations* highlights their interest in bead history, while at the same time bringing many fresh new designs and a brilliant approach to creating them. Each project consists of elements that are not only used in the artist-designed piece, but that can also be re-used in different arrangements or combined with other elements from other projects to create an incredibly versatile body of work.

I love this approach because it frees you from the engineering of the original project, while at the same time allowing you to stretch your own design aspirations and create finished pieces that are uniquely yours.

The pieces incorporate a wide variety of stitches, showcasing the technical accomplishments and deep beading knowledge of both artists. Personally, I delight in the projects incorporating Hubble and Albion stitch, developed by Melanie and Heather respectively because they utilise new techniques that contribute to our growth as beaders.

The imaginative narrative accompanying each of the main designs draws us into the historical background that was the initial inspiration for the book. You'll not only enjoy the stories and the projects themselves, but this book also serves as a reference to beadwork creation that will, by virtue of its approach, provide you with unlimited design options in your own work.

A huge thank you to Melanie and Heather for sharing your beady brilliance with us!

# CONTENTS

| | |
|---|---|
| vi | Introduction |
| viii | About the authors |
| x | From us to you |
| x | About our work |
| xi | How the book works |
| xii | Notes and abbreviations |
| 1 | **Project 1:** Aragon |
| 15 | **Project 2:** Cattern's Tallie pendant and cuff |
| 31 | **Project 3:** Anne Boleyn |
| 45 | **Project 4:** Walsingham Cypher necklace and bracelet |
| 55 | **Project 5:** Matins and Vespers |
| 69 | **Project 6:** Merels Token necklace |
| 77 | **Project 7:** The Nonsuch Tour de Cou |
| 89 | **Project 8:** Dotis Nomine necklace |
| 97 | **Project 9:** Pease Pod Chain of Office |
| 109 | **Project 10:** Gloriana Regnat necklace and bracelet |
| 123 | Elements Library |
| 137 | Gallery |
| 147 | Acknowledgements |
| 148 | Invitation to participate |

## ooo◉ooo  INTRODUCTION  ooo◉ooo

When two of the world's leading beadwork artists meet for an afternoon at the V&A, something exciting is bound to happen. Picture a rainy winter day in London, then the Arts & Crafts tiled interior of the Pointer Room at the museum café. In the corner a conversation is started, about collaboration, and the dream that it will grow into this book.

## ABOUT THE AUTHORS

Heather and Melanie have been friends for many years, meeting through their work for the Beadworkers Guild. They are passionate about researching, teaching and sharing the skills of beadwork.

Both teach internationally and have published intriguing new technique developments with their respective books on Albion stitch and Hubble stitch.

Conversations soon revealed more common ground, a love of history and historical reference as starting points for design, alongside the shared practice of creating a narrative around which to weave their beadwork. They also share the tenacity to work relentlessly towards an imagined objective.

## ∘∘∘⬤∘∘∘ FROM US TO YOU ∘∘∘⬤∘∘∘

As this is our book, our passion, we have departed from 'the usual'. We don't have pages of equipment lists, or material sources. We tell you what beads and needle size you will need at the start of each project. We have our own personal preferences for certain threads. Melanie recommends using 4lb Fireline and a size 13 needle, switching to a size 15 needle if necessary when working with size 15° Czech charlottes for her projects, but you must use the thread with which you are comfortable. Heather also recommends using the thread with which you are most familiar, her favourite being OneG. She works with a size 10 or 11 needle, with a size 12 on hand if working with size 15° seed beads. Most important of all, we have easy-to-follow instructions, lots of diagrams and photographs of finished beadwork.

We want you, our reader, to enjoy the journey of each piece as it was created, so at the beginning of each project, we have shared the stories we worked with in our imagination as we beaded. We have also included snippets and asides of random facts and quotes that we discovered and found fascinating, not necessarily bead related, but fun to know.

As experienced tutors, we both have our own unique, individual writing and teaching styles, which you will inevitably experience in this book, but we've worked hard to try and bring you a greater degree of continuity. Also, our Albion and Hubble stitches have their own terminology, which we've endeavoured to explain, whenever necessary, for those of you new to these techniques.

We want to participate in your journey too, so if you have any questions, or want to see more inspirational beading, or share your creative experiments, go to our 'Invitation to participate' section on page 148 so you can join our online community.

## ∘∘∘⬤∘∘∘ ABOUT OUR WORK ∘∘∘⬤∘∘∘

**The inspiration**

We took a journey back in time, to the English Renaissance (1450–1650), where we indulged our fascination with the royal characters of the era together with the artefacts they collected and the costume and jewellery they wore. Starting with Henry the VIII, of course, whose tempestuous reign saw the tearing down of an entire religious institution, enabling his multiple marriages. Then, sweet Edward IV, tiny and delicate and Lady Jane Grey who was Queen for just nine days. Queen Mary, ostentatiously bejewelled was followed by Elizabeth I, the virgin Queen, who ruled like a man with her mastery of political intrigue. Her portraits, each a carefully crafted political statement full of symbolism, also give us a formidable record of her courtly costume.

This period inspired us with its vast treasure trove of sumptuous fashion, and indulgence of exotic materials, silk, velvet, precious stones and pearls; made available through expanding international trade empires. Trading voyages to the Far East, as well as a generous helping of piracy and plunder, led to unimaginable wealth for some and a parade of flamboyant and extravagant aristocracy indulged themselves with ever-changing fashions. Yards and yards of hand-stitched lace, each lace ruff a year in the making, mounted jewels stitched to garments, gold chains, pomanders, pearls as big as doves' eggs hung from earlobes with a strand of black silk. The list is extensive and dazzling.

## The research

We started with real jewellery and a visit to the jewellery rooms at the V&A museum in London. We sat with the personalities of the period during a visit to the National Portrait museum, noting what each individual chose to display about themselves for posterity. We visited the 'London's Lost Jewels' exhibition at the Museum of London, where the Cheapside Hoard was displayed for the first time in a carefully curated exhibition that included a jeweller's shop of the period, the sounds and smells of London, and the exquisitely delicate enamelled and precious stone jewellery discovered under the floorboards of a Cheapside house. We walked through the dark panelled rooms of Montacute House in Somerset, where the evocative 'Wolfe Hall' was filmed. We gazed out of mullioned windows at Hever Castle, from where Anne Boleyn teased Henry VIII towards marriage.

History books and articles supplied the detail and for a while we discussed the various merits of aiguilettes and aigrettes, ouches and billiments. We explored the modes of attachments to partelets and peasecods. We defined a colour palette of the period, sought out commonly recurring motifs, all the while moving closer to a theme and to the real work ahead.

## The beadwork

Distilling the elements that make a style, a mood, an evocation of period from the inspiration sources is just the starting point. The beadwork itself may have its origins in the source, but it has many more tasks to perform. It must be wearable and sit well with our contemporary ways and lifestyles. It must be repeatable in easy steps and made from materials widely available and easy to source. We each do this instinctively as we work. Defining how we do it, so that we could bring our work together in a way that sits comfortably as a collection, was a challenge we resolved by setting a simple boundary. Each piece would be made of individual elements that could be separated and combined in different ways. The more we explored this concept, the more we could see how much fun this could be for other beaders.

Our designs are tried and tested, designed for beaders who are comfortable to work from a pattern and who have already mastered the basics. We recognise in many beaders we meet, a need for a stepping stone between following patterns and creating a design from scratch. Our elements system is designed to be that stepping stone, where there is safety in a pattern, but freedom to explore combinations of elements.

# HOW THE BOOK WORKS

## The finished designs and how to use the Elements Library

Each design is made of interconnecting elements. The designs are laid out as individual projects that can be worked from start to finish. We created the elements so that each one could stand alone, to be worked in repetition, or joined to any other element within the projects. To make this an easy process for you to explore, there is a library of all the elements with the page reference for the instructions.

If you choose a particular element from the library and wish to make more than one for a design you have in mind, we have provided a list of the requirements you would need to make a single element. Simply decide how many you want to make and multiply the quantities of the individual ingredients, much like scaling up a recipe to cook for more people.

To show you how much variety this piecing together of elements can create, our beadwork testers have each created their own combinations, and these are shown in the gallery.

It is our hope and wish that you will embrace the fun of creating your own combinations of our Renaissance-inspired elements, and enjoy the process of experimenting.

**Our techniques**

It was inevitable that we would use Albion and Hubble stitch; we love them for their versatility and continue to explore and develop them, but it is also true that we love all beading techniques so you will find herringbone and right angle weave, peyote, netting, brick and square stitch also thrown into the mix.

If you are new to our work, we have each published several books on our stitches, so please find out more on page 148.

## NOTES AND ABBREVIATIONS

Always snuggle the beads up after every stitch to ensure all loose or slack thread is taken up and that no thread is showing between stitches.

Maintain good thread tension throughout.

**Backstitch** – pass in the direction of the last stitch made, or towards where the thread is coming from.

**CRAW** – cubic right angle weave (CRAW beadwork here is described as units – each unit being a cube).

**HB** – herringbone.

**HorSO** – this is the horizontally spaced out Hubble stitch technique whereby a spacer bead is picked up between stitches and then completely ignored. It literally pushes stitches apart within the row.

**LHS** – left-hand side.

**P** – peyote.

**RAW** – right angle weave (you could think of the beads in each stitch as the points on the compass: north, east, south and west).

**RHS** – right-hand side.

**Spacer row** – beads placed between the tip beads of a row of Albion stitches.

**Stalk** – the number of beads used to create the length of an Albion stitch. These beads are passed back through to complete the stitch.

**Threadless side** – indicating you must pass through this bead from the side where there is no thread exiting. This is to balance a stitch when there is thread exiting the other side of the bead.

**Threadside** – this is the side of the bead from which the thread is emerging.

**Tip** – the bead used at the top of an Albion stitch. This bead is not passed through when completing the stitch. Tip beads can be single or multiple beads.

**VerSO2** – this is a variation of the vertically spaced out Hubble stitch technique (the instructions within will guide you).

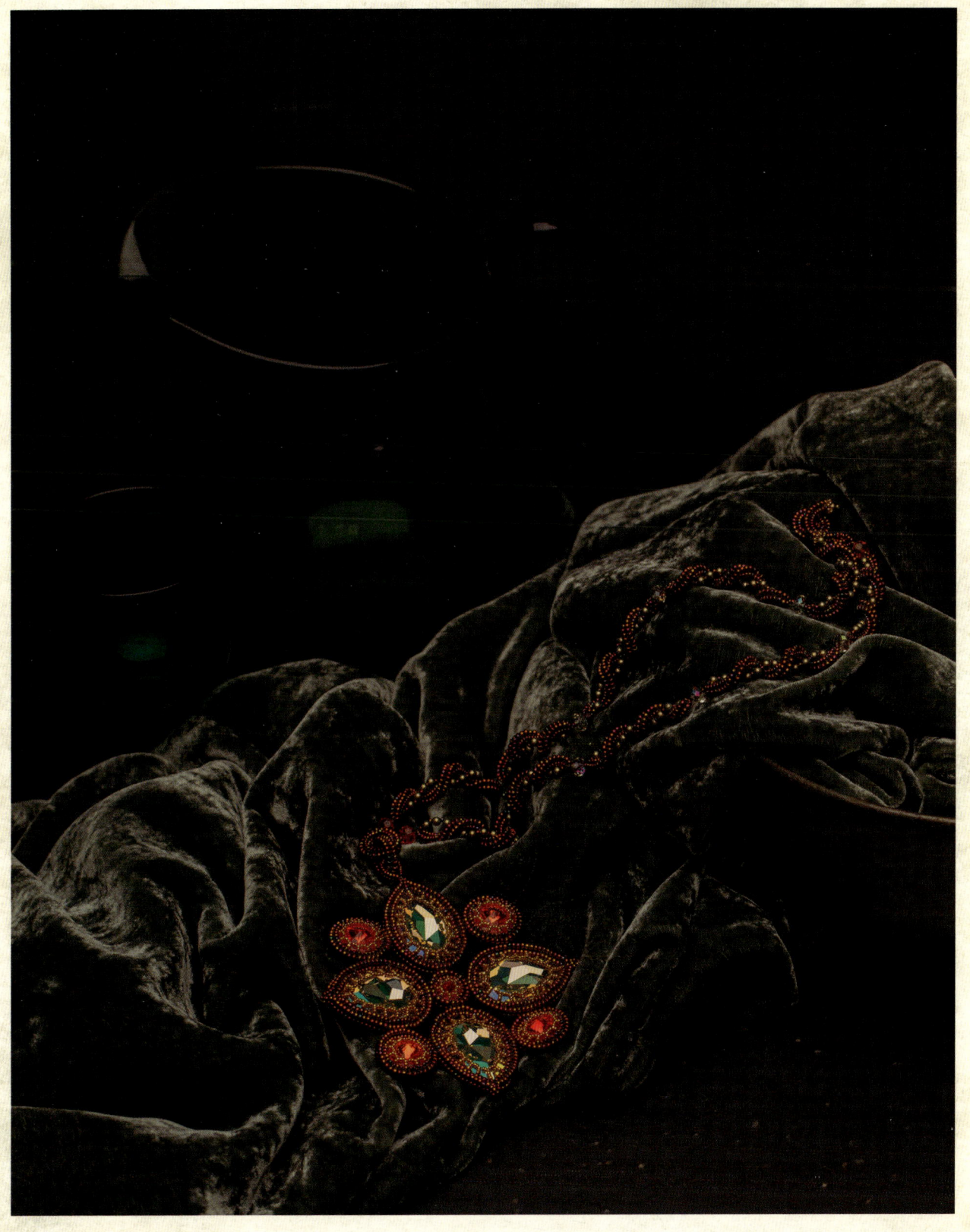

ARAGON

# ARAGON

April 30th, 1506, Windsor. The signing of the Intercursus Malus. The ink was barely dry when Felipe pursed his lips and angrily pushed back his chair from the table. Looking directly at the old king and seeing the smug grin slowly spreading across his face, he fought hard against the sudden, deep desire to drive a dagger into that wizened heart. Now the deal was done, Henry would export English textiles, duty free, to the horror of the Low Countries, and the dangerous Yorkist, Edmund De La Pole, would be handed back to England and locked away securely in the Tower; everything he had demanded, he had got. For his part, Henry would allow the return of Felipe and his wife, Juana, back to Castile; in other words, they were now free to go. He begrudged letting her go, with her startlingly beautiful blue eyes and auburn hair, but wanted nothing more than to see the back of that vile, peacock of a husband of hers. He had adored his beloved Elizabeth, who had left this life, three years ago, breaking his heart to the point where he had battled to find a reason to continue breathing, but England must come first. With his own wife gone, and the Crown Prince, his dear son Arthur, having died at Ludlow of the malign vapour, the monarchy needed strengthening, so he pondered the possibility of re-marriage himself. Arthur's widow, Catherine was a huge problem as her parents wouldn't allow her to marry her father-in-law, although they still hadn't paid all the promised dowry to England, but her sister Juana - now, she was quite a prospect, if it weren't for Felipe.

Felipe couldn't wait to leave this godforsaken, cold, bleak land, and go home, where life could go back to how it should be. For three months he had been cooped up here with Juana, who was stifling him with her constant simpering attention. He, Felipe El Hermoso, Philip the Handsome, wasn't called that for nothing; at home, he had the pick of the Castilian court ladies, and being a Habsburg, he commanded absolute respect and reverence, so no one questioned his comings and goings. His wife's explosive temper when she discovered his misdemeanours was something he had to deal with, but it was a worthwhile sport.

Henry pulled his cloak around his shoulders, feeling a chill in the air, and swept across the room to the window where Juana was watching a light rain falling over the gardens and distractedly touching the magnificent pendant that lay against her pale skin. The pendant had been a wedding gift from her father, King Ferdinand II of Aragon, and reminded her of that joyful time. Juana knew the meeting today was of great importance, and would guarantee their return home soon. Heartened at this, but saddened at leaving her dear younger sister behind, she resolved to set the pendant around Catherine's neck as a reminder of her love and her home. Ignoring the fact that Felipe was still seething behind him, Henry smiled jubilantly at Juana and, taking her hand, kissed it lightly and guided her to the door. They made their way along the corridor lined with rich tapestries to the banquet hall. This called for a celebration!

**Elements**: large pear drop, rivoli unit, chaton unit, rope, toggle ring and bar
**Techniques**: tubular herringbone, tubular twisted herringbone, brick stitch (modified), square stitch
**Completed necklace length**: 60cm/24"

**You will need**:

12g x Miyuki seed beads size 15° 462 (metallic gold iris) (A)
21g x Miyuki seed beads size 11° 462 (metallic gold iris) (B)
4 x Swarovski® pear drop fancy stones #4327 30x20mm (crystal luminous green) (C)
1.5g x Czech charlotte seed beads size 15° (24Kt gold-plated) (D)
4 x Swarovski® rivolis #1122 14mm (hyacinth) (E)
1 x Swarovski® xilion chaton #1088 ss39 8mm (hyacinth) (F)
120 x Swarovski® pearls #5810 3mm (crystal iridescent green) (G)
8 x Swarovski® briolettes #5040 6mm (crystal iridescent green) (H) (can substitute 6mm bicone/round crystal or other bead)
4 x Swarovski® crystal rounds #5000 6mm (fire opal) (J) (can substitute 6mm bicone crystal or other bead)

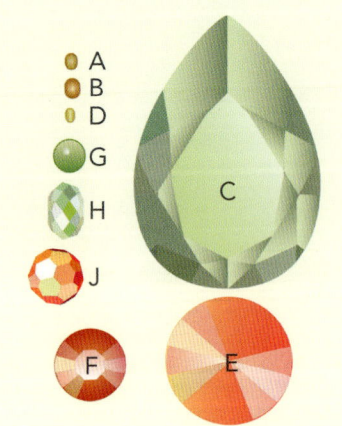

*Aragon*

> "Make haste, signor, come and see our mistress the princess arrayed and adorned; in short, as she ought to be: her damsels and she are all one flame of gold; all covered with pearls, diamonds, rubies and brocade, more than ten hands deep."
>
> Miguel de Cervantes, Don Quixote

## Pear drop unit (PDU) (Make 4)

1. With a wingspan of thread:

    a) Pick up 3A, pass through all 3 again and the 1st A bead picked up once more.
    b) Pick up 2A and pass through the bead from which the thread was emerging, in the same direction.
    c) To step up, pass through the adjacent A bead of the 1st 3A.

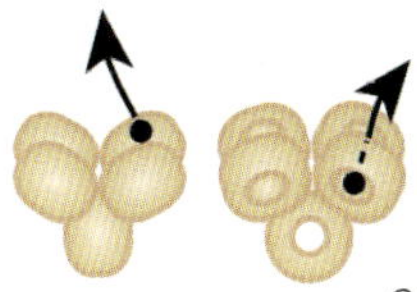

    *Step 1*

2. Fold the beadwork so that the 2 pairs of beads are pushed together; these are now HB (herringbone) base pairs, and the single bead in the centre is the pointed end of the PDU.

    In the 2nd diagram the beadwork is rotated 90° for ease of description.

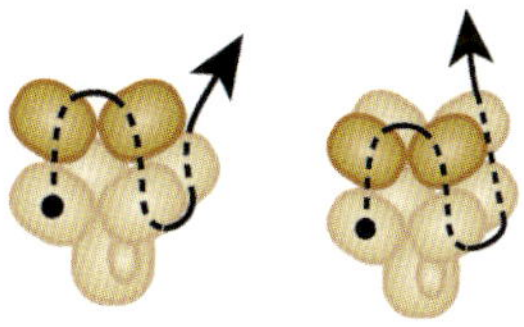

    *Step 2*

3. Using these 2 base pairs, make an HB row thus:

    a) Pick up 2A and pass down through the partner base pair bead.
    b) Pass up through the adjacent A of the other base pair.
    c) Repeat a).
    d) Pass up through the adjacent A of the 1st base pair and the 1st bead placed in this row. Remember, for normal HB, you will always have to step up through 2 beads – the bead of the row below and the 1st bead placed in the current row.

    *Rotated 180°*
    *Step 3*

4. Now we're going to work an HB row in B with A as spacer beads:

    a) Pick up 2B and pass down through the partner A bead of the row below.
    b) Pick up 1A and pass up through the adjacent A bead of the other pair.
    c) Repeat a).
    d) Pick up 1A and pass up through the adjacent A bead of the 1st pair and the 1st bead placed in this row.

— *Step 4* —

*Rotated 180°*

– 3 –

Aragon

5. Repeat step 4 using B for both the stitches **and** the spacer beads. This creates a V-shape where the point of the crystal will nestle.

*We will build a length of 2-stitch HB rope from one side of this V-shape, and join it onto the other side, making a tailored frame for C. But to do this we'll need two more beads on each side to form HB bases. Here the beadwork is shown from the side, viewing the outer columns, with the thread emerging from the left B bead. The beads of the opposite side of the V-shape are omitted, to prevent confusion.*

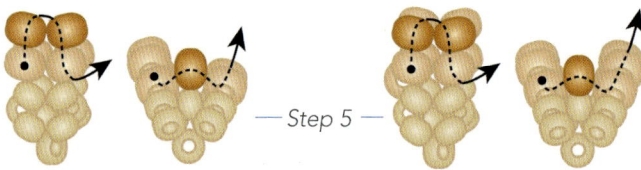

— Step 5 —

Rotated 180°

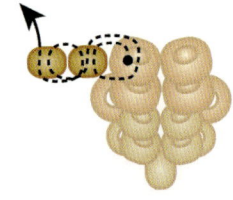

Step 6

6. Ladder stitch 2A beads onto the side of the B bead, snuggling each one properly into place.

7. Still looking directly at the outer columns, swing the new A beads around, so that they are above the spacer beads in the centre of the structure, and ladder stitch the last A onto the B bead on the right thus:

   a) Pass down through B and back up through the last A.
   b) Pass down through B again and on through the B below that, to emerge as in the diagram. **We'll call this row 1.**

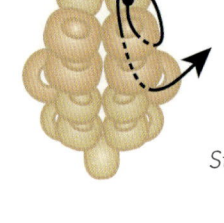

Step 7

8. Now we'll set up the other side. Turn the beadwork to view it from the front, as in the diagram. The thread is exiting a B at the left front. Pass through the spacer B bead, and up through the 2B of the right, front column.

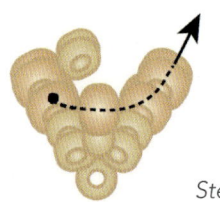

Step 8

9. a) Repeat steps 6–7a) on this side of the V-shape.
   b) Pass down through B again and up through the partner B, to emerge as in the diagram.
   c) Now is a good time to finish off the tail thread.

10. **Rows 2–19**: Viewing from the front, and using only B, work 18 rows, remembering to always step up through 2 beads.

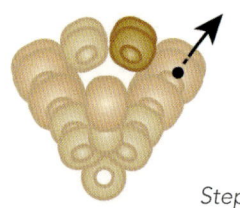

Step 9

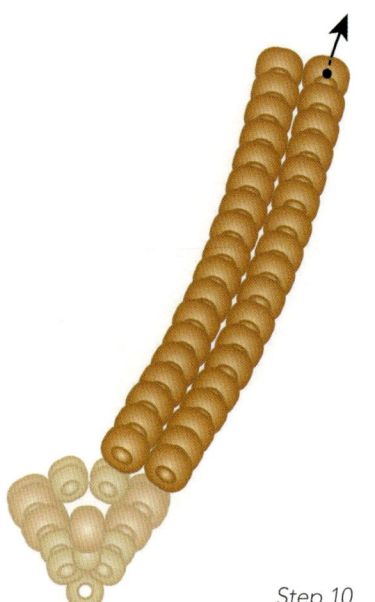

Step 10

> *"His Majesty, in addition to his wonderful presence, was adorned with a most rich collar, full of great pearls and many other jewels, in four rows, and in his bonnet he had a pear-shaped pearl, which seems to me something most rich. Your lordship has heard from many of this king's wisdom and ways. I can testify to this, and need add no more."*
>
> *Milanese ambassador Raimondo de Raimondi regarding Henry VII*

11. **Row 20**:

   a) 1st stitch – pick up 2B.
   b) 2nd stitch – pick up 2A.

   **Row 21**: Use B only.

   **Rows 22–43**: Repeat rows 20 and 21 eleven times. The beadwork will feel floppy, but don't worry as we'll take care of that in a minute.

12. **Rows 44–60**: Use B only. These rows mirror the opposite side of the structure.

13. The 2 pairs of A and B beads on the other side of the V-shape are actually row 61, so now we must make the join.

   a) **Row 61 (1st stitch)**: Align the working end of the HB rope with the B and A beads of the other side of the V-shape.
   b) With the thread emerging from the rope right, outer column B bead, pass down through the B of the V-shape right, outer column, and up the B of the left outer column.
   c) Continue up through the rope left, outer column B, to complete the stitch, and snuggle the 2 parts together.

14. a) **Row 61 (2nd stitch)**: Turn the beadwork so the join is on the left.
   b) Pass into the B bead of the inner column, and make the 2nd stitch using the awaiting A beads.
   c) The needle should now be exiting the upper side of the inner column, row 60 B bead, as in the diagram.

15. Pass around the entire inner column of beads, exiting the row 1 A bead, on the other side of the V-shape.

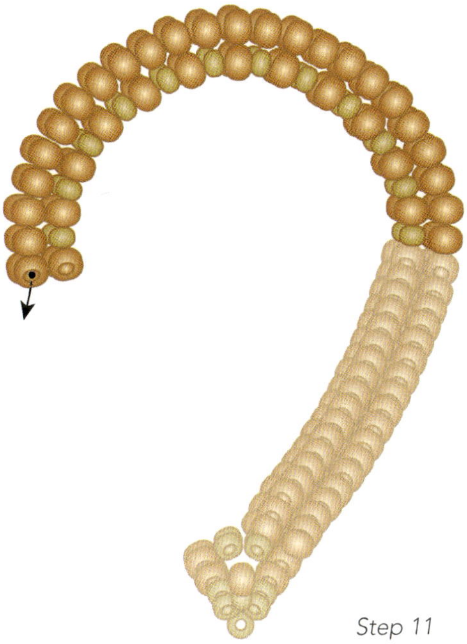

*Step 11*

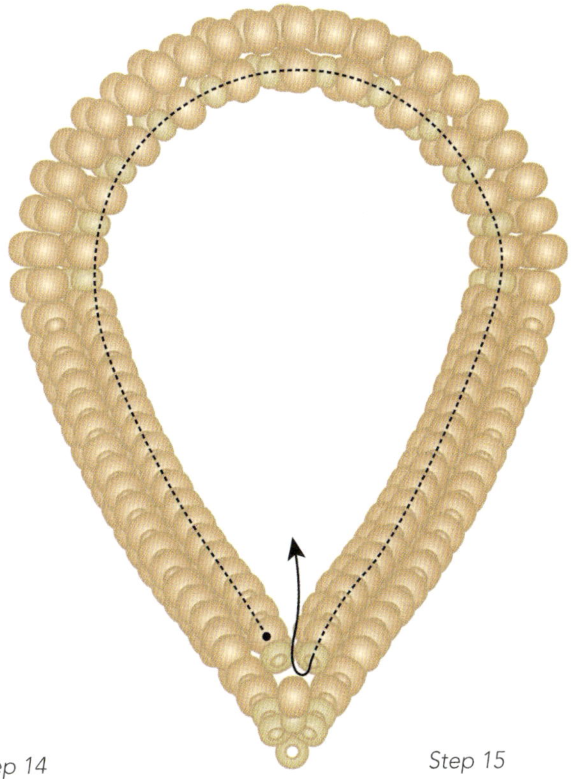

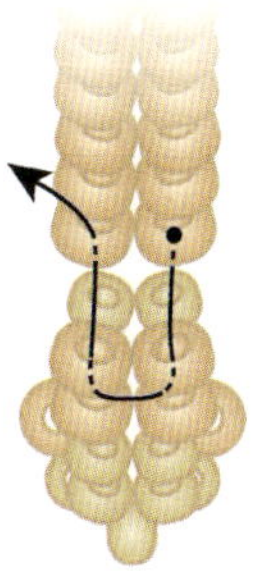

*Step 13*

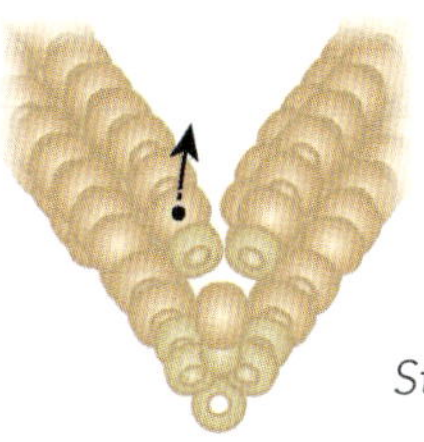

*Step 14*

*Step 15*

– 5 –

Aragon

**16** a) Pick up 1B and backstitch through the spacer B bead in the centre. Pass again through the B bead just picked up in the same direction as before.
b) Continue on through the A bead, of row 61, and the B bead of row 60, above it. This starts to firm up the structure.

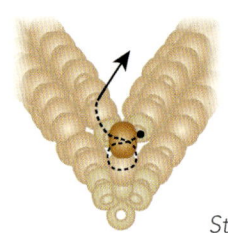
*Step 16*

**17** Turn the V-shape around to view from the other side. The thread must cross to this side now.

On this side, pass down the B of row 60, and A of row 61.

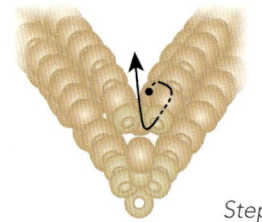
*Step 17*

**18** Repeat step 16, followed by step 15 (yes, in that order). Pass through the adjacent spacer B bead. This tightens up the beadwork considerably.

**19** Pick up 9A, backstitch through the 3rd B bead of the inner column, and pass back through the last 3A picked up, in the opposite direction.

Snuggle up, ensuring no thread is showing.

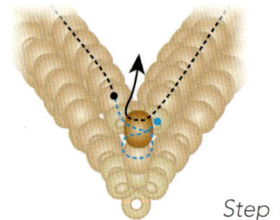
*Step 18*

**20** Pick up 5A, backstitch through the next anchor B (marked X), and pass back through the last 3A picked up, in the opposite direction.

**21** Repeat step 20 fifteen more times – but take extra care that you use the correct anchor beads for attachment, especially where A beads are positioned in the HB frame, tailoring the curl around. Also, be totally vigilant about snuggling up; you may be able to backtrack, using an awl or thick needle to pull and tighten each stitch, but it's easier to make sure you keep a good tension as you go along.

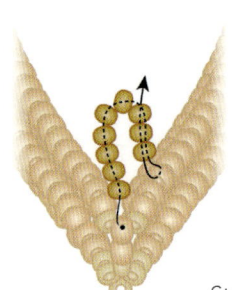
*Step 19*

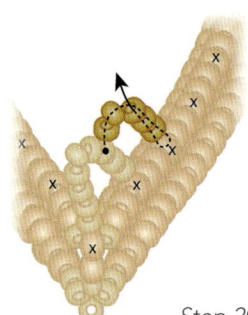
*Step 20*

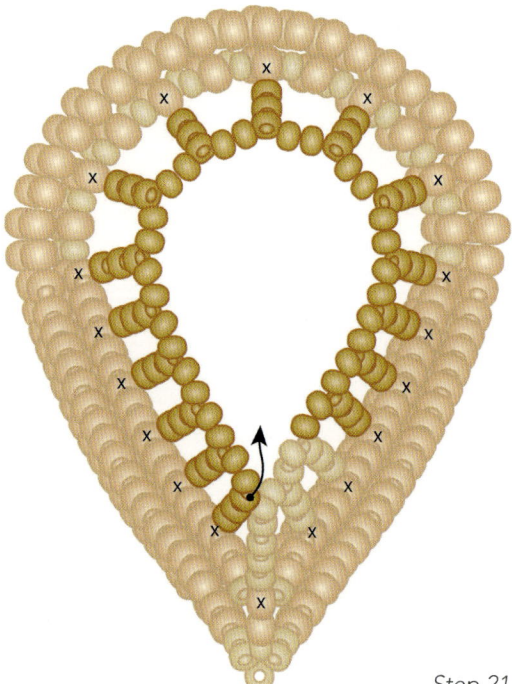
*Step 21*

> "He was dressed in armor worth a treasure chest, his shield encircled by large pearls, and he wore mail of solid gold. His helmet was more costly yet, due to a gem set in its work that was, if Turpin does not lie, a ruby of a walnut's size."
>
> *Matteo Maria Boiardo,*
> *Orlando Innamorato*

*Aragon*

**22** To close the row:

    a) Pick up 2A.
    b) Pass down through the 1st 4A picked up this row, in the direction of the B spacer bead.
    c) Backstitch through the B spacer bead.
    d) Pass back up through the 4A in the opposite direction.

**Important note**: Except for the 4A beads attached to the centre of the V-shape, for each stitch, 3A were shared 'up' (↑) beads and 2A were free 'along' (→) beads. So the pattern created was 3↑ & 2→ (hold that concept, as we'll use it in further elements). No surprise that I call this modified brick stitch method up-and-along, and it's perfect for trapping crystals and cabochons! Did you notice that you only had to pick up the → beads for the last stitch? That's because the ↑ beads were already in place with the first stitch.

*Step 22*

**23** a) Follow the threadpath of one of the stitches to either side of the 4↑ beads, down to the HB frame, and weave around to emerge from the central B spacer bead on the other side of the V.
    b) Press C firmly into place, as it can help you work the next row.

The next row is worked in size 15° Czech charlottes, so you may need to change to a size 15 needle. These beads are definitely not equal in size to a Japanese size 15° seed bead, in fact, on average they behave like an 18°, but can vary between 17° (eg those coated in precious metal) and 19° (eg gunmetal and some dark bronze). So if, after working this final row, the trap is a little loose (even though you've really worked at snuggling everything tightly), try modifying the numbers of up-and/or-along beads as suggested at the end of the next step. In the diagram, each stitch has been numbered. There are also three sets of highlighted B beads which mark the connection points for assembling Aragon; those marked **O** will attach to the ChU, and those marked **O** attach to RUs. Ignore them for now! The final diagrams for RU and ChU will be similarly marked to aid assembly.

*Step 23*

Aragon

**24**  a) Stitch 1: Pick up 10D, backstitch through the anchor B, and pass back up through the last 3D picked up, in the opposite direction.

b) Stitch 2: Pick up 6D only, backstitch through the next anchor B, and pass back up through the last 3D picked up, in the opposite direction.

c) Stitches 3–17: Work as for 2nd stitch.

d) Stitch 18: To close the row, pick up 3D and work the same threadpath as in step 22 for the underside. (Except for the 18th stitch, this pattern is 3↑& 3→.)

Loose trap? Try the following stitch pick-ups, but maintain the 3↑ part of each stitch:

1: 9D; 2–3: 5D; 4–6: 6D; 7–12: 5D; 13–15: 6D; 16–17: 5D; 18: Close with 2D.

e) Finish off all threads, keeping the working thread on one PDU only – this will be used to make the SBL (see page 11).

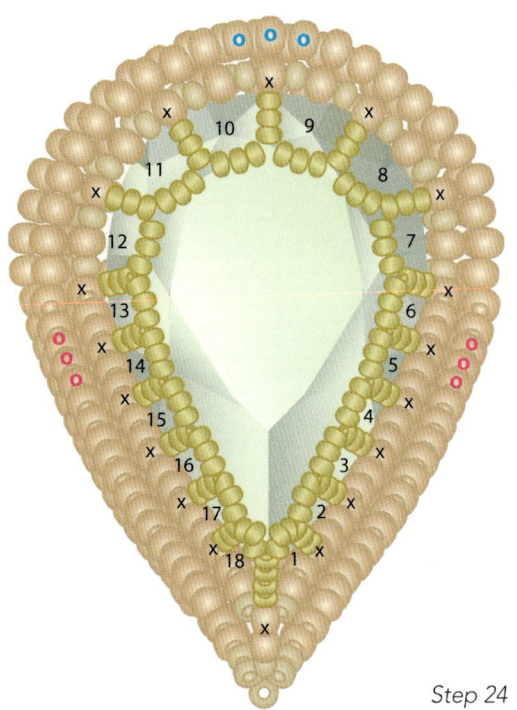 

*Step 24*

## Rivoli unit (RU) (Make 4)

**1**  Here's a neat HB start: Maintaining a moderate tension, with 1.5m/60" of thread and leaving a tail thread of 15cm/6", pick up 4B, 4A and pass through the 1st 2B again.

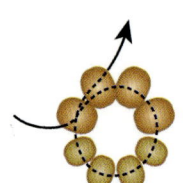

*Step 1*

**2**  a) Pick up 2B, pass down through the next B.
b) Skip 1B, 1A and pass through the next A.
c) Pick up 2A, pass through the next A.
d) Skip 1A, 1B and pass through the next B and the 1st B placed in this row.
e) You may have to coerce the beads a little into the HB formation – giving you **3 ready-made rows**, shown far right. The thread may be emerging from the left or the right B bead, depending on which hand you use and which direction the structure adopted when you snuggled it up.

**3**  Make 1 stitch in B and 1 stitch in A for every row, and remembering always to step up through 2 beads, work rows 4–36.

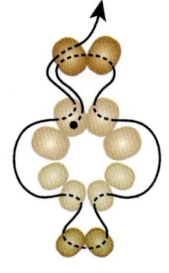 

*Step 2*

Aragon

4. Follow steps 13–14 of the PDU to join rows 36 and 1 together.

5. Weave on to emerge from the right side of an A bead, as in the diagram. Do not run the thread around the inner columns!

6. **Underside, stitch 1**: Pick up 5A, backstitch through the next anchor A, pass back up the last 2A picked up, in the opposite direction. (The pattern is 2↑ & 1→.)

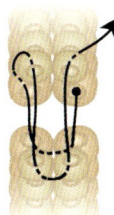

*Step 4*

7. a) **Stitches 2–11**: Pick up 3A, backstitch through the next anchor A, pass back up the last 2A picked up in the opposite direction.
   b) **Final stitch** – closing the row: Pick up 1A, pass down through the 1st 2A picked up in this row, towards the frame, backstitch through the anchor A, and pass back up the 2A in the opposite direction.

*Step 5*

*Step 6*

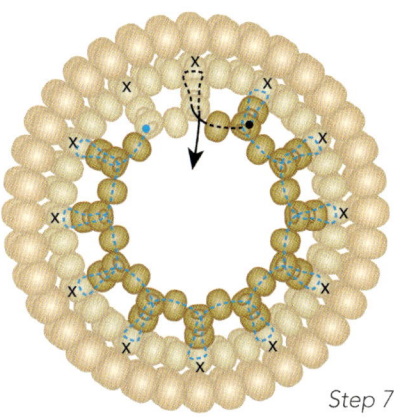

*Step 7*

8. Weave around the up-and-along stitch to either left or right, and on into the frame, to exit an A on the top side of the frame, corresponding with an anchor A on the underside.

9. a) Press E, face-up, firmly into the centre of the frame as it will facilitate a good grip on the beadwork and support the structure.
   b) Using D, work an up-and-along row in 2↑ & 2→ pattern. The stitch pick-ups are as follows: 1: 6D; 2–11: 4D; 12: Close with 2D (12 stitches in total).
   c) Weave around to exit a B bead as in the diagram ready to be used for connection. Designate this B as the 1st in the 3 pairs to be attached to the side of the PDU.
   d) Finish off the tail thread. The beads marked O are for attachment to the PDU.

*Step 8*

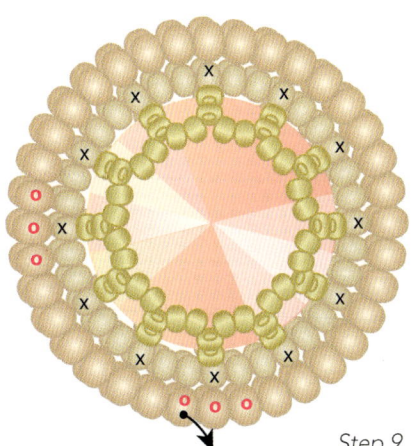

*Step 9*

– 9 –

*Aragon*

## Chaton unit (ChU) (Make 1)

**1** With 1.5m/60" of thread and leaving a tail thread of 15cm/6", again maintain a moderate tension and work steps 1–5 of the RU, bearing in mind that, for step 3, you only need to make rows 4–24.

**2** a) The up-and-along pattern is 1↑& 1→, and is worked in A (8 stitches in total). Pick-ups are as follows: 1: 3A; 2-7: 2A; 8: Close the row with 1A.
b) Weave around to emerge from an anchor A on the top side of the frame, corresponding with an anchor A used for up-and-along on the underside.

**3** a) Using D, work an up-and-along row in 2↑& 1→ pattern. Pick-ups are as follows: 1: 5D; 2–7: 3D; 8: Close the row with 1D.
b) Weave around to exit a B, as in the diagram, ready for connection. If you find this row hard to snuggle up, it could be a size problem with the charlottes again. The simple alternative is to work the row pattern as 1↑& 2→ instead.
c) Finish off the tail thread. The beads marked O are for attachment to the round ends of the PDUs.

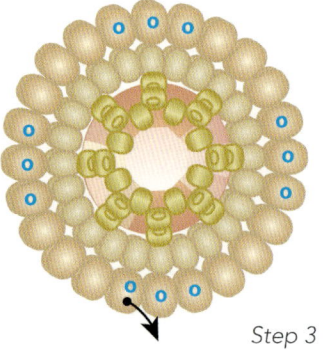
*Step 3*

## Assembling the pendant

**1** Bring the ChU and PDU close together so that the beads marked O in the diagram correspond with each other. We'll be using square stitch for the join.

a) Pass into the corresponding B of the PDU in the direction away from the next ChU connection bead.
b) Pass back into the ChU B bead and continue on through the 2nd B.
c) Repeat steps a)–b) for the 2nd and 3rd corresponding pairs of B beads.

**2** Pass through the 3 B beads of the PDU and the ChU.

**3** Turn over the beadwork and pass into the ChU B bead, corresponding with the last connection B used on the top side. Now work steps 1–2 on this side of the beadwork and finish off.

**4** Attach the remaining 3 PDUs to the ChU in the same way.

**5** Using the same square stitch method of connection, each RU is attached to a side of 2 different PDUs by matching up the beads marked O in the diagram.

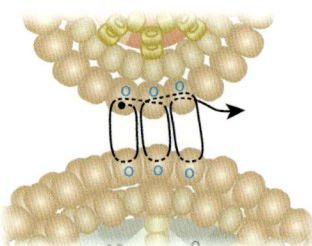
*Step 1*

*Step 2*

## Toggle ring (Make 1) and bail rings (Make 2)

**Toggle ring**: Using 0.75m/30" thread, make a 24-row ring and finish off the tail thread only. Add a connection link thus:

a) Weave through to emerge from a B.
b) Pick up 9A and pass through the partner B of the same outer stitch.
c) Pass again through the 1st B, to emerge as in step a).
d) Pass around the little circuit again and finish off.

**Bail rings**: Make one 24-row ring and finish off both the working and tail threads. Work the 24 rows of the second ring, but post one end of the beadwork through the centre of the first ring before joining the two ends of the second ring together.

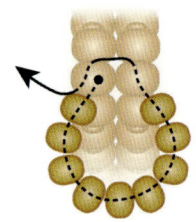
*Toggle ring*

Aragon

## Small bail link (SBL)

**1** With 50cm/20" thread, weave into the PDU frame and down to exit the A bead at the very tip of the PDU.

a) Pick up 2A and pass through the tip A again in the same direction as before, making a ring.
b) Step up through the 1st A just picked up. We'll call this pair of beads **Row 1**.

*Step 1*

**2** **Row 2**:

a) Pick up 2A and pass down through the partner A of row 1.
b) Pass back up through the 1st A of row 1, step up through the 1st A bead just picked up.

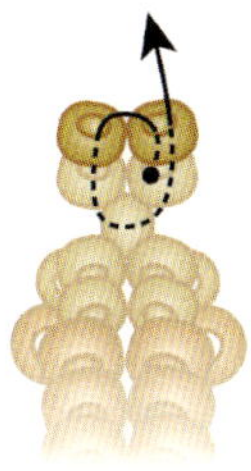

**3** **Rows 3–20**: Work as for row 2, picking up 2A, anchoring them in the 2 beads of the row below and stepping up out of the 1st new bead.

*Step 2*

**4** Connect the SBL with the interlinked bail rings thus:

a) With the thread exiting the right-hand column, pass through the central space of one of the linked bail rings.
b) Ensuring the SBL column isn't twisted, position row 20 against the tip bead to reflect row 1, and pass through the tip bead.
c) Pass back through the central space of the bail ring, in the opposite direction.
d) Pass into the left-hand column, continue through it to the end.

**5** a) Pass through the tip bead, turn and pass back up through the right-hand column.
b) Weave into the PDU and finish off.

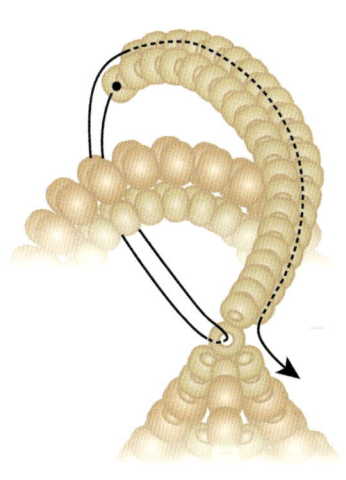

*Step 3*

*Step 4*

Aragon

## Twisted rope (Work 2 ropes, each 5 sections long)

**1** With a very long wingspan of thread and leaving a tail thread of 20cm/8", use A beads to work steps 1–2 as for the PDU. Count these 2 HB base pairs as **Row 1**.

**2** Each section of the rope is worked in twisted HB, so it's really important that you remember to step up through **only one bead**. The completed section will coil with the B beads outside and the A beads inside.

**Row 2**:

a) Stitch 1 (outer): 2B.
b) Stitch 2 (inner): 2A and step up through the 1st B of stitch 1.

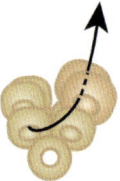
*Step 2*

**3** **Rows 3–45**: Work as for row 2. As you progress the rope section will feel loose, but it will coil up after step 5.

*Step 3*

**4** **Row 46**: Work both stitches in A only.

**5** Make a picot thus:

a) Stitch 1 (outer): pick up 1A.
b) Pass down through the partner HB bead.
c) Pass up into the 1st A of the inner stitch.
d) Stitch 2 (inner): pass through the A picked up in stitch 1, in the opposite direction.
e) Pass down through the partner HB bead.

*Step 4*

**6** a) Pass down the entire adjacent inner column of A beads.
b) Cross to the other inner column, avoiding the picot bead at the end, and pass up the entire 2nd inner column.
c) Pass through the picot bead.
d) Pass down through the 1st A of the 1st inner column, to emerge as in the diagram.
e) Snuggle up tightly and watch the rope twizzle round.

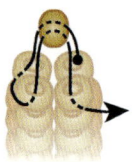
*Step 5*

*Step 6*

Aragon

**7** In the diagram the HB rope is shown as linear, to clarify the threadpaths. Working only on the inner stitches and with the thread exiting the underside of the A bead of row 46:

a) Pick up (1A, 1G) 12 times, plus 1A (in total 25 beads – a pearly snake).
b) Maintaining the taut spiral of HB, loosely wind the pearly snake inside the spiral so it appears to pass straight through the centre (don't overwind, it's only about 1.5 turns to get it inside the spiral).
c) Secure the snake by passing through the corresponding A of row 1.
d) Following the threadpath, pass through the end picot bead.
e) Pass through the other A bead of row 1, back towards the snake.
f) Pass through the 25 beads of the snake.
g) Continue through the 2nd A of row 46 and the picot bead.

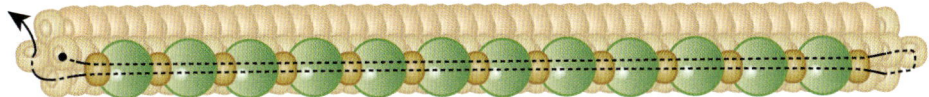

*Step 7*

**8** a) Pick up 1A, 1H, 2A.
b) Missing out the last A picked up, pass back through A, H, A and the picot A at the end of the rope section.
c) Now pass again through the A, H, 2A picked up. That completes one rope section.

*Step 8*

**9** To commence a new section, simply start again from step 1, building 2 HB base pairs onto the A bead from which the thread is now emerging – the only difference is you won't need to pick up 3A, you'll only need to pick up 2A as you already have 1A present on the completed rope section. **Note**: When you make the 5th (end) rope section follow steps 1–7 only!

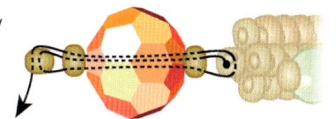

*Step 10*

**10** Pendant end: To complete this end of the rope, repeat step 8, substituting 1J for 1H.

Keep the working thread ready for attachment.

**11** **Connection at the pendant end**:

a) Pass under 2 adjacent threads of the outer stitches on the linked bail ring that is not connected to the SBL, and back through the end A bead, from the threadless side.
b) Pass back under the 2 threads, weave into the pendant.
c) Finish off.
d) We'll call those 2 threads we used 1 and 2. Count on to threads 7 and 8 and attach the 2nd completed rope in the same way.

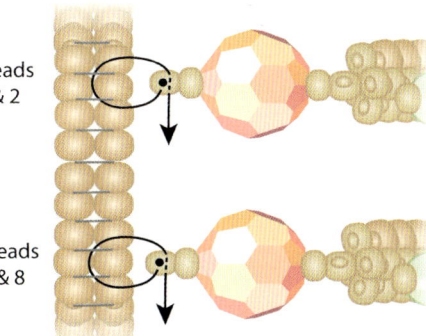

*Step 11*

**12** **Toggle end**:

a) Using the tail thread, repeat step 10.
b) Pick up 9A and pass again through the A, from which the thread was emerging, making a link.
c) Pass around the link once more.
d) Finish off by weaving back into the rope.

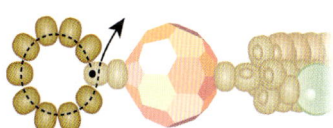

*Step 12*

### Toggle bar (Make 1)

**1** This is worked in normal HB, so remember to step up through 2 beads. With 65cm/25" of thread, leaving a tail thread of 20cm/8":

   a) Work steps 1–2 as for the RU – setting up the 1st 3 rows.
   b) Work a further 10 rows (13 in all).
   c) With the needle exiting a B of the 13th row, pass down into the adjacent A bead.
   d) Continue along the entire column of A beads, to emerge from a row 1 A bead.
   e) Turn and pass along the other entire column of A beads.
   f) Snuggle up, making the arc solid.

Step 1

**2** a) To secure the pearl embellishment at the end of the bar, work steps 13–14 as for the Anne Boleyn toggle bar (page 44), using 1G, 1D.
   b) Weave around so that the thread is emerging from an end B, as in the diagram.

**3** Make a perky picot embellishment thus:

   a) Pick up 2D and pass down the partner B bead.
   b) Pass back up the 1st B and on through the 1st D picked up.
   c) Pick up 1D, pass down through the adjacent D and the B below.
   d) Cross to the inner stitches and pass up the adjacent A bead.

Steps 2–3

**4** To make the 2nd picot:

   a) Pick up 2D.
   b) Pass down the adjacent B bead.
   c) Pass back up the A bead and on through the 1st D picked up.
   d) Pick up 1D, pass down through the adjacent D the B below.
   e) Pass back up the A bead again.

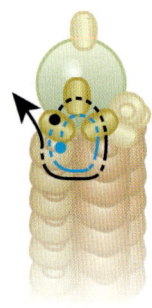
Step 4

**5** The threadpaths for the 3rd and 4th picots will be in the same direction as for the 1st and 2nd picots respectively.

**6** Weave along to exit a row 7 A bead, at the centre of the arc.

**7** The connection link is set on the side of the bar, so that it lies flat against the toggle ring when closed.

   a) With the thread exiting the right side of the arc A, pick up 9A.
   b) Pass into the right side of the B bead of the same row, directly above.
   c) Pass back through all 9A in the opposite direction.
   d) Pass through the arc A, from the threadless side.
   e) Finish off the working thread.

Step 7

**8** Using the tail thread, work steps 2–5 to embellish this end of the toggle bar, and finish off.

### Links

Joining the loop of the toggle ring with the looped end of the rope requires a single link. Work this link as detailed in step 15 of Anne Boleyn (page 44), using 11A.

Work another link to join the loop of the toggle bar to the other rope.

CATTERN'S TALLIE
PENDANT AND CUFF

# CATTERN'S TALLIE PENDANT AND CUFF

'Over two, under one, round three and twist, pin and prick, knot and bind', the little sentence repeated hour after hour as the lacemaker bent to her work. Fine linen threads as thin as gossamer wound out from bobbins that danced under her quick fingers. Every two hours another inch of intricately patterned lace was completed, and lay with a glistening edge of spun gold. This commission was for a pair of ruffled cuffs, dyed a delicate shade of grey, to match the new gown, the gold thread edging the deep rich colour of ripened straw. Twelve yards had been ordered and the finished gown had to be ready in time for her ladyship's new portrait.

The grey and gold lace cuffs can be seen in the painting *Portrait of a lady in a black dress with gold trim and jewelled cap*, attributed to the circle of Master of the Countess of Warwick. Lace was as expensive as jewellery and these cuffs were the starting point for the Cattern's Tallie pendant. There are also directions to make a matching cuff.

Catherine of Aragon was exiled to Ampthill in Bedfordshire, where she is said to have taught and supported local lacemakers. It's possible that the lacemaker's holiday, Cattern's day (25th November), is named after her. On Cattern's day small dough cakes flavoured with caraway seeds were baked to celebrate. There is lots of evidence that 'Keeping Cattern' was celebrated before this time, as November 25th is St Catherine's Day, the patron saint of unmarried women. By extension she became the patron saint of all forms of needlework as this was the main form of employment for maids and spinsters.

A tallie is a woven section in bobbin lace, usually an oval form.

The Master of the Countess of Warwick was an anonymous English painter who was named thus to identify a group of paintings thought to be by the same artist in a similar style to a portrait of Anne Russell, Countess of Warwick. Anne served Queen Elizabeth I in her privy chamber and was a favourite, 'Most beloved and in greater favour than any other woman in the kingdom'.

**Elements**: ruffle bead, caged drop bead, caged round pearls, chain

**Techniques**: Albion stitch, netting, peyote stitch

**Completed length**: necklace 54cm/21¼", pendant 10cm/4"

**You will need**:

15g x Miyuki seed beads size 11° 457 (metallic bronze) (A)
10g x Miyuki seed beads size 11° 4202F (galvanised matte gold) (B)
10g x Miyuki seed beads size 11° 4201F (galvanised matte silver) (C)
10g x Miyuki seed beads size 11° 4204 (galvanised champagne gold) (D)
2g x Miyuki seed beads size 8° 457 (metallic bronze) (E)
3g x Miyuki seed beads size 15° 457 (metallic bronze) (F)
3g x Miyuki seed beads size 15° 4204F (galvanised matte gold) (G)
32 x CzechMate half tile 2-hole beads (matte lila vega) (H)
68 x Swarovski® pearls #5810 3mm (crystal bronze pearl) (J)
1 x tear drop bead 14x27mm (irridescent pearl) (K)
4 x Swarovski® pearls #5810 10mm (crystal cream pearl) (L)

*Fascinating fact:*

*Elizabethan ruffs were made of cambric (linen) or lawn (cotton). Unlike the rough linen fashionable today, Elizabethan linen was very fine. One surviving lace ruff has 50 threads per centimetre.*

*Fascinating fact:*

*The Elizabethan fashion for ever more outrageously goffered lace ruffs and cuffs led to a huge demand for skilled lace makers. Lace was worked in 3-inch widths; a 9-inch deep ruff would require three pieces of lace to be stitched edge to edge. A moderate ruff would need 9 yards of lace, or 45 yards stitched edge to edge, taking over a year to make.*

## Ruffle bead (Make 1)

The ruffle bead foundation is worked as a flat band of Albion stitch, then the ends are brought together to form a tube. Because of this the foundation row will start with the (H) 2-hole beads included. As you work the foundation, keep the thread tension up so that the beads snuggle together.

Albion stitch is a way of working with picots, an individual stitch is described in two parts, the stalk and the tip. The thread passes back through the stalk beads and the tip bead will flip onto its side. Stitch tips are joined with beads between them, this is called a spacer row, and forms a new foundation row to work more stitches from.

1. Use a stop bead and pick up 2A, 1H, 3A, 1H, 3A, 1H, 3A, 1H, 2A (17 beads in total).

2. Now to work the 1st row of Albion stitch. Place a stitch over the 17th, 13th, 9th, 5th and 1st A beads of the base row. Work each stitch to have 3A stalk, 1A tip. **Note**: the thread path for the 1st stitch differs from that of the remaining stitches.

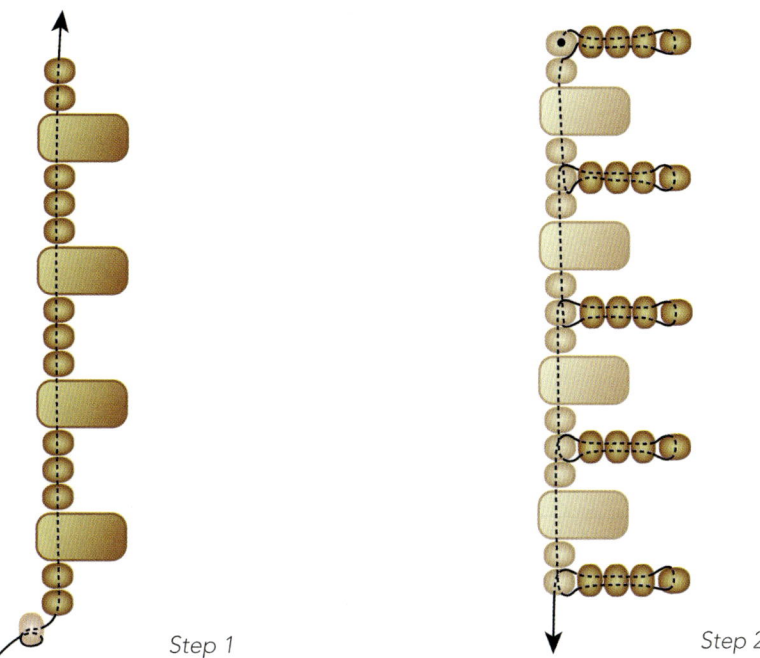

Step 1       Step 2

Cattern's Tallie pendant and cuff

**3** Add the spacer row of 1A, 1H, 1A between each tip bead.

Continue working, repeating steps 2 and 3 until there are 7 completed rows ending with a step 3.

**4** Fold the beaded strip to bring the start row and end row together. Pick up 3A, pass through the end bead of the start row, pass back through the 3A.

Pass through the beads of the end row to exit the next tip bead.

Repeat the step to link the 2 rows together at each tip bead.

Adjust the H beads so that they all stick out from the surface of the beaded tube. Finish off the thread and tail.

Now to embellish the apertures of the tube. The embellishment will show between the ruffles.

**5** The diagrams show these steps working from the bottom edge of the tube towards the top edge. With a 1.5m/60" thread, secure the thread to the beadwork and exit a tip bead on the end of a row. Pick up 1F, 1J, 1F, pass through the 1A, 1H, 1A beads at the side of the aperture.

**6** Pick up 1F, pass through J. Pick up 1F, pass through the next tip bead on the side row of the same aperture.

Repeat to embellish each aperture of the tube, making sure that the H beads stick outwards and your thread doesn't snag on them as you work. Weave the thread and any tails back into the beadwork to finish off.

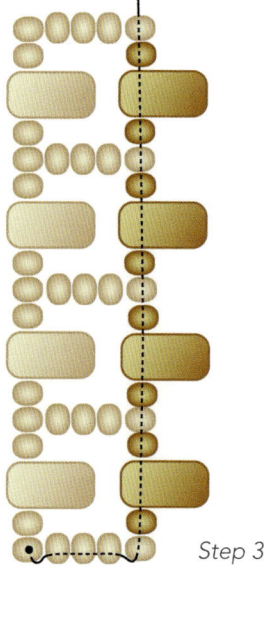

Step 3

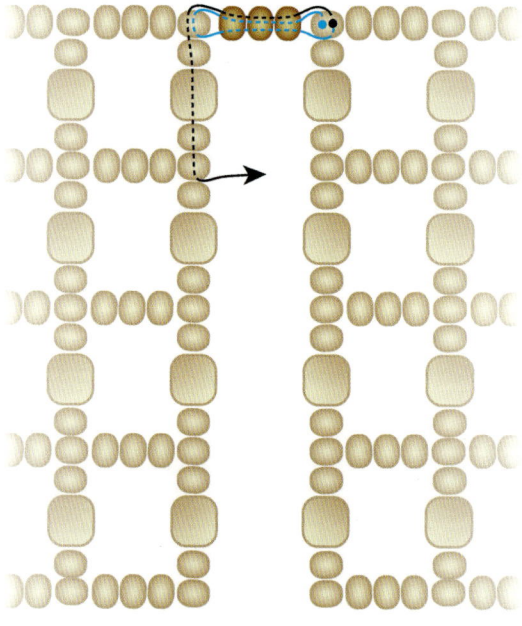

Step 4

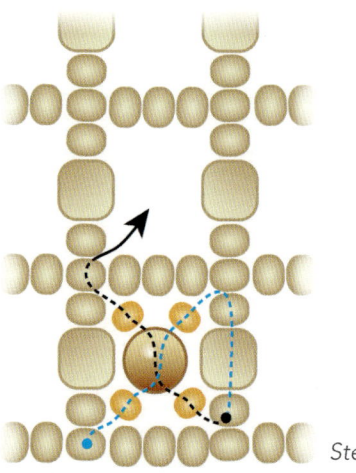

Step 5

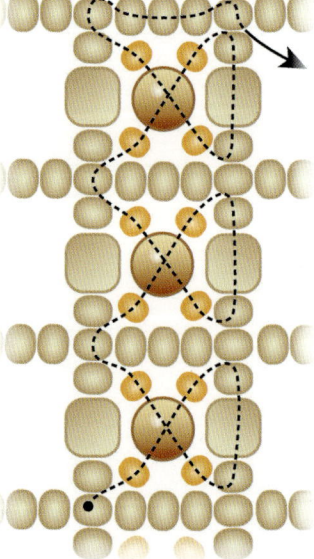

Step 6

Cattern's Tallie pendant and cuff

## The Ruffle

All the beads for the first row, to begin the peyote stitch foundation, will join into a continuous loop. The first row is peyote stitch, which will tighten this thread, so allow room for the beads of the next row, by easing up on the thread tension.

### Ruffle row 1:

1. With a 1.5m/60" length of thread, leave a 15cm/6" tail and use a stop bead. Pass through the 2nd hole of an H bead on the end of a row.

2. Place 3B, between each H bead of the row.

3. At the end of the row, place 7B between this and the end H bead of the next row.

4. Keep working up and down the rows until all the H beads are linked.

   At the end of the last row, pick up 7B and pass through the H bead started from. Now the beads form a continuous wave around the tube.

   Keep the stop bead in place, and release it to ease off the thread (if you need to).

5. a) Exit 1H, peyote stitch single B beads until you are back at the start. The thread will always pass through the H beads in this row.
   b) Step up at the end of the row to exit the 1st bead added at the start of this row. Remove the stop bead.

### Ruffle row 2:

6. Now we combine peyote stitch and netting:

   Place 1G, 1D, 1G into 1st peyote space, place 1D into next peyote space. Repeat until you reach the end of the row (single D beads will sit above H beads).

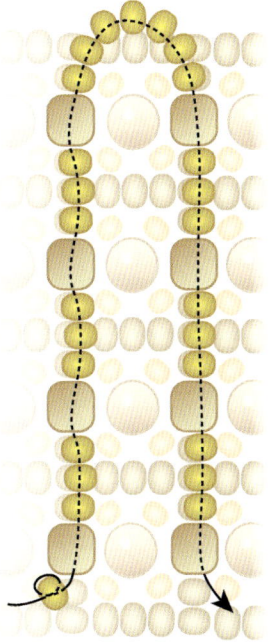

*Steps 1–3*

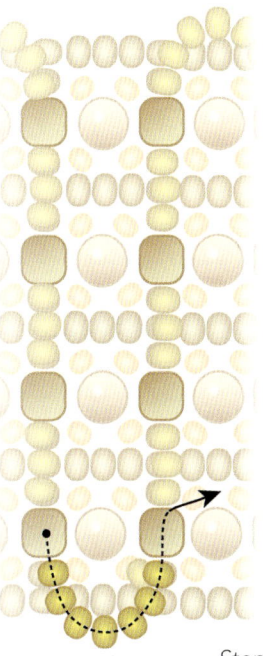

*Step 4*

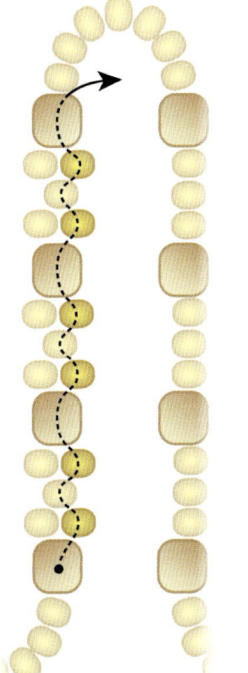
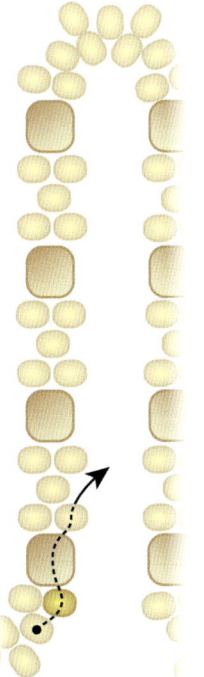
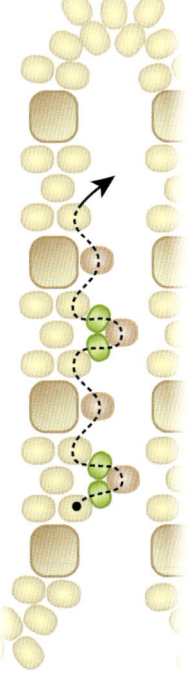

*Step 5a*  *Step 5b*  *Step 6*

– 19 –

*Cattern's Tallie pendant and cuff*

**Ruffle row 3:**

7. Peyote stitch 2G between each D bead of the previous row.

**Ruffle row 4:**

8. The last row is netting, and again the sets alternate: place 3E over single D beads, and 3C over the D of the 1G, 1D, 1G sets.

9. Pass through the beads of the last row a 2nd time, omitting the centre bead of each set of 3 beads. This will help the beads lie in neat triangles and strengthen the edge of the beadwork.

**End caps**

These are worked from the edge beads at each end of the base tube.

1. Attach a new thread and exit a centre bead of a stitch on one edge of the tube.

2. Pick up 1D, 1J, 1E stalk, 1A tip. Pass back through 1E, 1J, pick up 1D, pass through the next centre A bead of the next stitch on the base edge. Pull the thread up and the edge 3A beads will pull in slightly, which is just how you want it to be as this creates a slight decrease.

3. Repeat step 2, to place a stitch between each centre A bead on the edge (8 stitches in total).

4. Pass up through the beads to exit a tip bead, add the spacer round of 1A between each tip bead.

   Secure this round by passing through the beads a 2nd time. Exit a tip bead.

5. Place a stitch over each tip bead: 1C stalk, 1A tip. Step up to exit a tip bead.

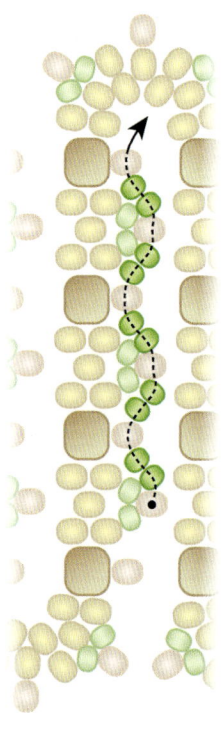

*Step 7*

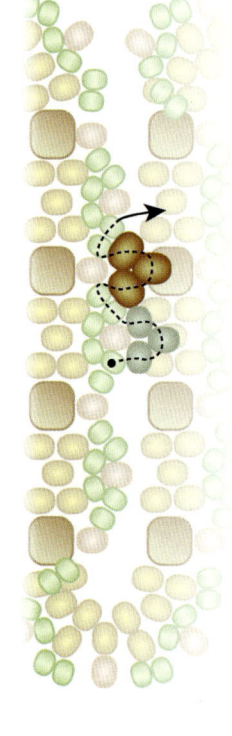

*Step 8*

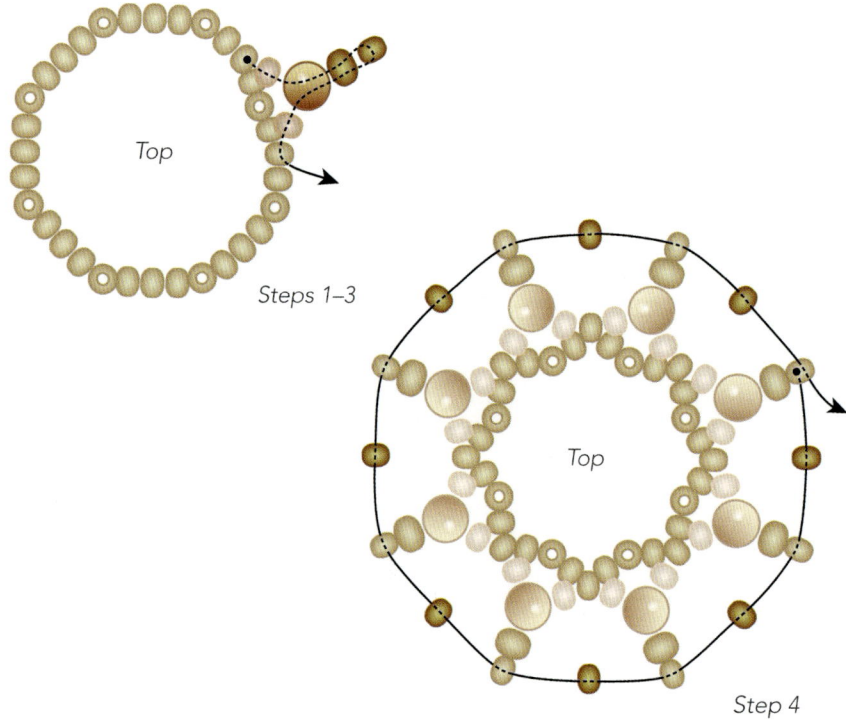

*Steps 1–3*

*Step 4*

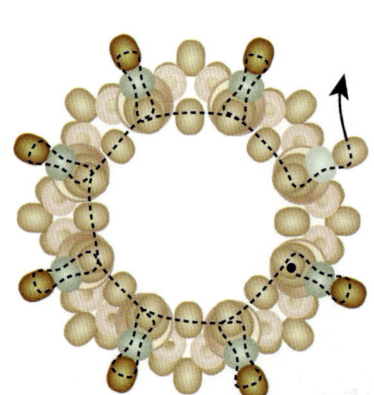

*Step 5*

Cattern's Tallie pendant and cuff

6. Pass through all the tip beads to draw them into a neat ring.

7. a) Stitch 1J across the aperture, then weave through the beads to exit 1C. Now to make a loop across the top of the end cap. There are 8C (stalk beads of the last round of stitches), 4 will be used to attach the loop, leaving 2 spare on either side.
   b) Exit 1C, with the needle pointing downwards. Pick up 1A, then pass through the next 1C, with the needle pointing upwards

8. a) Pick up 1D, 1B, 9F, 1B, 1D. Pass down through the 3rd C from the start point.
   b) Pick up 1A, pass up through the next C.

9. Pick up 1D, then pass back through 1B, 9F, 1B. Pick up 1D, pass down through 1C started from in step 8.

10. Retrace the threadpath to strengthen the loop. Finish off the thread tails.

    Repeat all the end cap steps at the other end of the base, weave the thread and tails back into the beadwork, then leave this piece to one side.

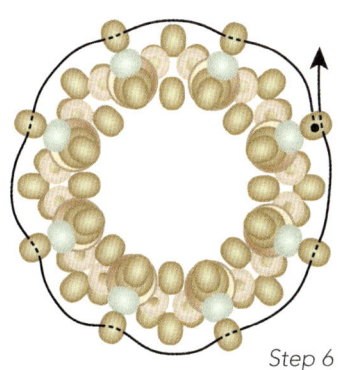
*Step 6*

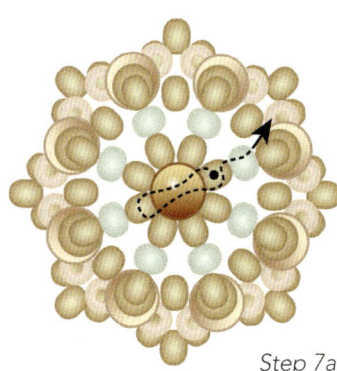
*Step 7a*

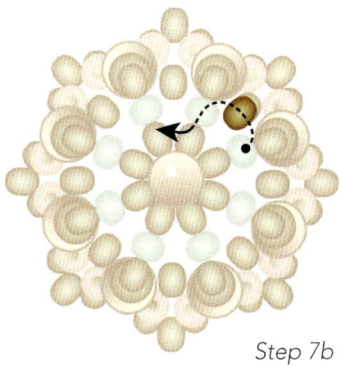
*Step 7b*

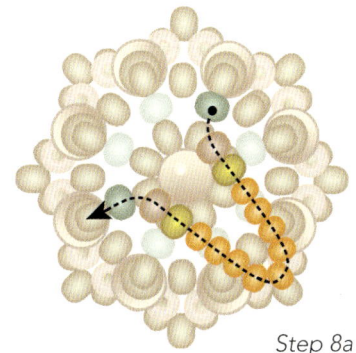
*Step 8a*

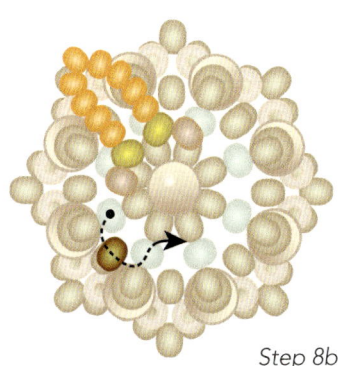
*Step 8b*

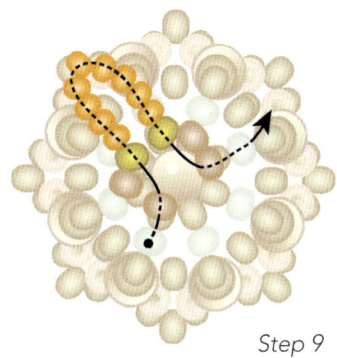
*Step 9*

> "I seek a pearl of rarest worth,
> By the shore of some bright wave:
> Such a gem, whose wondrous birth
> Radiance to all nature gave."
>
> Remy Belleau
> "The Pearl", to the Queen of Navarre

## Caged drop bead pendant (Make 1)

For this element a cage of netting is worked over a tear drop shaped bead. Keep the thread tension easy for the netted section, you can always go back through the rows to tighten further if needed.

1. With 1.5m/60" thread, leave a 30cm/12" tail long enough to make a loop like the one on the end of the ruffle bead. Pick up 8A and secure in a ring. Exit a bead on the ring.

2. Place an Albion stitch over each bead on the ring, 1C stalk, 1A tip.

3. Add a spacer round of 1A between each tip bead.

4. a) Place a stitch over each tip bead of the previous round: 1E stalk, 1J, 1A tip, 1D, 1A. This time the stitch has three tip beads, so you will just pass back through the stalk beads as usual.
   b) Step up to exit 1D centre tip bead.

5. Pick up 3A, 1B, 1D, 1C, 1D, 1B, 3A, pass through the next 1D centre tip bead. Repeat to join each centre tip bead. At the end of the round step up to exit the centre 1C bead of the 1st set.

6. Pick up 1D, 1B, 3A, 1D, 3A, 1B, 1D, pass through the centre 1C bead of the next set of the previous round.

   Repeat until you are back at the start, then step up to exit the centre D bead of the 1st set added.

*Step 1*

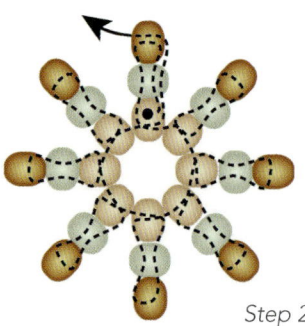

*Step 2*

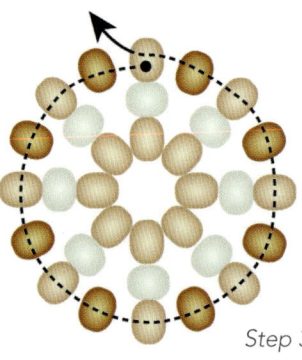

*Step 3*

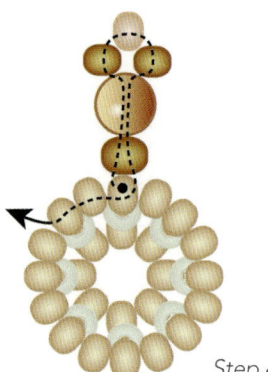

*Step 4a*

*Step 4b*

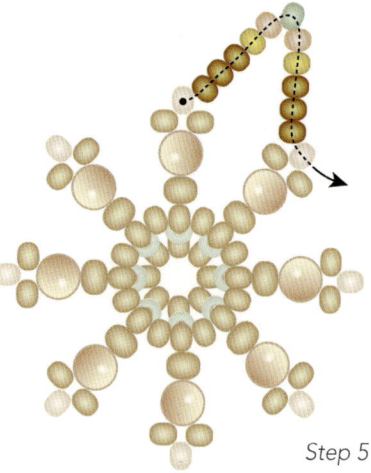

*Step 5*

*Step 6*

Cattern's Tallie pendant and cuff

**7** Place 1D between each centre 1D bead. Put K into the beadwork, fat end uppermost; the hole of the K is not used. Draw the ring of beads tight. (**Note**: wrangle the beads until they settle around the drop bead neatly. Pass through the round of D beads a 2nd time to tighten it.

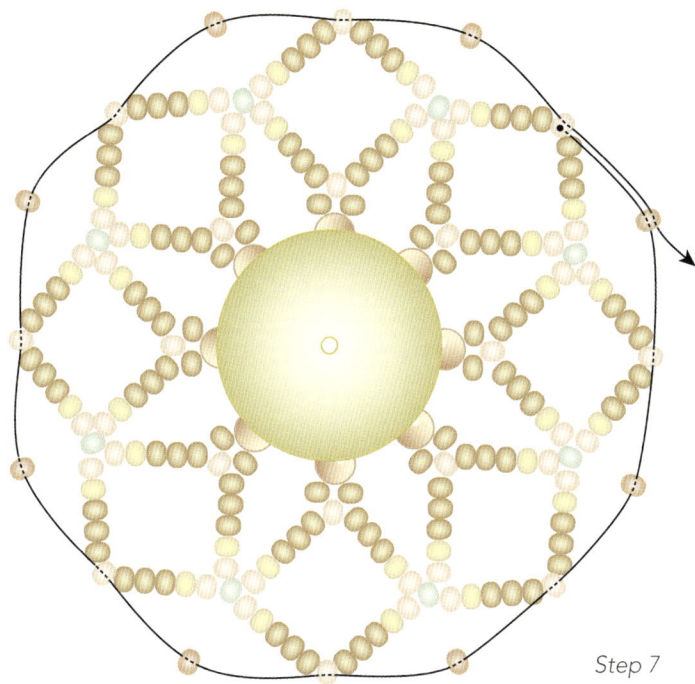

*Step 7*

**8** Place a stitch over alternate beads of the round. 1C stalk, 1A tip.

**9** Step up to exit the tip bead, then pass through all the tip beads to join them into a neat ring.

**10** Stitch 1J across the ring of beads. Return to the thread left at the start and make a loop exactly as for the ruffle bead... but... remember to pass the beads through the ruffle bead loop before securing them to form the link. Weave the thread and tails back into the beadwork and finish off.

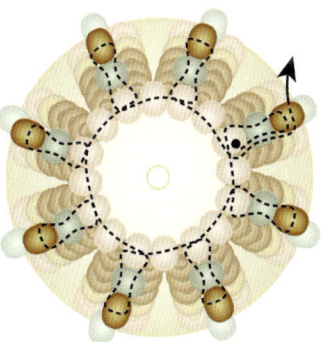

*Steps 8–9*

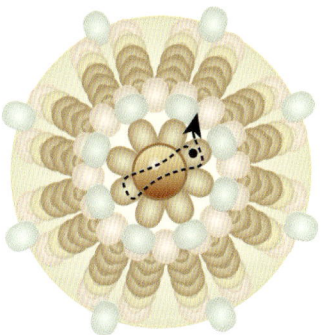

*Step 10*

– 23 –         *Cattern's Tallie pendant and cuff*

## Caged pearl (Make 4)

Now the pendant section is completed, next are the beaded 10mm pearls that form the base of the necklace. Each bead is worked in the same way, then linked with beaded chain.

With a very long wingspan, leave a 30cm/12" tail, as for the caged drop pendant.

1. Make a ring of 8A, then place a stitch over each bead on the ring, 1C stalk, 1A tip.

2. Add a spacer round of 1A between each tip bead.

3. a) Place a stitch over each tip bead of the previous round, 1E stalk, 1B, 3A tip.
   b) At the end of the round step up to exit centre A bead of stitch tip.

4. Place 1D, 1C, 1D, between each centre A tip bead.

   At the end of the round step up to exit the centre C bead of 1st set added.

5. Place 1D, 1A, 1D, between each centre C bead of previous round.

   At the end of the round step up to exit 1D bead of 1st set added.

6. Pick up 1A, 1B, 1E stalk, 1A tip, pass back through 1E, 1B, pick up 1A, pass through 2nd D of 1st set of previous round. Pass through 1C and 1D of next set to be in place to repeat the stitch.

   Continue round until you have 8 stitches, then step up to exit 1A tip bead. Place an L into the beading. The hole of the L is not used.

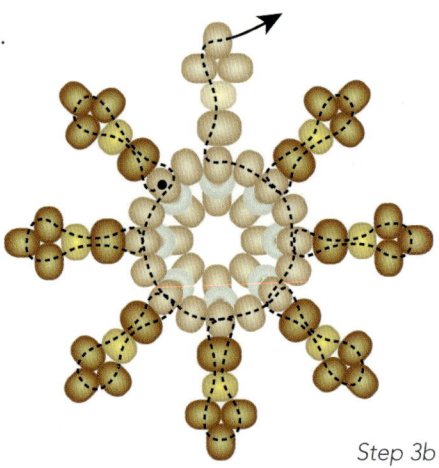

*Steps 1–3*

*Step 3b*

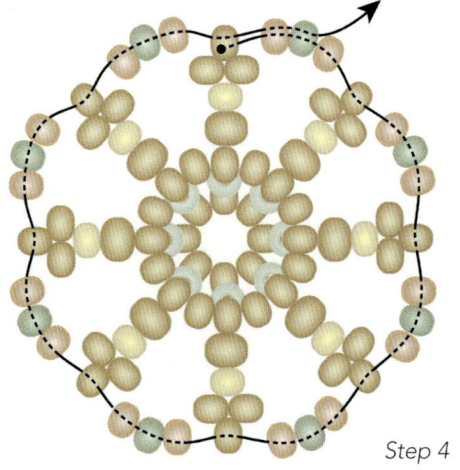

*Step 4*

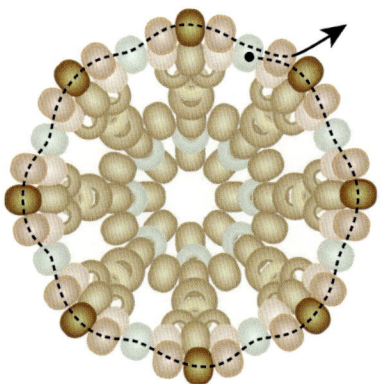

*Step 5*

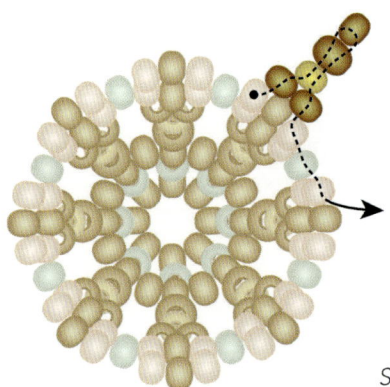

*Step 6*

*Cattern's Tallie pendant and cuff*

7. Add a spacer round of 1A between each 1A tip bead. Pass through the beads a 2nd time to secure them into a neat ring.

8. a) Place a stitch over tip beads of the previous round, 1C stalk, 1A tip.
   b) At the end of the round step up and pass through all the tip beads.
   c) Stitch a J across the aperture. (See figure 10 on page 23.)

9. Add a loop exactly as for the drop bead and end caps of the ruffle bead. Weave the thread and tails back into the beadwork to finish off.

   Work steps 1–9 three more times, so you have 4 caged pearls in total.

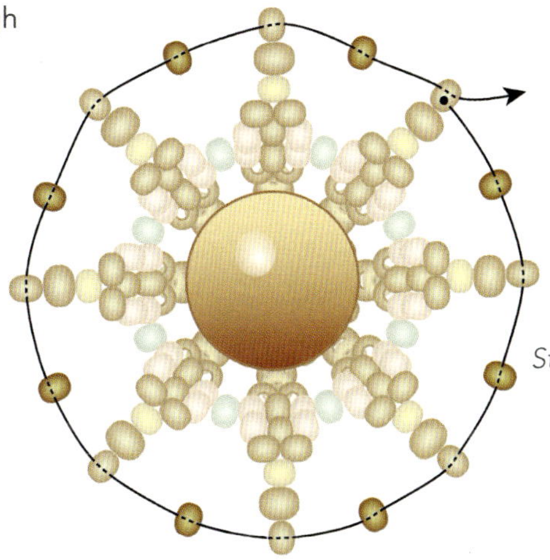

*Step 7*

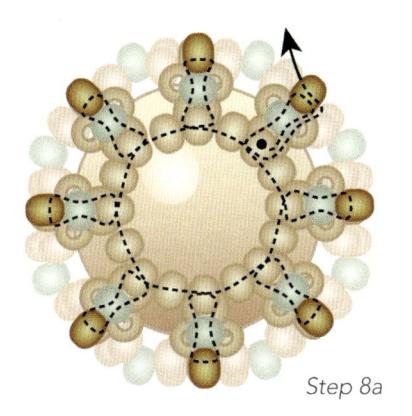

*Step 8a*

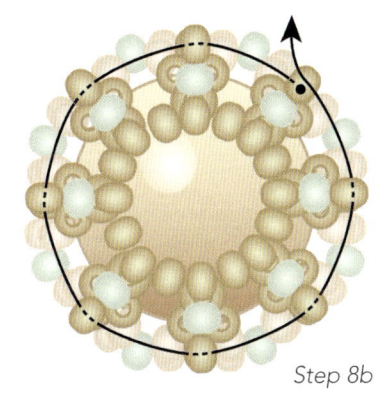

*Step 8b*

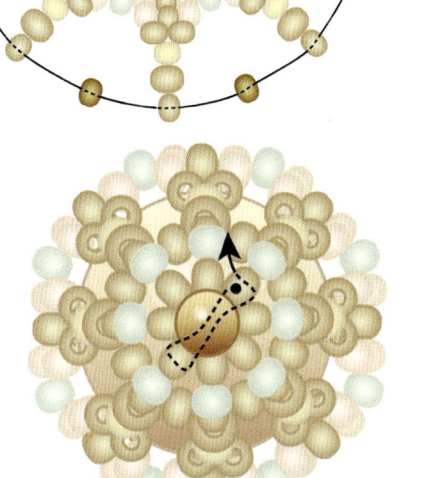

*Step 8c*

## Chain

**Centre section**:

1. With 50cm of thread, leave a 15cm/6" tail. Pick up 1E, 1D, 1C, 15F. Pass needle and thread through a loop at the end of a caged pearl.

   Pass back through 1C, pick up 1D, pass back through 1E.

2. Pick up 3A, 3B, 3C, 3B, 3A, 1E, 1D, 1C, 15F.

   Slide the ruffle pendant on to the strand of beads, then pass needle and thread through a loop at the end of another caged pearl.

3. Pass through 1C, pick up 1D, then pass back through all the beads to the start point and secure the thread tails. (You can weave through all the beads of the chain section a 2nd time to strengthen it.) Finish off the thread tails.

*Step 1*

*10mm pearl*

*10mm pearl*

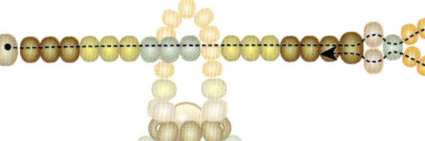

*10mm pearl*

*Ruffle pendant*

*Steps 2–3*

Cattern's Tallie pendant and cuff

**Side sections**:

A second chain section joins the other two caged pearls, one each to each of the caged pearls of the centre section. This section is then repeated, linking through the end loops of F beads, until the necklace sides are the required length. The sample has seven links to each side after the second caged pearl.

Start with a wingspan of thread, this will be enough to make several chain sections. Allow yourself a 15cm/6" tail for finishing the thread end for each chain section.

1. Pick up 1E, 1D, 1C, 15F. Pass needle and thread through a loop at the end of a caged pearl.

   Pass back through 1C, pick up 1D, pass back through 1E.

   Pick up 2A, 2B, 2C, 2B, 2A, 1E, 1D, 1C, 15F.

2. Pass through the loop of the next caged pearl. Pass back through 1C, pick up 1D, pass back through all the beads to the start point and secure the thread tails. (You can weave through all the beads of the chain section a 2nd time to strengthen it.) Finish the thread tails by weaving back into the beads.

   As you work, pass the 1st loop of a new chain section through the closed loop of the previous one.

   Attach a jump ring through the last end loop of each side, and attach a clasp to one of the jump rings (or both, if you use a push-shut-style clasp).

*Steps 1–2*

*Fascinating fact:*

*Piccadilly in London is so named after the popular short ruff known as a Piccadillie, which was made by a tailor who had premises on that street.*

Cattern's Tallie pendant and cuff

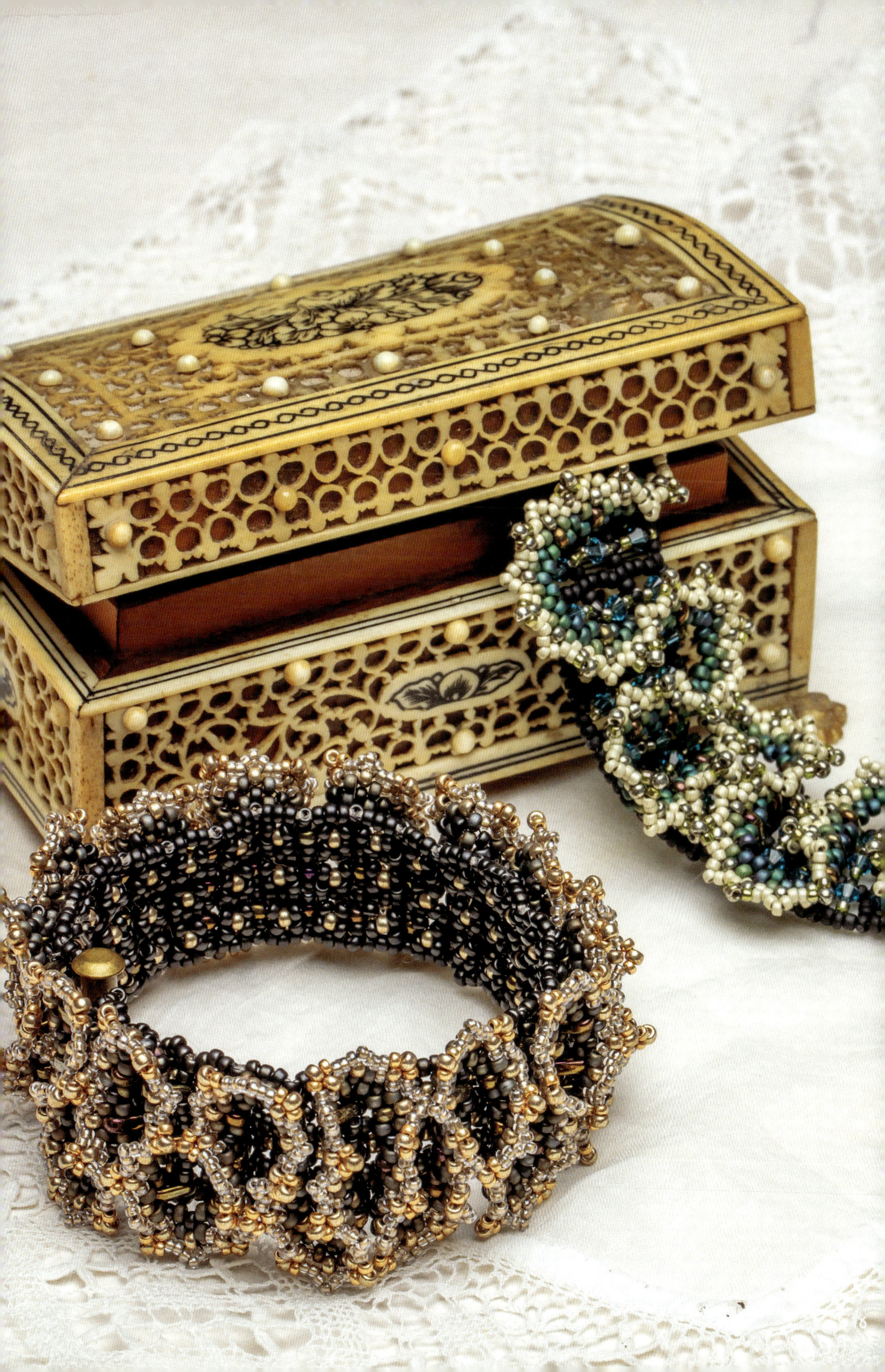

## Cattern's Tallie Cuff

**Completed cuff size**: 27 rows plus clasp rows 18cm/7¼". To add more length please note 3 rows = 2cm/⅞": The steps to make the cuff are the same as for the ruffle bead (page 17), but the start row has fewer beads and the colour sequence of seed beads used is slightly different.

### You will need:

15g x Miyuki seed beads size 11° 2011 (matte metallic charcoal) (A)
6g x Miyuki seed beads size 11° 2002 (matte metallic silvergrey) (B)
6g x Miyuki seed beads size 11° 4204 (duracoat galvanised champagne gold) (C)
5g x Miyuki seed beads size 15° 1001 (silver lined crystal AB) (D) (orange in diagram)
5g x Miyuki seed beads size 15° 4204 (duracoat galvanised champagne gold) (E) (green in diagram)
87 x CzechMate half tile 2-hole beads (gunmetal iris) (F)
3-loop sliding clasp

### Make the base

1. With a long wingspan of thread and leaving a 40cm/16" tail (to be used later to work a row of stitches and attach the clasp), position a stop bead. Pick up 2A, 1F, 3A, 1F, 3A, 1F, 2A and push them down to the stop bead.

2. Now add the stitches; these are worked in the same way as for the ruffle bead (page 17).

3. Continue working until the bracelet is the required length (sample has 29 completed stitch and spacer rows). Finish off this thread tail, but leave the long one at the start.

### Embellish the base

It's fine to skip this step if you want a lighter, more airy bracelet, but the embellishment adds strength to the base and adds a studded texture that can just be seen beneath the lacy ruffle.

1. Start at the end without the tail and leave a similar length tail. Exit the end bead of the last row.

2. Pick up 1A, 1C, 1A. Pass through 1A, 1F, 1A at the side of the same aperture.

3. a) Pick up 1A, pass through the 1C of step 2, pick up 1A and pass through the next tip bead of the end row.
   b) Repeat to embellish each aperture of the row, then weave through the beads of the base to start the next row of embellishment. Keep working until each aperture has a little diagonal cross embellishment.

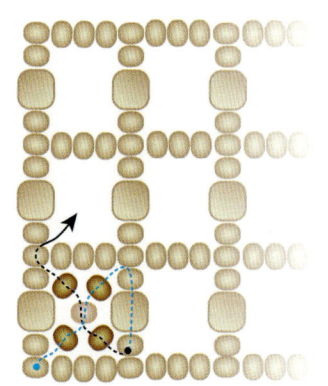

*Steps 1–3*

*Cattern's Tallie pendant and cuff*

## The ruffle for the bracelet

To start the ruffle, the second holes of the F beads are joined with a strand of seed beads. This forms the base row for the peyote stitch and netting ruffle. Because the bracelet has ends, whereas the ruffle bead was a tube, the start and finish of each ruffle row is slightly different.

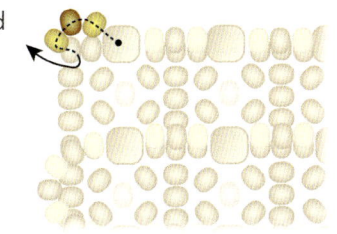

**Ruffle row 1:**

1. a) Use a stop bead, (you may need to ease this starting thread later if you tend to bead with a tight tension). Exit the end bead of the 1st row with F beads on the base.
   b) Pick up 1B, 1A, 1B, pass through the 2nd hole of the 1st (nearest) F bead.

2. Place 1B, 1A, 1B, between each F bead of the row.

3. At the end of the row place 1B, 1A, 1B, 1A, 1B ,1A, 1B (7 beads) between this and the end F bead of the next row. Now you will work back across the F beads of this row.

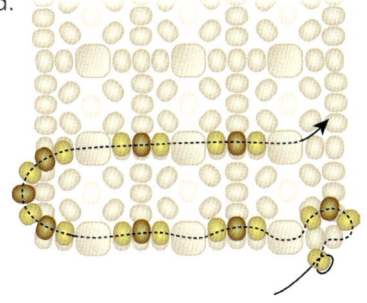

*Step 1*

*Steps 2–3*

**Ruffle row 2:**

4. a) Working in B beads, peyote stitch along the new row of beads, placing the beads so that you pass through the F beads. The diagram shows the turn to get started, the 1st straight row, and the 1st end curve.
   b) Turn at the end of the row through the bead of the base row, then step back up to exit the last peyote stitched bead.

**Ruffle row 3:**

5. Now we combine peyote stitch and netting:

   a) Place 1D, 1C, 1D, into the 1st peyote space, place 1C into the next peyote space. Repeat until you reach the end of the row (single C beads will sit above F beads).
   b) Turn at the end of the row to exit the last C bead added.

*Step 4a*

*Step 4b*

*Step 5a*

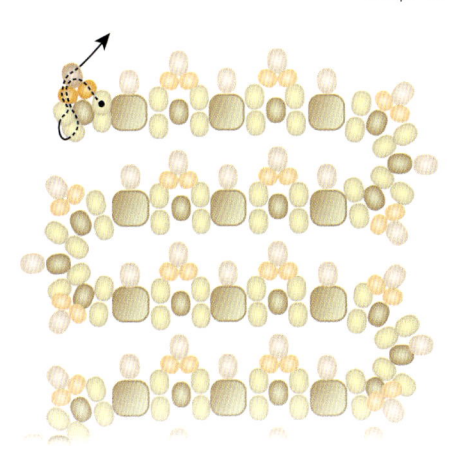

*Step 5b*

### Fascinating fact:

*Ruffs were often stiffened with dyed starch. Pink, and yellow were popular, as was blue, until Elizabeth decreed her disfavour of the colour because it was the colour of the flag of Scotland. It is said that thereafter only prostitutes wore blue starched lace.*

**Ruffle row 4:**

**6**    a) Peyote stitch 2D between each C bead of the previous row.
b) At the end of the row, turn through the beadwork to exit the last 2C added.

**Ruffle row 5:**

**7**    The last row is netting, and again the sets alternate:

a) Place 3D over single C beads (1C of step 5), and 1E, 1C, 1E over the (1D, 1C, 1D of step 5) C beads.
b) Turn and step up to exit the last bead of the last set of 3 beads added.

**8**    Pass back through the beads of the last row a 2nd time, omitting the centre bead of each set of 3 beads. This will help the beads lie in neat triangles and strengthen the edge of the beadwork.

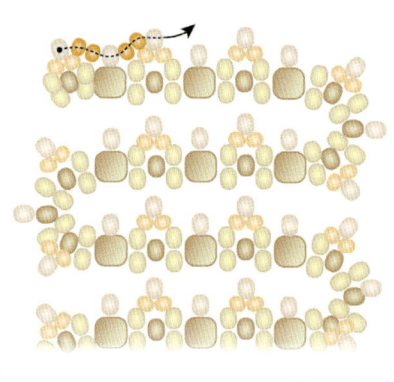

*Step 6a*

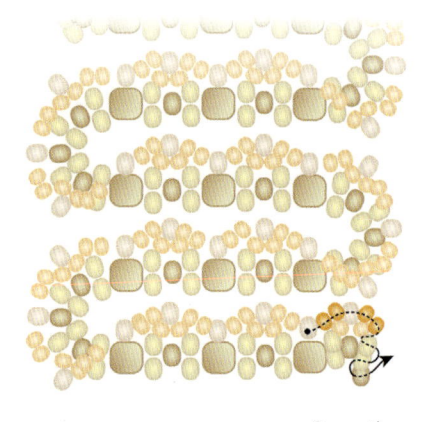

*Step 6b*

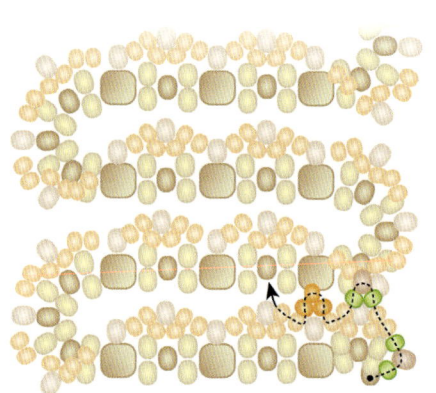

*Step 7*

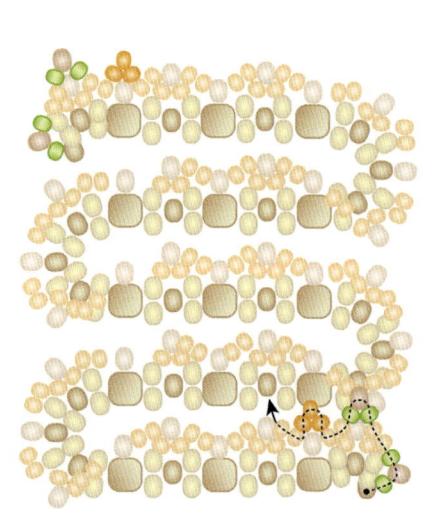

*Step 8*

## Attaching a clasp

The bracelet is fastened with a vertical loop clasp, and a row of stitches is added to each end to hold the clasp loops in place.

**1**    Thread a needle on to 1 of the 40cm/16" tails and work a stitch over each tip bead of the end row, 1A stalk, 1A tip. Step up to exit the tip bead of the last stitch. (Diagrams show base without the ruffle).

**2**    Work a spacer row. Pick up 3A and pass the needle through the 1st loop of the clasp and the next tip bead. Repeat to capture the next 2 loops of the clasp and the next 2 tip beads.

**3**    Turn through the beadwork and retrace the threadpath through the spacer row to strengthen it. Finish off the thread tail. Repeat at the other end of the bracelet with the 2nd set of loops on the clasp.

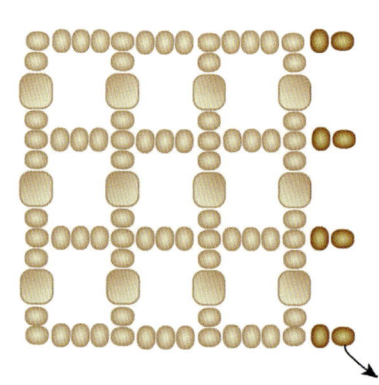

*Step 1*

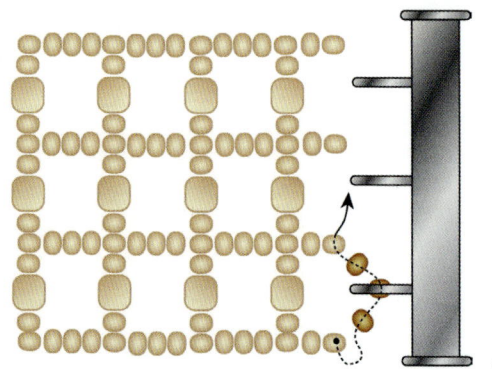

*Step 2*

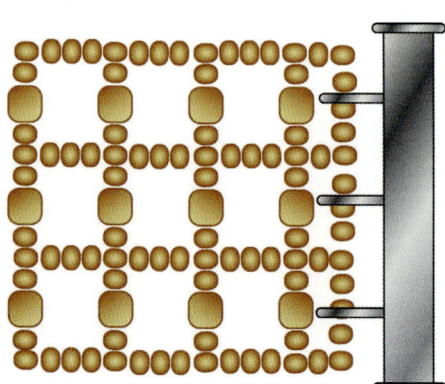

*Step 3*

*Cattern's Tallie pendant and cuff*

– 30 –

ANNE BOLEYN

## ANNE BOLEYN

November 14th, 1532 – St Erkenwald's Day. Dr Rowland Lee visibly trembled and, although the bitter wind had chilled him to the bone en route to the chapel, a trickle of sweat falteringly made its way down his cheek. Every fibre of his being was silently screaming that this was wrong, but to protest risked the King's fury and a slow, agonising death. As the witnesses stood silently in the soft candlelight, darting nervous glances at one another, the iron ring of the chapel door creaked suddenly, and the door swung open allowing in a freezing blast. All heads turned to see Henry and Anne tumble in, stifling their laughter and, still bristling with passion and anticipation, attempting to adopt the sober mood of the little gathering. William, Henry's groom, followed them in and closed the great oak door, then bowed low as his master gently took Anne by the hand. Even now she doubted the reality of this night and wondered if it was a dream as Henry led the way up the aisle, never taking his eyes from hers. As they reached the altar, Henry paused and turned to his beautiful queen-to-be. He drew a velvet pouch from his cloak and placed it into Anne's hands, loosening the silk tie so that the contents spilled forth into her cupped palms. The jewels sparkled and gleamed in the flickering light and she could see the detailed royal rose symbols of the combined families that represented the throne of which she was going to become part. She raised her eyes to meet Henry's and smiled as they turned to take their vows.

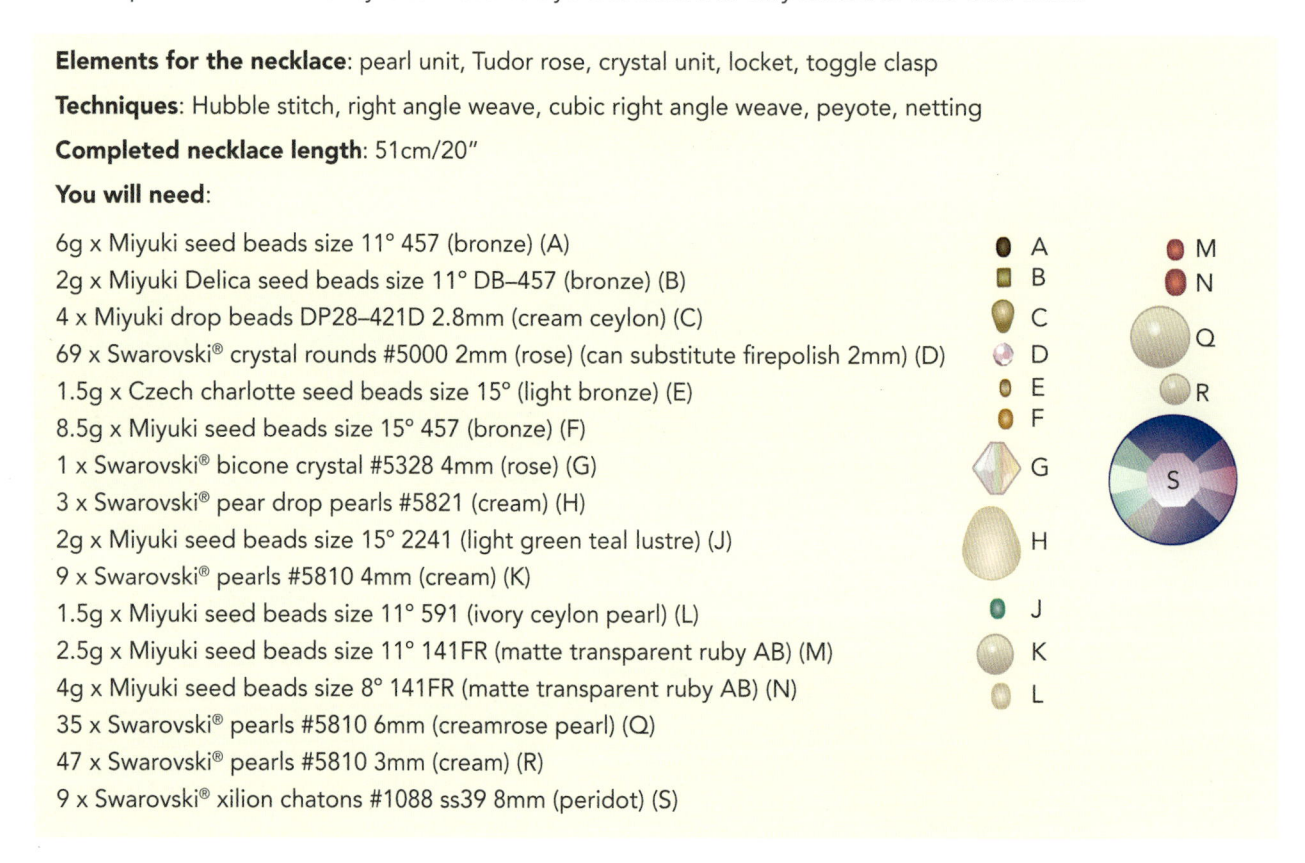

**Elements for the necklace**: pearl unit, Tudor rose, crystal unit, locket, toggle clasp

**Techniques**: Hubble stitch, right angle weave, cubic right angle weave, peyote, netting

**Completed necklace length**: 51cm/20"

**You will need**:

6g x Miyuki seed beads size 11° 457 (bronze) (A)
2g x Miyuki Delica seed beads size 11° DB–457 (bronze) (B)
4 x Miyuki drop beads DP28–421D 2.8mm (cream ceylon) (C)
69 x Swarovski® crystal rounds #5000 2mm (rose) (can substitute firepolish 2mm) (D)
1.5g x Czech charlotte seed beads size 15° (light bronze) (E)
8.5g x Miyuki seed beads size 15° 457 (bronze) (F)
1 x Swarovski® bicone crystal #5328 4mm (rose) (G)
3 x Swarovski® pear drop pearls #5821 (cream) (H)
2g x Miyuki seed beads size 15° 2241 (light green teal lustre) (J)
9 x Swarovski® pearls #5810 4mm (cream) (K)
1.5g x Miyuki seed beads size 11° 591 (ivory ceylon pearl) (L)
2.5g x Miyuki seed beads size 11° 141FR (matte transparent ruby AB) (M)
4g x Miyuki seed beads size 8° 141FR (matte transparent ruby AB) (N)
35 x Swarovski® pearls #5810 6mm (creamrose pearl) (Q)
47 x Swarovski® pearls #5810 3mm (cream) (R)
9 x Swarovski® xilion chatons #1088 ss39 8mm (peridot) (S)

> *"No more to you at this present, mine own darling, for the lack of time, but that I would you were in mine arms, or I in yours, for I think it long since I kissed you."*
>
> *From Henry's love letter to Anne*
> *16th September 1528*

Anne Boleyn

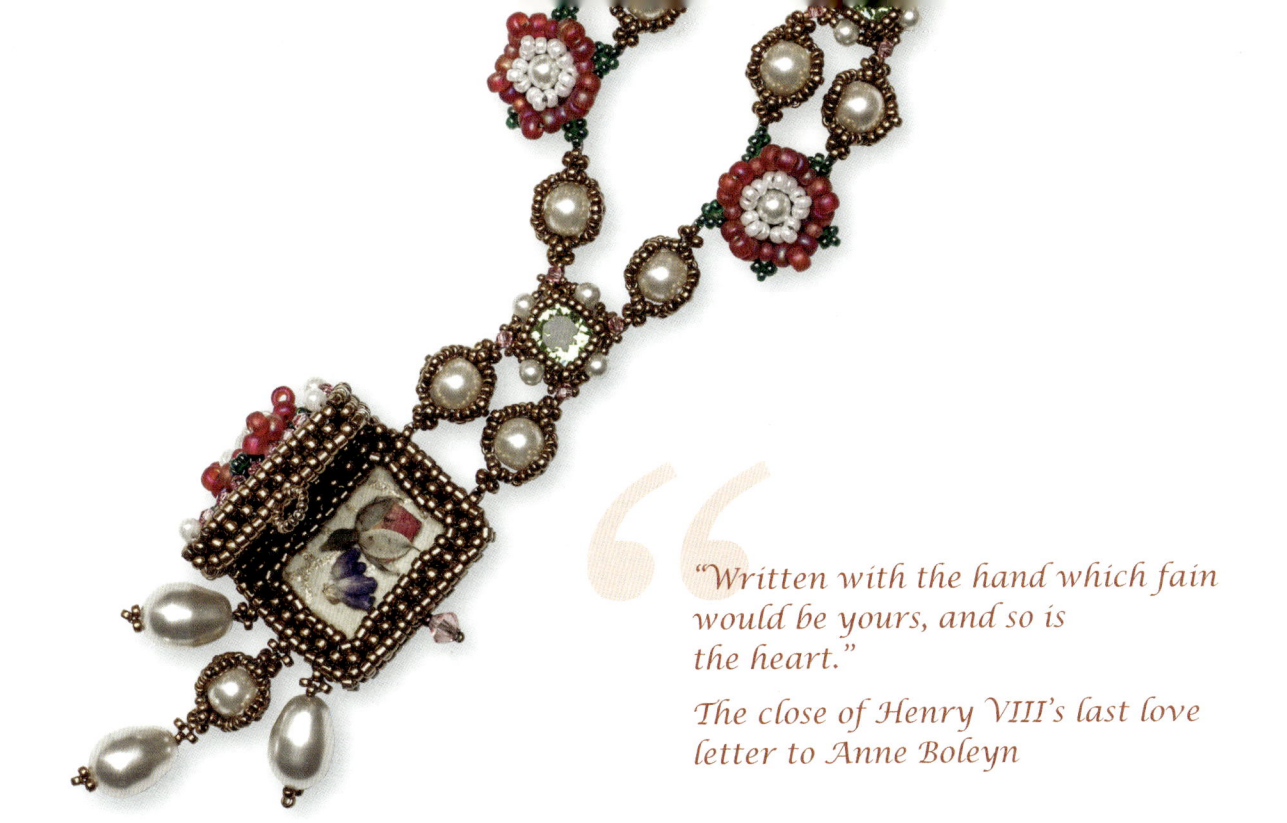

> "Written with the hand which fain would be yours, and so is the heart."
>
> The close of Henry VIII's last love letter to Anne Boleyn

## Locket

### Locket front (door) (make 1)

1. With a wingspan of thread, using A beads and working in CRAW, build a rectangular frame 7 CRAW units wide and 9 CRAW units long. Take care not to twist the beadwork as you join the last unit onto the 1st. Weave around to emerge as in the diagram.

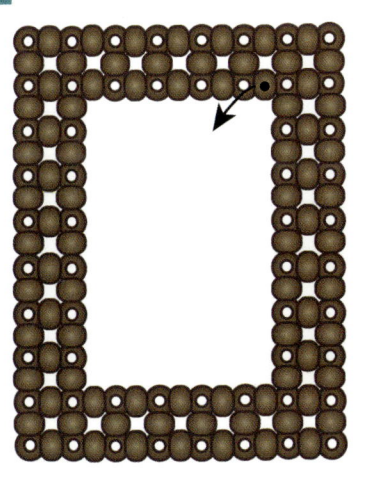

2. This is a reinforcing peyote row.

    a) With the thread emerging from a south bead, pick up 1B and pass through the south bead of the next stitch.
    b) Repeat a) 3 more times.
    c) To turn the corner, pick up 1B and pass down through the east bead of the neighbouring stitch. This B will sit at 45° to the rest.
    d) Continue placing B beads around the inner edge of the frame.
    e) Weave through to the back of the beadwork and reinforce the inner edge on the other side.
    f) Weave up to emerge from one of the north beads.

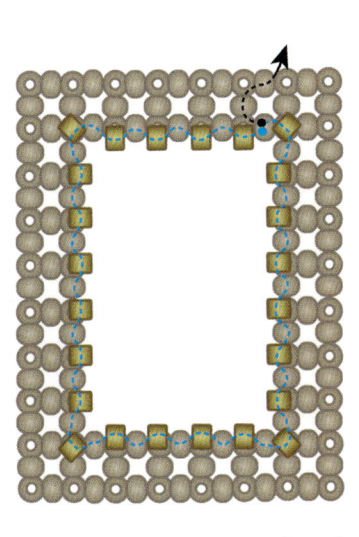

*Step 1*

*Step 2*

Anne Boleyn

**3**
a) Using B, add a P row around the outer edge on this side of the beadwork.
b) Weave through to the other side of the beadwork and add the P row around the corresponding outer edge.
c) Weave back to the 1st side to emerge as in the diagram.

**4** We're going to use a quick start for the fill-in RAW stitches.

a) **Stitch 1**: Pick up 2A and work a RAW stitch using the 2A in place at either side of the corner.
b) Pass through the adjacent B bead and on through the next A bead.
c) **Stitch 2**: Pick up 2A and work a RAW stitch.
d) Repeat step b).
e) **Stitches 3–4**: Repeat steps c) and d) 2 more times.
f) **Stitch 5**: Pass down through the west bead, pick up 1A and complete the RAW stitch.
g) Pass through the corner B bead and down through the next A, B and A beads.

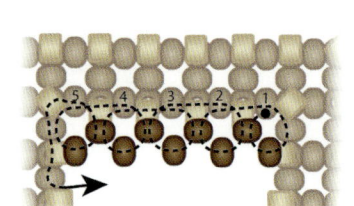

*Step 3*

**5**
a) Fill in the rest of the RAW stitches (5 stitches by 7 rows), monitoring the 5 stitches in each row. **Note**: The 6 beads marked X, are for positioning the TR (Tudor rose) later.
b) Weave on to exit the east bead of the end stitch on this face of the beadwork (just below the corner B bead), as in the diagram.

*Step 4*

**6** Pick up 1C and pass up through the west bead of this end stitch.

**7** Pick up 1D and pass up through the west bead of the 2nd stitch.

**8**
a) Repeat step 7 four more times.
b) Position 1C in the same way at the corner.
c) Weave around the corner stitch of the frame, to emerge as in the diagram.
d) Rotate the frame through 90° to work along the side, so that you can still make the same passing motion with the needle.
e) Continue positioning D beads down the side to the next corner.

**9** Complete the frame embellishment with the C and D beads. Weave on to emerge from the top of the end stitch east bead, as in the diagram.

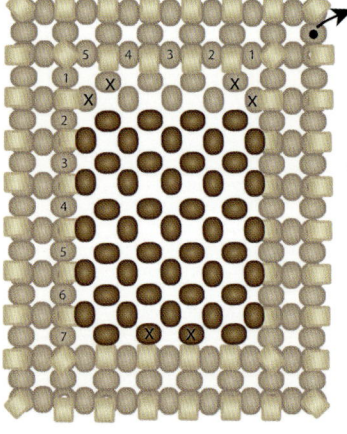

*Step 5*

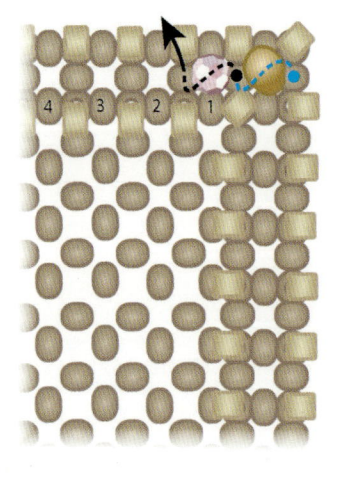

*Steps 6–7*

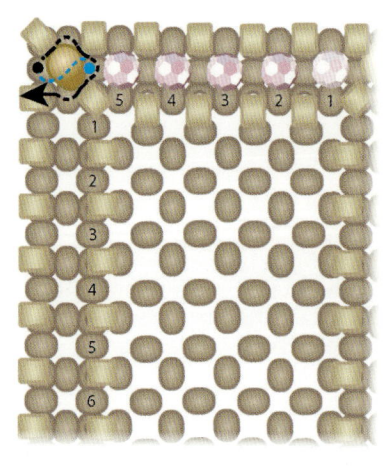

*Step 8*

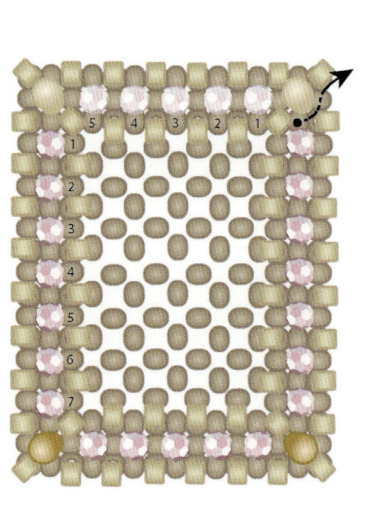

*Step 9*

Anne Boleyn

**10** Turn the beadwork so you are looking at it from the side, as in the diagram.

Weave down to emerge from the 5th A bead (the central one) along the edge.

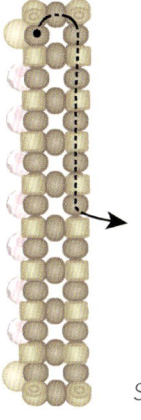

**11** a) Pick up 15E and pass into the A bead again, making a ring.
b) Pass around all 15E and A once more.
c) Don't finish off, as you may need to adjust the loop size, when you've made the locket back, with its button.

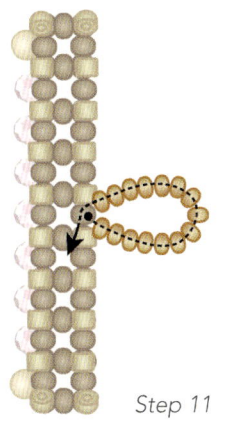

**Locket back**

**12** a) Work steps 1–3a only.
b) Now weave through to emerge from an A bead at the non-reinforced edge. Place the completed locket front on your work mat, embellished side down and set the locket back beside it, long sides together, with the non-reinforced edge towards you. The 2 adjacent long sides are going to be hinged together by sharing the B beads along that edge.
c) Work a P row around the outside edge, sharing the B beads of the locket front on one long side only – do not share any of the corner beads as this will not allow free movement of the hinge.
d) Weave through to emerge from an A bead at the inner edge of the back of the locket back.

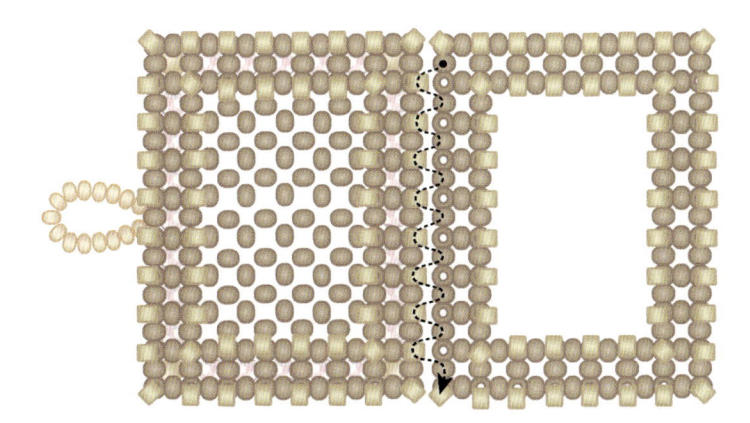

*Step 10*

*Step 11*

*Step 12*

**13** Work steps 4–5 to fill in the RAW panel at the back of the locket. Once complete, the little recessed area is a great place for an image, pressed flowers or maybe a tiny lock of hair!

**14** Button closure on the locket back:

a) Weave down from the top edge to emerge from the north A bead of the 5th RAW stitch down on the outer edge of the locket back.
b) Pick up 1F, 1G, 1E.
c) Missing out the E bead, pass back through G and F in the opposite direction.
d) Continue on through the adjacent A bead as in the diagram.

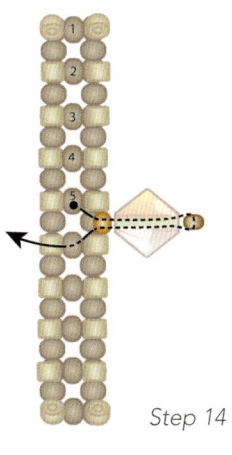

**15** a) Follow the threadpath through F, G and E, and back again.
b) Pass through the original A bead as in the diagram.
c) Snuggle up so that the little button sits perfectly and firmly in the centre between the 2 A beads. It may help to grip E with finger and thumb, while pulling the working thread.
d) Following the threadpath in the diagram, weave down to the bottom edge of the frame to exit the south A bead, as in the diagram.

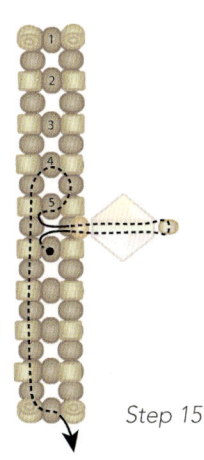

*Step 14*

*Step 15*

*Anne Boleyn*

**16** Let's add the dangles! With the locket open like a little book in front of you, focus only on the bottom edge of the locket back.

Weave around to exit bead 1, as in the diagram, then add a connector bead thus:

a) Pick up 1F and pass down through bead 2.
b) Pass back through F in the opposite direction.
c) Pass through bead 1 from the threadless side.

*Step 16*

**17** Pass into the newly positioned F bead.

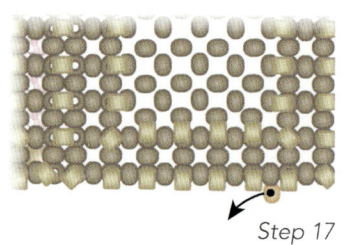

**18** Pick up 3F and work a RAW stitch, stepping up out of the south bead.

*Step 17*

**19** a) Pick up 1H, 3F and pass back through H in the opposite direction.
b) Continue on through the south, west and north beads of the RAW stitch, as in the diagram.
c) Weave on to exit bead 3 (see step 16 diagram), ready to add another connector bead.

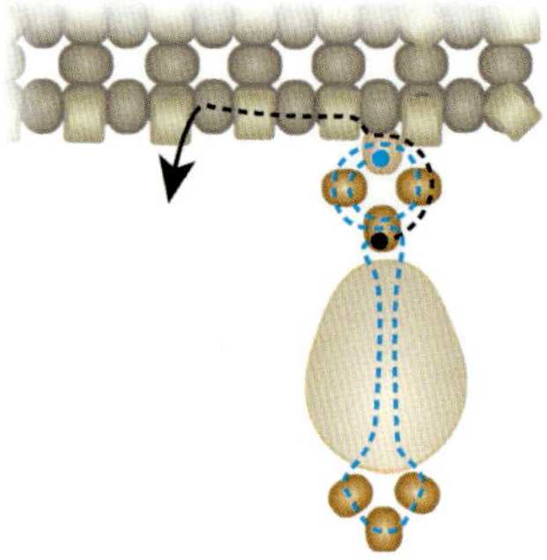

**20** a) Repeat step 16 to add the connector bead between beads 3 and 4.
b) Weave back into the locket base and on, to emerge from bead 5 (in case you're wondering, we'll work the central dangle last).
c) Repeat steps 16–19 to add another pearl dangle between beads 5 and 6, and finish off.
d) Now, for the central dangle we'll attach a PU (Pearl unit) (instructions on page 39) thus: using either the working thread or the tail thread of a PU, pick up 1F, pass through the central connector bead on the locket bottom (between beads 3 and 4), pick up 1F and pass through the PU bead from which the thread is emerging, making a RAW stitch.
e) Repeat the circuit and weave into the locket base to finish off.
f) Using the awaiting thread at the other end of the PU, follow steps 18–19 to add a pearl drop, but weave into the PU to finish off.

*Steps 18–19*

**21** a) The TR embellishment is sewn into position in the front locket panel using leaves at 'clock face positions' 10, 2 and 6.
b) Make a TR (instructions below) and bring the working thread to emerge from the tip of the 10 o'clock leaf and the tail thread from the 6 o'clock leaf.
c) Refer to step 5 diagram which shows beads marked X; these will be used to secure the TR leaves.
d) Place the TR on the front panel of the locket with the working thread leaf positioned at the top, left-hand corner.
e) Secure the leaf by weaving down through the 2 corner beads of the front panel, and back into the leaf tip.
f) Weave on, via the TR or the panel beads, to the leaf tip bead positioned at the top, right-hand corner (2 o'clock) and secure it as for the 1st leaf, in the beads marked X. Finish off.
g) Using the tail thread emerging from the 6 o'clock leaf, secure it by weaving through the 2 central beads marked X at the bottom edge of the panel, and back into the leaf tip bead.
h) Finish off in the panel beads and locket bottom edge.

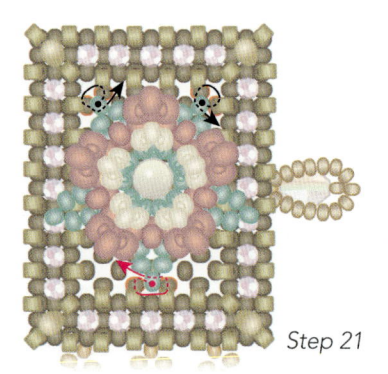

*Step 20*

*Step 21*

Anne Boleyn

22. The locket itself is attached to 2 PUs, via 2 connector beads on the top edge of the locket back.

   a) Using step 16 diagram as a guide, work a new thread (0.25m/10") into the top edge of the locket back, to emerge from the A bead at position 1.
   b) Add an F connector bead at position 1–2, and another at 5–6.
   c) Finish off.

## Tudor rose (TR) (Make 9)

1. With 1m/40" thread and pick up 5J. Pass through all 5J again and the 1st J once more, making a ring.

2. This is a row of circular Hubble stitch and the 5J are the awaiting body beads:

   a) Pick up 2J (arm beads), pass again through the body bead below and on through the 1st of the 2J just picked up.
   b) Pick up 1J (head bead) and pass down through the awaiting arm bead.

3. a) Pick up 2J and backstitch through the body bead on the ring.
   b) Continue on through the 1st of the 2J just picked up, in the same direction as before.
   c) Repeat step 2b) to complete the 2nd Hubble.

4. a) Complete the remaining 3 Hubble stitches and close the row by passing up the arm of the 1st Hubble and on through the head bead as in the diagram.
   b) Secure this join by passing around all 4 beads of the 1st Hubble stitch again. The beadwork has become cup-shaped.

5. a) Pick up 1K and pass through the next-but-one head bead.
   b) Pass back through K in the opposite direction.
   c) Pass through the head bead adjacent to the one from which the thread was emerging.

6. a) Using L, work another row of Hubble on the heads of the previous row. Close the row in exactly the same way as in step 4 (pass up into the arm bead and on through the head bead).
   b) Finish off the tail thread (except if you are using this TR as the embellishment on the locket front), but keep the working thread.

7. Viewing the beadwork from the back, weave down to emerge from the closest J head bead.

8. I've rotated the diagram so we can start from the top. This is a HorSO Hubble stitch row where a spacer bead will be introduced between each stitch. The 1st stitch is a normal Hubble. Work step 2 using M beads.

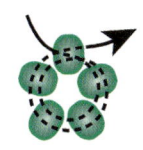

*Step 1*

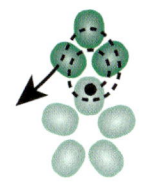

*Step 2*

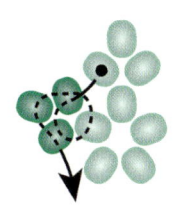

*Step 3*

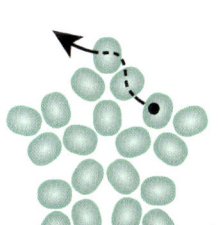

*Step 4*

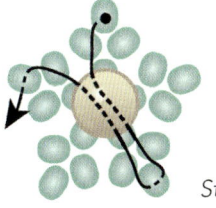

*Step 5*

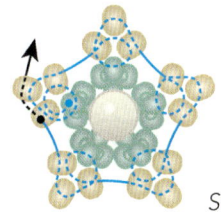

*Step 6*

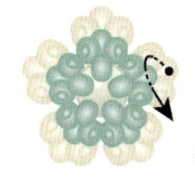

*Step 7*

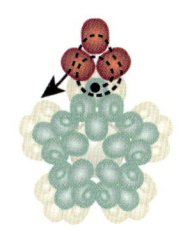

*Step 8*

Anne Boleyn

**9**    a) Pick up 3M and backstitch through the next J head bead.
b) Ignoring the 1st M, pass through the 2nd M picked up in the same direction as before. The spacer bead simply sits between the stitches, pushing them apart.
c) Pick up 1M and pass down the awaiting arm bead.

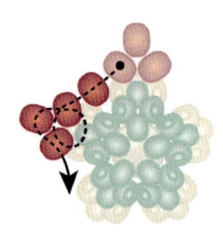

*Step 9*

**10**    a) Repeat step 9 three more times.
b) To close the row, pick up 1M (the final spacer) and pass up into the arm and head bead of the 1st Hubble in the row, as in the diagram. This row hugs the previous row very snugly.

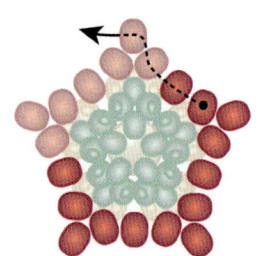

**11**    View the beadwork from the front. More HorSO Hubble, but this time worked in N, with M as the spacer beads.

a) Make the 1st Hubble stitch with N on the M head bead.
b) Pick up 1M, 2N and backstitch through the next head bead.
c) Pick up 1N and pass down the awaiting arm bead.

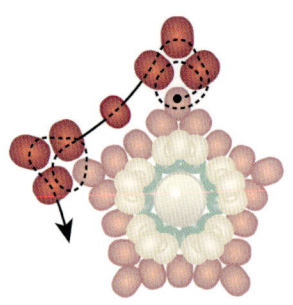

*Step 10*

**12**    a) Repeat step 11 three more times.
b) To close the row, pick up 1M (the final spacer) and pass up into the arm and head beads of the 1st Hubble in the row, as in the diagram.

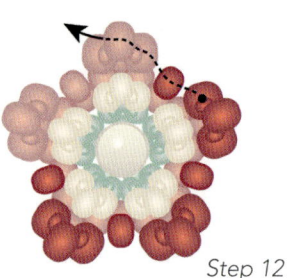

**13**    View the beadwork from the back, and weave down to emerge from the closest M spacer bead of the row below.

**14**    Now for the leaves, which are single, 3-drop Hubble stitches.

a) Pick up 6J, pass through the M from which the thread was emerging, and on through the 1st 3J picked up.
b) Pick up 1J, pass down through the adjacent 3J and on through the M bead below.
c) Weave on via the next Hubble stitch to emerge from the next M spacer bead, as in the diagram.

*Step 11*

**15**    a) Repeat step 14 four more times.
b) Finish off.
c) For the TR embellishment on the locket front, leave a tail thread of 20cm/8"; keep the working and tail threads and weave both through to exit leaf tip beads, ready for attachment.
d) The 4 leaf tips marked with an X, will be connection beads for PUs.

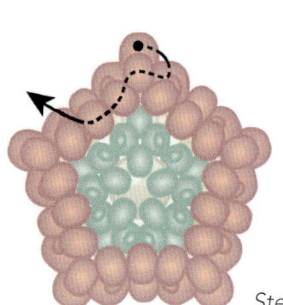

*Step 12*

*Step 13* 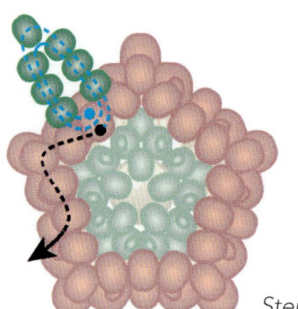      *Step 14* 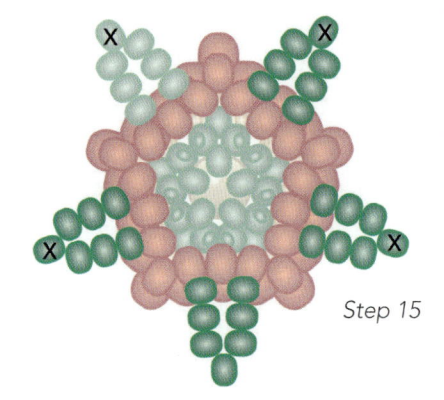      *Step 15*

*Anne Boleyn*

## Pearl unit (PU) (Make 35)

1. With 0.5m/20" thread, a size 15 needle and leaving a tail thread of 15cm/6", pick up 12F, and pass through the 1st 3F picked up, making a ring. If you are making the 2 PUs to be placed at either end of the necklace, then use 0.75m/30" thread and leave a tail thread of 0.25m/10".

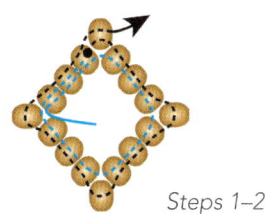

2. a) Pick up 1F and pass through the next 3F beads, making sure the new F bead clicks properly into place between the F beads of the ring.
   b) Repeat step a) 3 more times.
   c) Step up into the 1st bead placed in this row, as in the diagram.

   *Steps 1–2*

3. a) Pick up 1E, 2F, 2E, 2F, 1E.
   b) Pass through the 1st E and F again. Do not be tempted to pass through the corner bead of the 1st square. The new beads will hang at the side.
   c) Snuggle up so that there is no thread showing, but it's very important to remain aware from which side of the corner bead the thread is emerging.

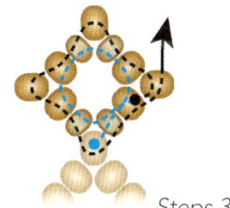

   *Steps 3–4*

4. a) Pick up 1F and pass through 1F, 1E.
   b) Pick up 1F and pass through 1E, 1F.
   c) Pick up 1F and pass through 1F, 1E.
   d) Pass through the corner F bead of the 1st square, from the threadless side, ensuring the 2nd square is perfectly balanced/set on the 1st square.
   e) Pass through E, F and the corner F, as in the diagram.

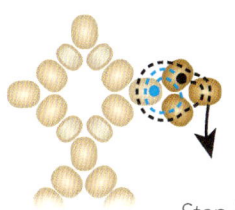

   *Step 5*

5. Now to build a Hubble stitch structure over the top of the 2nd square thus:
   a) Pick up 2F.
   b) Pass through the corner bead from which the thread was emerging, making a tiny ring.
   c) Continue on through the 1st F of the pair just picked up.
   d) Pick up 1F and pass through the adjacent F of the pair.
   e) Pass through the corner bead, the 1st of the 2F pair and the head bead, to emerge as in the diagram.

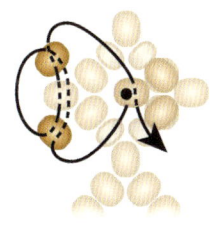

   *Steps 6–7*

6. Pivot the Hubble stitch inwards to the centre of the square.

7. We now have to build an inverted Hubble onto the opposite corner bead:
   a) Pick up 1F.
   b) Pass through the corner bead opposite, from lower to upper side.
   c) Pick up 1F.
   d) Pass through these 3 beads again in the same order.
   e) Pass through the 1st Hubble head bead from upper to lower side, so that the 2 stitches share the head bead.

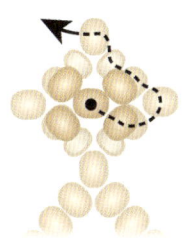

   *Step 8*

8. Weave through:
   a) the adjacent F,
   b) underneath into the corner F bead of the square, and
   c) the next F, E and F **of the square**, to emerge, as in the diagram.

9. The 3rd square is the same as the 1st.
   a) Pick up 12F and pass through the 1st 3F again – do not be tempted to pass through the corner of the 2nd square.
   b) Pick up 1F and pass through the next 3F.
   c) Repeat step b) twice more.
   d) Pass through the corner bead of the 2nd square, from the threadless side.

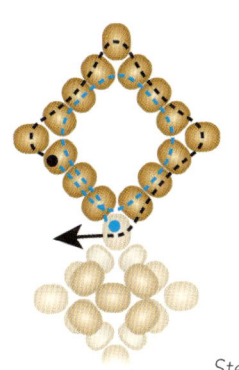

   *Step 9*

Anne Boleyn

**10** Weave around to emerge from the corner bead, as in the diagram.

**11** Repeat steps 3–4a.

**12** Curl the beadwork around so that the 1st square corner bead is positioned where the 4th square needs it. **Note**: The Hubble structure on the 2nd and 4th squares must be on the outside of the beadwork when it's curled round. You may find it helpful to curl it around an awl or straw to help you to see exactly which direction to pass the needle.

    a) Pass through the corner bead of the 1st square.
    b) Continue through E and F of the 4th square.
    c) Pick up 1F.
    d) Pass through the adjacent F, E and the corner bead shared by squares 3 and 4, as in the diagram.

**13** a) With the thread emerging right of the shared corner bead, pick up 1Q.
    b) Pass through the corner bead shared by squares 1 and 2, in the direction right to left.
    c) Draw up the thread as if to snuggle the Q bead into position inside the structure, but continue to push it through and out the other side.
    d) Pass back up through Q, and through the corner bead from the threadless side, so that the threadpath completes a circuit.
    e) Snuggle Q into the structure, taking up all the slack thread.

**14** a) Weave on through the E, F and the corner F of square 4.
    b) Repeat steps 5–7, to complete the little Hubble structure, mirroring the 2nd square.

**15** The working thread should be emerging from the shared head bead on the Hubble structure, and this will be used to connect the PU to other elements. Weave the tail thread around to emerge from the shared head bead on the opposite side of the pearl, to be used for attachment too.

Each connection to another element is made by a reinforced ladder stitch thus:

    a) Pass into the connection bead of the other element and back into the shared head bead of the PU from which the thread was emerging.
    b) Pass around this tiny, 2-bead circuit once more for reinforcement.
    c) Weave into the back of the other element and finish off.

*Step 10*

*Step 11*

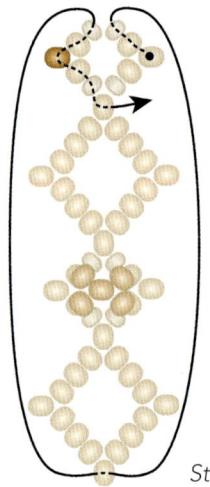

*Step 12*

*Step 13*

*Step 15*

Anne Boleyn

## Crystal unit (CU) (Make 9)

**1**
  a) With 0.5m/20" thread and size 13 needle, pick up 20F, and pass through the 1st 5F once more, making a ring.
  b) Pick up 1F and pass through the next 5F.
  c) Repeat b) 3 more times.
  d) Step up into the 1st F bead placed in this row.

**2** Make a Hubble stitch thus:

  a) Pick up 2F (arm beads), pass through the corner bead below and on through the 1st of the 2F picked up.
  b) Pick up 1F (head bead) and pass through the awaiting arm bead.
  c) Pass into the corner bead below.

*Step 1*

**3**
  a) Push the Hubble stitch towards the back of the beadwork, so you can easily see the corner bead.
  b) Make a 2nd Hubble stitch on the corner bead, by following steps 2a)–b) only (this is double Hubble, where 2 stitches share one body bead). Ensure the thread is emerging from the arm bead, as in the diagram.

**4** Pick up 1F and pass through the 3F of the Hubble at the back. Pick up 1F and pass through the 3F of the Hubble at the front. These 2 'joining' beads bond the 2 Hubbles together, making a double Hubble angle (DHA).

*Step 2*

**5** Push the DHA towards the back of the beadwork, so you can easily see the corner bead. Pass through the corner bead below and weave on through 5F of the side of the square and the next corner F, as in the diagram.

**6**
  a) Repeat steps 2–5 twice more, then steps 2–4 once more, to make a DHA at each of the remaining corners.
  b) Pass through the corner bead below and weave up to emerge from the front Hubble head as in the diagram.

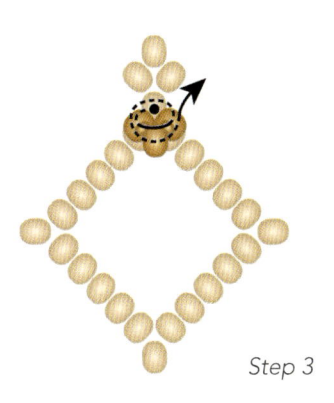

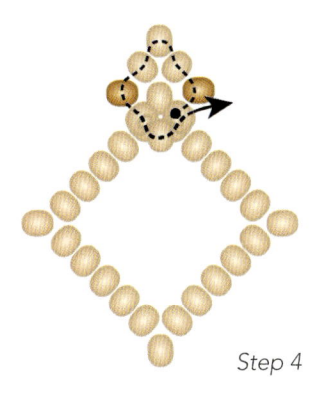

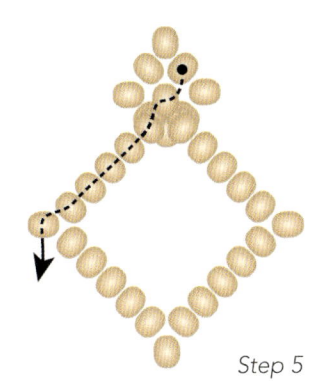

*Step 3*

*Step 4*

*Step 5*

*Step 6*

*Anne Boleyn*

7) Pick up 5F and pass through the inner Hubble head of the next DHA.

8) Repeat step 7 three more times, slipping the chaton, face-up, into the little trap, before you snuggle everything up.

Pass around this entire circuit again for security.

9) With the thread emerging from the inner Hubble head bead, weave through:

   a) the adjacent arm bead,
   b) the corner bead below,
   c) the arm, head and arm bead of the outer Hubble,
   d) and up through the 'joining bead', to emerge from its upper side as in the diagram.

10) Pick up 1E, 1R, 1E, and pass down through the closest 'joining bead' of the next DHA, spanning the gap between them.

11) a) With the thread emerging from the underside of the 'joining bead', pick up 1E, 1D, 1E.
    b) Pass up through the other 'joining bead' (from the underside to the top side) of this DHA. Ensure the new beads sit in the 'seat' of the DHA, and don't get caught underneath.

12) Repeat steps 10–11 three more times. Weave on to emerge from the nearest corner bead at the back of the beadwork, and finish off. The 4 corner beads marked X, will be the connection beads for PUs.

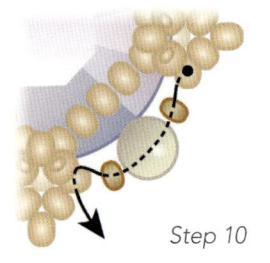

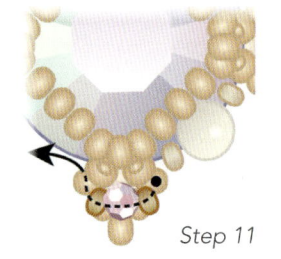

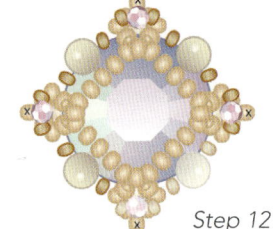

*Step 7*

*Step 8*

*Step 9*

*Step 10*

*Step 11*

*Step 12*

## Toggle clasp – ring and bar

**Ring (make 1)**

1) With 1m/40" thread and size 13 needle:

   a) Pick up 18F, pass again through the 1st 2 picked up, making a ring.
   b) Pick up 1F and pass through 2F, snuggling the new bead in place.
   c) Repeat step b) 8 more times.
   d) Step up by passing into the 1st F placed in this row.

2) a) Following steps 2–4 of the CU, build a DHA onto the bead from which the thread is emerging.
   b) Pass into the body bead below, on through 2F and the next body bead.
   c) Build a DHA onto this bead, but instead of picking up the 1st joining bead (as in step 4 of the CU), share the joining bead of the previous DHA, then continue on to pick up a new joining bead to complete the other side of this DHA.
   d) Weave into the body bead below, on through 2F and the next corner bead, ready to build the next DHA.

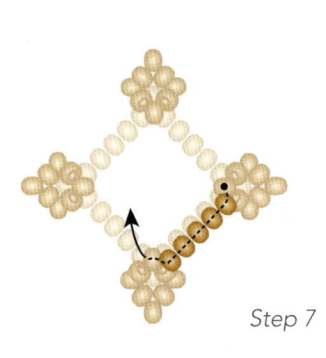

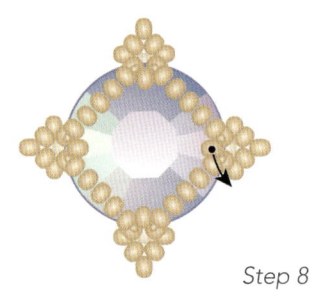

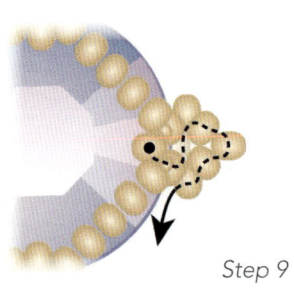

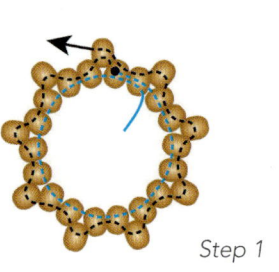

*Step 1*

*Step 2*

Anne Boleyn

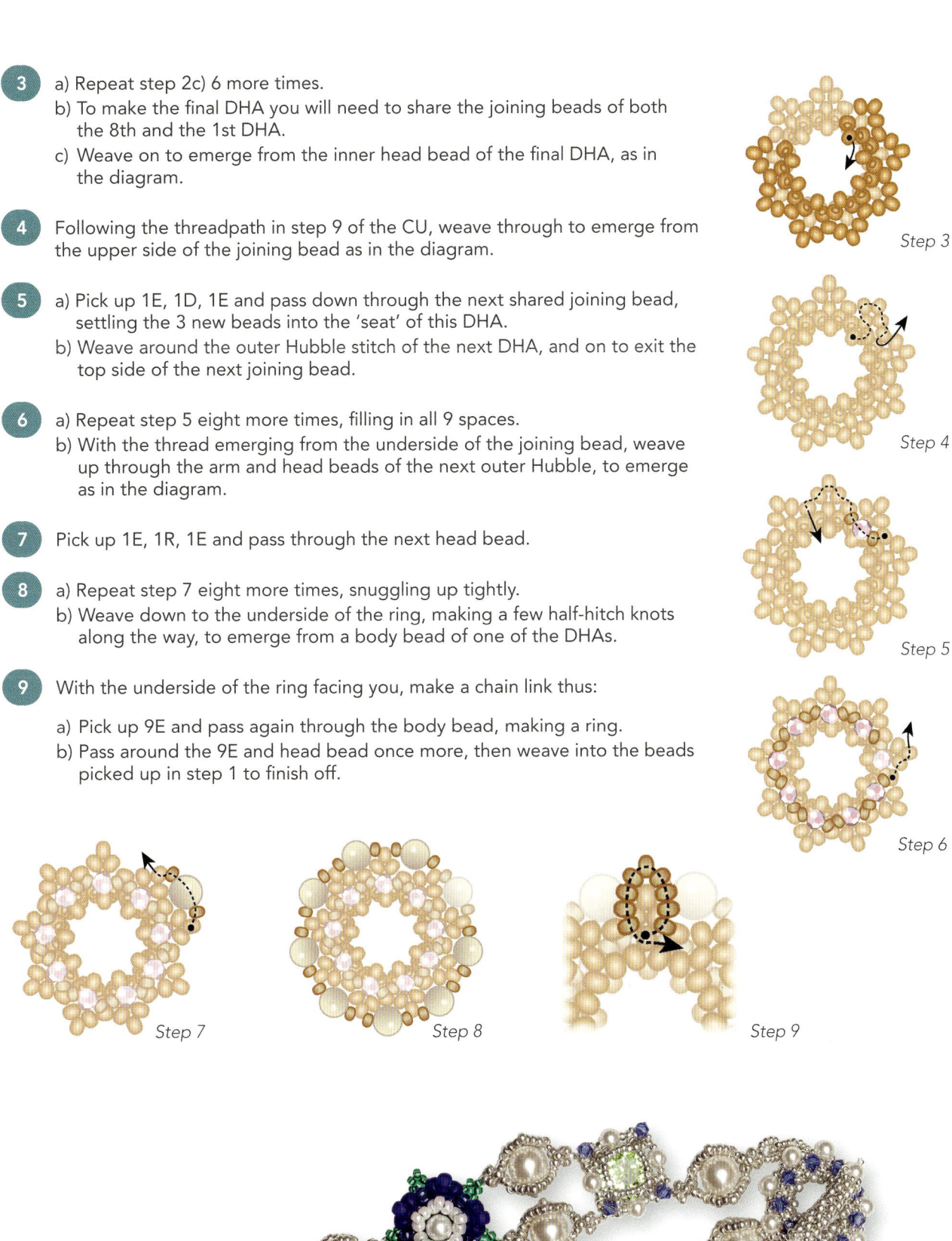

3. a) Repeat step 2c) 6 more times.
   b) To make the final DHA you will need to share the joining beads of both the 8th and the 1st DHA.
   c) Weave on to emerge from the inner head bead of the final DHA, as in the diagram.

*Step 3*

4. Following the threadpath in step 9 of the CU, weave through to emerge from the upper side of the joining bead as in the diagram.

5. a) Pick up 1E, 1D, 1E and pass down through the next shared joining bead, settling the 3 new beads into the 'seat' of this DHA.
   b) Weave around the outer Hubble stitch of the next DHA, and on to exit the top side of the next joining bead.

*Step 4*

6. a) Repeat step 5 eight more times, filling in all 9 spaces.
   b) With the thread emerging from the underside of the joining bead, weave up through the arm and head beads of the next outer Hubble, to emerge as in the diagram.

7. Pick up 1E, 1R, 1E and pass through the next head bead.

*Step 5*

8. a) Repeat step 7 eight more times, snuggling up tightly.
   b) Weave down to the underside of the ring, making a few half-hitch knots along the way, to emerge from a body bead of one of the DHAs.

9. With the underside of the ring facing you, make a chain link thus:

   a) Pick up 9E and pass again through the body bead, making a ring.
   b) Pass around the 9E and head bead once more, then weave into the beads picked up in step 1 to finish off.

*Step 6*

*Step 7*

*Step 8*

*Step 9*

– 43 –

Anne Boleyn

**Bar**

**10** With 0.75m/30" thread and size 13 needle, pick up 10F, and work a strip of peyote, 8 rows in all.

**11** Roll the strip ends together and zip up peyote-wise, then weave around to emerge from an end bead.

**12** a) Turn the little tube to look at it end on. Make a half-hitch knot around one of the adjacent, peyote end threads.
b) Make a 2nd half-hitch knot on the same thread, beside that previous knot.

**13** a) Pick up 1R, 1E and, missing out the E, pass back down through R and under the peyote end thread opposite. Don't snuggle up yet!
b) To reinforce this, retrace the path through R and E in reverse.
c) Pass under the thread where the 2 knots were and down 1 of the end F beads.
d) Snuggle up tight!
e) Optional – at this point you can weave up through the next F bead and add tiny picots of 3E between each of the 4 beads around the tube end, framing the pearl slightly at its base (see steps 4–6 of the Aragon toggle bar on page 14).

**14** a) Weave down peyote-wise, to emerge from the 6th F.
b) Pick up 11E and pass through the 5th and 6th F beads again in the same direction, to make a loop.
c) Weave on to emerge from an end F bead.
d) Repeat steps 12–13.
e) Finish off.

**Links**

**15** a) Using 0.5m/19" of thread and size 15 needle, pick up 11E and pass through the toggle bar loop.
b) Leaving a tail thread of about 15cm/6", pass the needle through all 11E and the toggle bar loop again, to form a ring.
c) Snuggle up, ensuring the beads of this new link are totally independent of the loop beads.
d) Work around the 11E making half-hitch knots between alternate beads, and finish off the working thread.
e) With the tail thread, work around the 11E as you did with the working thread, but in the opposite direction, and finish off.

**16** a) With the extra-long tail thread of one of the 2 end PUs, pick up 11E, pass through the new toggle bar chain link, and the end E bead of the PU from which the thread was emerging, making a loop.
b) Pass around this little circuit once more, weave into the PU and finish off.

**17** Repeat steps 16–17 for the toggle ring and the other end PU.

Refer to images on pages 40 and 43 to aid complete construction.

*Step 10*

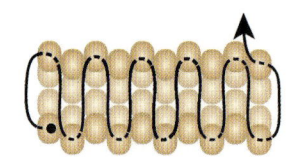

*Step 11*

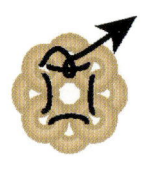

*Step 12*

*Step 13*

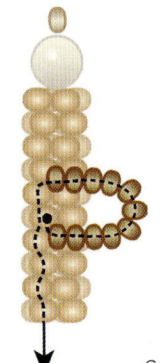

*Step 14*

WALSINGHAM CYPHER
NECKLACE AND BRACELET

# WALSINGHAM CYPHER NECKLACE AND BRACELET

When the old manor house was restored, a workman pulled at the rotting wood panelling of the long hall. It was to be replaced with new, the old used as a template. Behind the dark oak he found a linen bag, wedged between the lath and plaster. The historian was called and the bag opened with great excitement amid the dust and rubble. Out tumbled a jewelled chain, marked at intervals with diamond shaped panes. The historian smiled, knowing that at last they had found the long lost Chain of Office worn by the spymaster's daughter. It is said that Kit Marlowe lifted it from her jewellery box as a dare to show his stealth. One tiny note in her diary hinted that the loss of the necklace was great indeed for with it she memorised her most cunning cypher, one which was never broken during her lifetime. But now… perhaps… it would be.

There is a portrait of Frances, Countess of Wessex, painted by Robert Peake the Elder in 1594 (present collection unknown). The Countess was a skilled code breaker and worked for her father, the famed Elizabethan spymaster Sir Francis Walsingham. In this portrait she is wearing several ornate chains, darkly mysterious and painted as though the metal is oxidised. She was the inspiration for this design. It was fun to imagine a secret code worked into the sequences of elements.

Sir Francis Walsingham was Elizabeth I's spymaster for over 20 years. His network of spies reached right across Europe to the Middle East. He developed a school for spies and worked tirelessly for his Queen. It is said that she was not entirely comfortable with the almost puritanical and clever ways with which he uncovered plots and counter plots.

It is true that she rarely funded his work and he was left to pay for most of it himself.

**Necklace**
**The necklace elements**: square chaton motif, three-pane link/two-pane link, glass ring link, flat ribbon link. The beads at the tips of the square chaton motifs are used to join the other elements, so these are worked first.
**Completed length**: necklace 80cm/32", pendant section 8cm/3⅛"
**You will need**:
6g x Miyuki seed beads size 11° 401F (matte black) (A)
10g x Miyuki seed beads size 15° 1051 (galvanised metallic silver) (B)
5g x Miyuki seed beads size 15° 457 (metallic dark bronze) (C)
10g x Miyuki seed beads size 8° 457 (metallic dark bronze) (D)
10g x Miyuki cube beads 457 1.8mm (metallic dark bronze) (E)
8 x Swarovski® chatons #1088 ss39 8mm (erinite) (F)
7 x Czech glass rings 9mm (green) (G)

*Fascinating fact:*

*Spying was rife, and much time was devoted to passing messages in code. Some were simple alphabet cyphers; more complex ones used symbols and zodiac signs. Others required sheets of paper with holes punched in them to reveal a sequence of letters in a written manuscript. Invisible ink was also popular, with the use of citrus juice or milk, which would darken when the paper was held over a flame.*

*Walsingham Cypher necklace and bracelet*

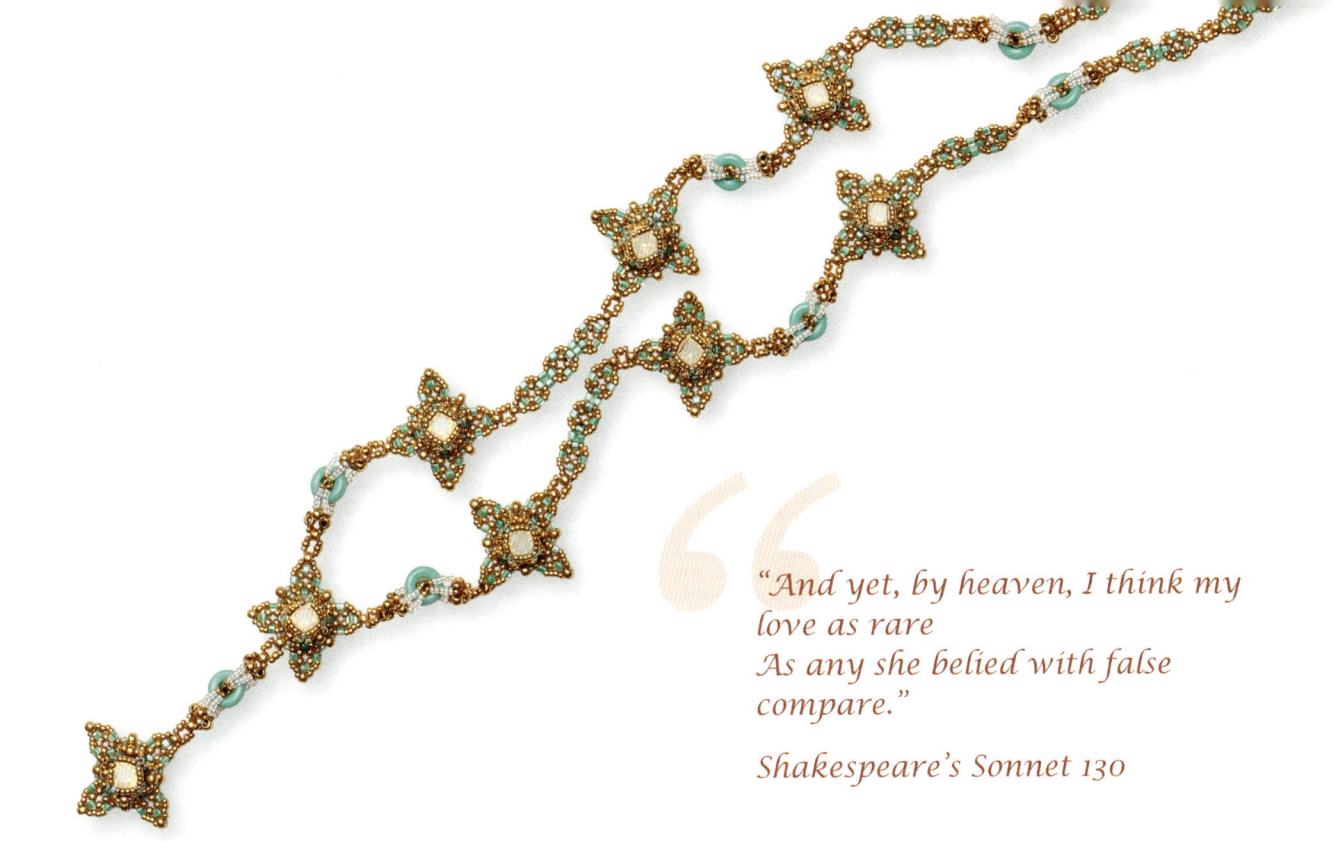

> "And yet, by heaven, I think my love as rare
> As any she belied with false compare."
>
> Shakespeare's Sonnet 130

### Square chaton motif (Make 8)

The base of the square motif is made of five panes and the centre one is embellished with stitches to hold the chaton in place. Each of the four outer panes is joined to its neighbour with beads.

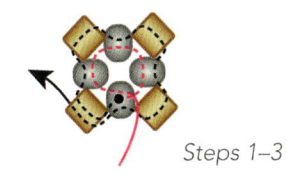

*Steps 1–3*

1. Use a 1.5m/25" length of thread, allow a 15cm/6" tail, then pick up 4A and secure them in a ring. Bring the needle out of 1A.

2. Pick up 1E, pass through the next 1A of the ring.

3. Repeat step 2 until there is 1E between each A bead, then step up to exit the 1st 1E added. The beads should lie flat, so ease off the thread tension if they do not.

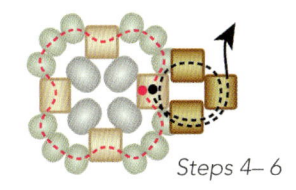

*Steps 4–6*

4. Pick up 3B, pass through the next 1E.

5. Repeat step 4 until you have 3B between each 1E. Finish with the thread coming out of 1E. This completes the 1st pane; now you are in place to start the next pane.

*Steps 7–8*

6. Pick up 3E and pass back through the 1E started from. Then pass through 2 of the 3E just added.

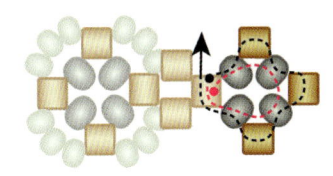

7. Pick up 4A, pass back through the 1E and 1A of the 4A just added.

8. Place 1E between each A bead, then step up to exit the original E bead.

9. Place 3B between each 1E (red threadpath), then stitch forward through 3B, 1E, 3B.

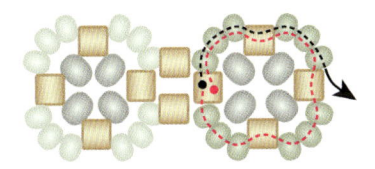

*Step 9*

10. Pick up 1B, 1D, 1B. Pass through the next 3B. Then weave through the beads to exit the next 1E of the 1st pane.

Repeat the steps to make a pane coming from each of the E beads of the 1st pane.

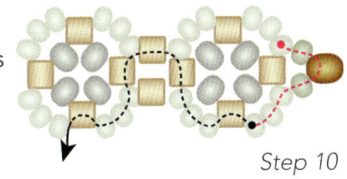

*Step 10*

Walsingham Cypher necklace and bracelet

**Link the panes**

Each of the four outer panes is joined to its neighbour through the centre B of the 3B nearest the centre pane. So, to be in place, exit the centre B on the last pane worked.

1. Pick up 1C, 1D, 1C, pass through the centre B of the next pane. Pick up 1C, 1D, 1C, pass back through the bead started from in this step.

2. Weave through the beads to the next centre bead and repeat step 1.

3. Repeat steps 1 and 2 until all 4 panes are linked together. Weave through the beads to exit one of the 1st E beads added to the centre pane.

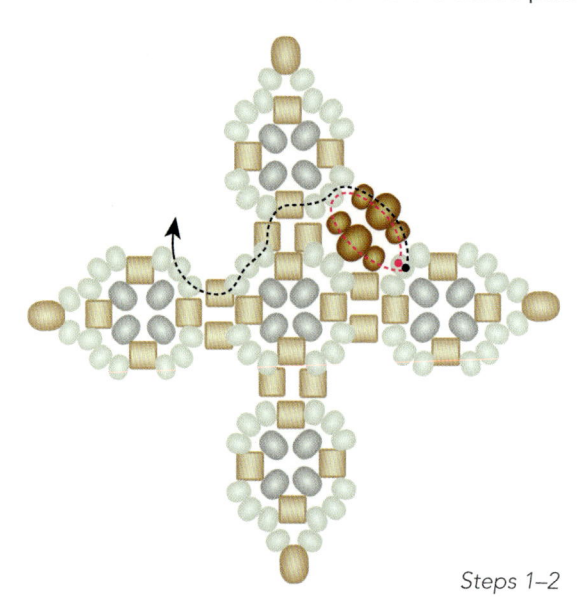

*Steps 1–2*

**Add the chaton**

The chaton is attached directly over the centre pane, working from just the 4 E beads and sets of 3B beads that form the inside edge of the centre pane.

1. Pick up 1B stalk, 3C tip, pass back through the 1B and then the 1E started from.

   Yes, the thread will show a little bit over the edge of the E beads. This is fine, just pull your thread up firmly so the new beads are secure and centred over the E.

2. Weave through 3B and 1E of the inside edge.

3. Repeat steps 1 and 2 until back at the start. Step up to exit the centre 1C of the 1st 3C added.

4. Pick up 4B, pass through the next centre C. Repeat until you are back at the start.

*Steps 1–3*

*Step 4*

> *Fascinating fact:*
>
> *The Museum of London is planning to open a permanent display of the Cheapside Hoard in its new museum in Smithfield in 2021. Smithfield, a marketplace since 1175, was also where many of the Crown's enemies were executed, before public executions were moved to the more accessible Tyburn Fields.*

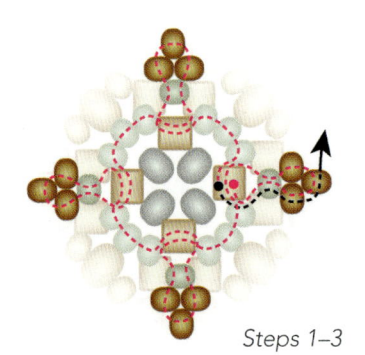

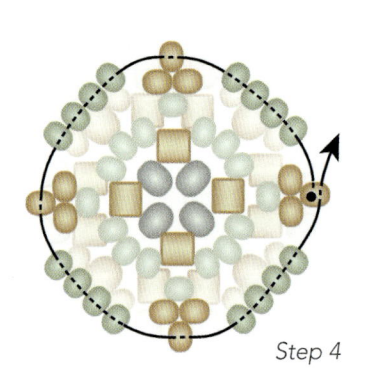

Walsingham Cypher necklace and bracelet

**5** Place the chaton, face up, inside this ring of beads, then weave through the ring of beads a 2nd time, pulling firmly to close the ring securely over the top of the chaton.

*Step 5*

**6** Pass through 2C of a set of 3C (so the thread is coming out of the bottom of the bead). Pick up 3B, step down to pass through the centre B of the 3B of the pane directly below. A full layout diagram is shown on pages 51 and 52. You can follow it exactly, or combine the elements as you choose.

**7** Pick up 3B, then pass through the next 3C of the chaton bezel.

Repeat to link each 3C of the bezel through the centre B beads of the centre pane, with sets of 3B. Finish off the start tail, but leave the working thread in place. You can use it to join the elements once you have made more of them.

Make 7 more square chaton motifs.

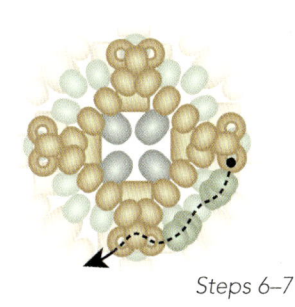

*Steps 6–7*

### Three-pane link (Make 4)

This is a centre pane with just two additional panes positioned so that they lie in a row. The two end panes have 1B, 1D, 1B over the end E beads.

### Two-pane link (Make 4)

This is made in the same way as a three-pane link, but with just one pane added to the first pane.

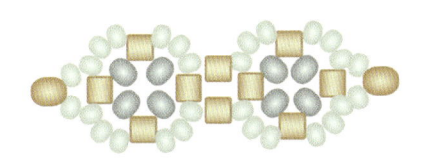

Walsingham Cypher necklace and bracelet

## Glass ring link (Make 7)

Four loops of beads are linked through the centre of a 9mm Czech glass ring (G). The centre beads of pairs of loops are then linked together. The threadpath for this element may seem a little unusual, until you have completed the first one.

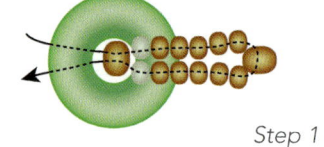

1. Pick up 1D, pass the needle through 1G. Pick up 1B, 5C, 1D, 5C, 1B. Pass back through the 1D started from, and through the 1G.

   Hold the beadwork so that this loop of beads stays on one side of the G.

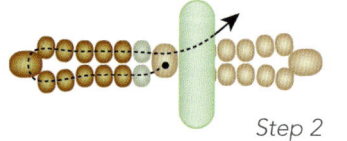

2. Pick up 1B, 5C, 1D, 5C, 1B. Pass back through the 1D started from. There should be one loop of beads either side of the centre D bead; and, therefore, one loop either side of the G.

3. a) Pass through 1B, 5C, 1D of the 1st loop of beads then fold both loops so they meet at the edge of the G.
   b) Pick up 1B, 1D, 1B. Pass through the 1D at the top of the 2nd loop. Pick up 1B, 1D, 1B, pass back through the 1D started from in this step.

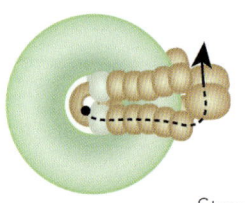

4. Weave through the ring of B and D beads to secure it, then exit 1D added in step 3 (the new D, not the D of the loop).

5. Pick up 1B, 1D, 1B and pass through the 2nd 1D added in step 3.

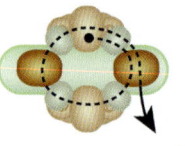

6. Pick up 1B, pass back through the 1D of step 5. Pick up 1B, pass back through the 1D started from in step 4.

7. Weave back to exit the D bead of step 1, then repeat steps 2 to 6, to add the 2nd pair of loops.

   Finish off the thread tails.

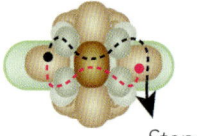

*Step 1*

*Step 2*

*Step 3a*

*Step 3b*

*Steps 4–6*

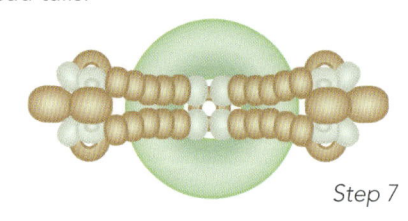

*Step 7*

## Flat ribbon link

This is a simple variation of right angle weave which works into a flat ribbon that is very comfortable to wear at the back of necklaces. To start, exit 1D at the end of a three-pane element.

1. Pick up 1C, 1A, 1C, 1D, 1C, 1A, 1C. Pass back through the 1D started from. Then pass through 1C, 1A, 1C, 1D.

2. Pick up 1B, 1A, 1B, 1D, 1B, 1A, 1B. Pass back through the 1D started from. Then pass through 1B, 1A, 1B, 1D.

   Repeat steps 1 and 2 until the flat ribbon is the right length for you, then finish off the thread.

   A jump ring can be passed through the last stitch of the ribbon and a clasp attached to the jump ring.

*Steps 1–2*

*Walsingham Cypher necklace and bracelet*

## Joining the elements

Each element is joined to the next with a simple right angle weave stitch of 1C, 1A, 1C. Pass through 1D of the next link: 1C, 1A, 1C. Pass back through 1D started from. Each join is reached by weaving through the beads of an element, or by joining a new thread if needed.

The centre square chaton element has three glass ring elements joined to it, two from adjacent corners and one from the linking D bead between the other two corners (shown on next page).

All three glass ring elements have one square chaton element linked through one corner. The sequence for the necklace sides, which are worked from the opposite corners of the two square chaton elements joined to the corners of the centre square is: three-pane element, square chaton element, glass ring element, square chaton element, two-pane element, glass ring element, three-pane element. The end of the two-pane element has a flat ribbon element worked from it, which can be made as long or short as needed.

*Side section layout of necklace. (See next page for centre section layout.)*

*Centre section layout of necklace.*

The flat ribbon section can be worked to adjust the necklace to the right length.

*Walsingham Cypher necklace and bracelet*

## Bracelet

**You will need:**

6g x Miyuki seed beads size 11° 4479 (duracoat moody blue) (A)
5g x Miyuki seed beads size 15° 4203 (duracoat galvanised metallic gold) (B)
10g x Miyuki seed beads size 15° 460 (metallic plum iris) (C)
10g x Miyuki seed beads size 8° 460 (metallic plum iris) (D)
10g x Miyuki cube beads 460 1.8mm (metallic plum iris) (E)
8 x Swarovski® xilion chatons #1088 ss39 8mm (siam) (F)
10 x Czech glass rings 9mm (transparent red) (green in diagram) (G)
3-loop sliding clasp 20mm in length (antique bronze)

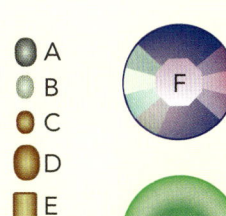

The bracelet uses a simple variation of both the square chaton element and the glass ring element of the necklace. For this variation the glass ring element shares a D bead. The bracelet shown measures 18cm/7" not including clasp.

### Square chaton motif variation (Make 8)

The techniques are the same, just the number of panes is changed to give an alternatively shaped element.

1. Make a centre pane and add sets of 3E to each E of the pane. On 2 opposite sets of E exit the side E: pick up 3B, pass through the top E. Pick up 3B, pass through next side E.

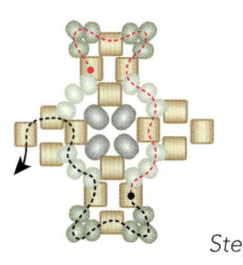

2. Add a pane to the 2 remaining (also opposite each other) sides of the centre pane. Add 1B, 1D, 1B to end E bead of each of these 2 panes.

3. Join the centre B beads of the 2 panes through the centre B beads embellishing the sets of E beads.

   Exit a centre B, pick up 1C, 1D, 1C, pass through next centre B. Pick up 1C, 1D, 1C, pass back to bjead started from.

4. Add a chaton over the centre motif as before. (Full instructions are on pages 48–49.)

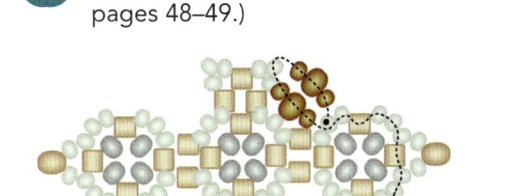

*Step 1*

*Steps 2–3*

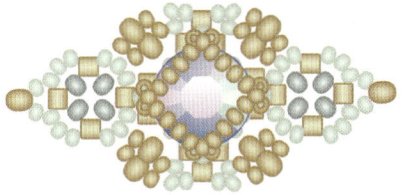

*Step 4*

Walsingham Cypher necklace and bracelet

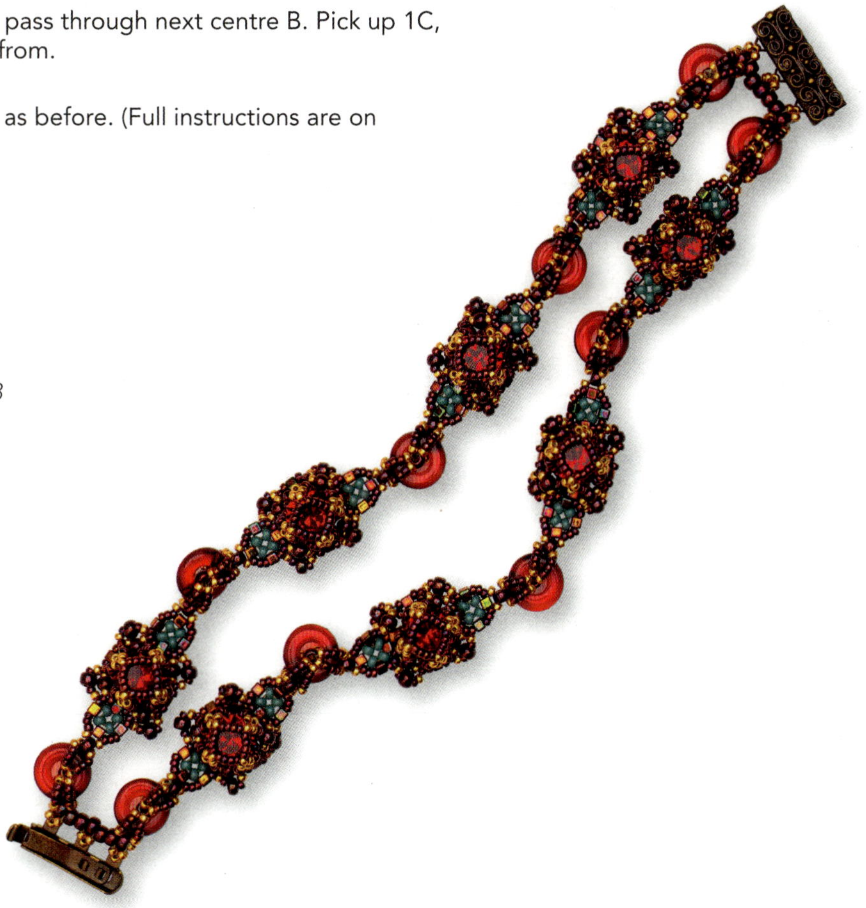

## Glass ring variation (Make 10)

To create the bracelet there is a glass ring link, which is less elaborate than the one used in the Walsingham Cypher necklace.

This one is linked through and shares the D beads at the tips of the square chaton motif.

1. Pick up 1D, pass through the glass ring. Pick up 1B, 3C, 1B and pass through the 1D of a square chaton.

2. Pick up 1B, 3C, 1B and pass through the 1D started from in step 1, from the same side and the glass ring.

3. Flip the piece over and repeat to add a 2nd loop. Then return to the centre D bead again.

4. Repeat to add 2 more loops through the 1D of step 1 and 1D of the next square chaton motif. Each glass ring will sit between 2 square chaton motifs. Check that both chatons face the same way.

(**Note**: end the bracelet with a glass ring; the last loop will need a centre 1D: pick up 1B, 3C, 1B, 1D, 1B, 3C, 1B, return through the centre 1D. Pick up 1B, 3C, 1B and pass through the 1D of the loop just created. Pick up 1B, 3C, 1B and return to the centre 1D.)

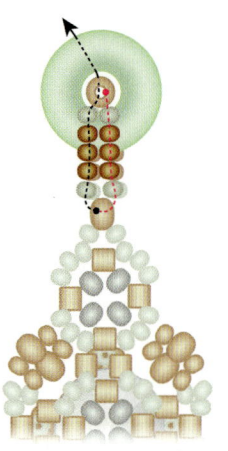

*Steps 1–2*

*Step 3*

## Add a clasp

1. To add a clasp, exit the 1D at the end of the loop of the last glass ring. Pick up 5D and pass through the 1D of the other end of the loop of the glass ring.

2. Pick up 1C and pass back through 1D.

3. a) Pick up 3C and pass back through the 1D.
   b) Pick up 3C and pass back through the 1D again, then step up through 2C.

4. Slide the clasp loop between the sets of 3C and stitch the centre C of each set together through the clasp loop.

   Repeat on the centre D and end D.

*Steps 1–2*   *Step 3a*   *Step 3b*    *Step 4*

*Walsingham Cypher necklace and bracelet*

MATINS AND VESPERS

## MATINS AND VESPERS

August 4th, 1537, Château du Louvre. Marie de Guise rose an hour before cockcrow, true to habit, and two ladies-in-waiting helped her step into a loose, black robe. She took a deep breath as Blanche carefully tied the ribbons at the back, while Amée dressed her hair with a modestly jewelled band. When she was ready, the little group quickly made their way to the chapel, as a soft glow was beginning to spread behind the trees on the hills. The two young ladies rustled softly into position in the pews behind their dear Marie, and knelt as Matins began.

Her fingers moved lightly along the necklace adorning her neck, and each time they rested upon a pearl, Marie whispered a short prayer. She offered thanks that King Francis refused to agree to the marriage proposal from that dreadful Henry of England; why, the man treated his wives abominably, first banishing one, then beheading the second! However, Francis seemed much too keen that she should marry James to cement the alliance between France and Scotland. She did not want to leave her family and comfortable home for that grey, misty land with bland food and austere palaces. Her heart was heavy with sorrow as she still mourned the loss of her beloved husband, Louis, just two months before, and her body was weary with the weight of the child within her belly. She had not felt movement from the child for some days now; this thought brought her focus away from prayer and she became aware of a dull, continuous ache in her back. She drew herself up with some effort and, clutching the cross on her necklace, kissed it as she turned to her ladies and signalled that it was time to leave. Today was the day and, if it was a boy, she would name him Louis.

**Elements**: square rivoli, lattice rope, bail, toggle bar, ring and links

**Techniques**: Hubble stitch variations – basic, VerSO2, HorSO, inverted, wave; RAW, netting

**Completed necklace length**: 60cm/24"

**You will need**:

18g x Miyuki seed beads size 15° 456 (gunmetal iris) (A)
8g x Miyuki seed beads size 11° 456 (gunmetal iris) (B)
50 x Swarovski® pearls #5810 3mm (crystal iridescent purple) (C)
6 x Swarovski® cushion square fancy stones #4470 12mm (crystal paradise shine, cyclamen opal, siam AB, padparadscha AB, olivine glacier blue) (D)
29 x Czech charlotte seed beads size 15° (light bronze) (E)
3 x Swarovski® pearls #5821 11x8mm (crystal powder almond) (F)
42 x Swarovski® pearls #5810 6mm (10 x crystal iridescent purple, 8 x crystal mauve, 8 x crystal burgundy, 8 x crystal bordeaux, 8 x crystal rosaline) (G)

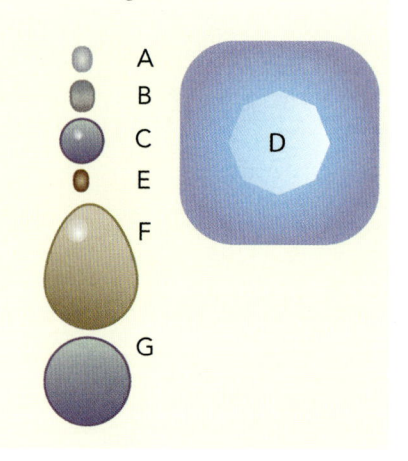

> "Oh, thou art fairer than the evening air
> Clad in the beauty of a thousand stars;
> Brighter art thou than flaming Jupiter
> When he appear'd to hapless Semele;
> More lovely than the monarch of the sky
> In wanton Arethusa's azured arms:
> And none but thou shalt be my paramour."
>
> Christopher Marlowe (1564-1593),
> The Tragical History of Doctor Faustus.

> "I trust she will prove a wise Princess. I have been much in her company, and she bears herself very honourably to me, with very good entertaining."
>
> Margaret Tudor (mother of James V of Scotland) wrote of Mary de Guise to Henry VIII in July, 1538

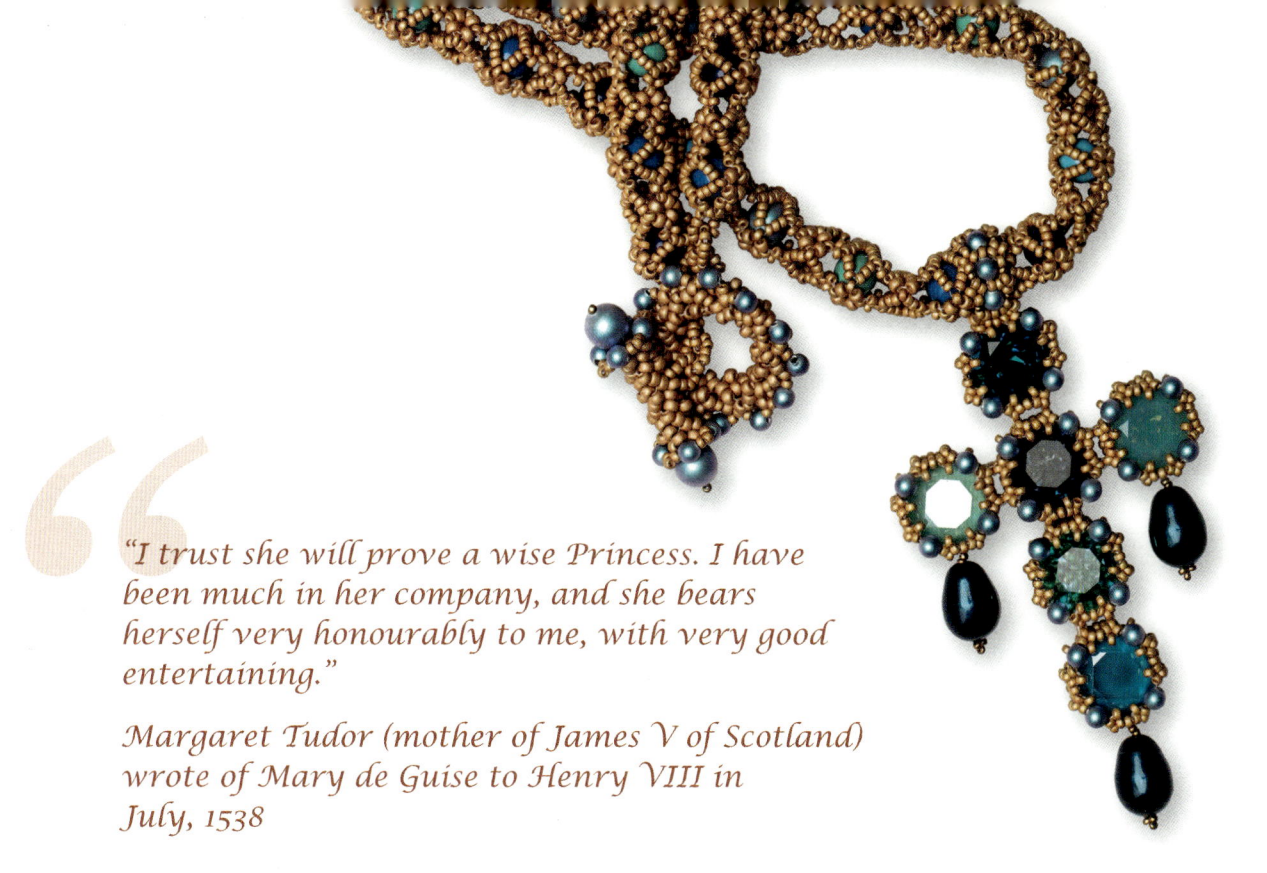

## Square rivoli (SR) (Make 6)

**Row 1 (Back):**

1. **1st stitch**: We're going to make a VerSO2 Hubble stitch, which starts with a normal body (as for a basic foundation stitch) – two arm beads and a body bead, but instead of just adding a head bead, we will pick up a further two extension beads. With 0.75m/30" thread, pick up 3A and pass again through the 1st A picked up, making a ring.

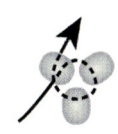

   *Step 1*

2. **1st stitch cont.:**

   a) Pick up 3A (the usual head bead, spacer bead, future head bead – in that order).
   b) Missing out the future head bead, pass back through the spacer bead in the opposite direction.
   c) Pass through the head bead, in the same direction as before. **Note**: It is absolutely imperative that the pass is made in the correct direction. The hole of the usual head bead must lie horizontally in the same plane as the body and future head beads; if it doesn't, then the trap will not fit the crystal.
   d) Pass through the awaiting arm bead.
   e) Snuggle up by gripping the future head bead between thumb and forefinger and pulling the working thread tightly. This completes the 1st VerSO2 stitch.

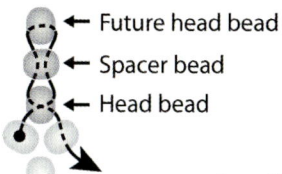

   ← Future head bead
   ← Spacer bead
   ← Head bead

   *Step 2*

3. **2nd stitch**: Pick up 4A, miss out the 1st A picked up and pass through the 2nd A again, in the same direction. **Note**: Again, here it is very important that this pass is in the correct direction. The 1st A picked up is the spacer bead; notice that it was simply ignored (that's the HorSO bit).

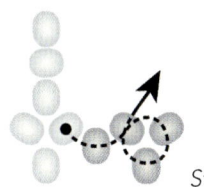

   *Step 3*

4. **2nd stitch cont.**: Repeat step 2 and snuggle up tightly. The acid test, to see if you're properly snuggled up, is to hold the working thread in one hand and the tail thread in the other and pull – if you don't see any thread between the stitches, then it's perfect. If you do see thread, then snuggle up a bit more!

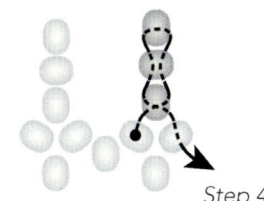

   *Step 4*

Matins and Vespers

**5** **3rd stitch**: Make a basic Hubble stitch and snuggle it up so tightly that it flips upside down.

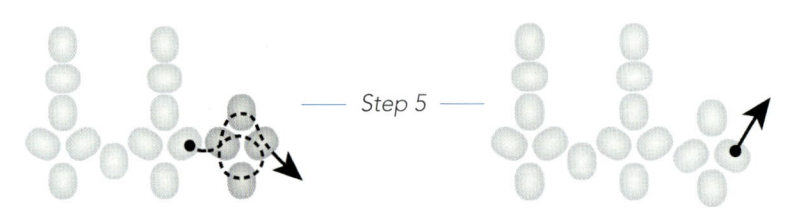

— Step 5 —

**6** a) Repeat steps 1–5 three more times. The actual beadwork won't look as neat as the diagram, but it will all behave once the 2nd row is underway.
b) Join the ends together by passing up through the arm and head beads.
c) For security, pass around the 4 main beads of the 1st stitch (2nd arm, body, 1st arm, head), then continue up through the spacer and finally exit the future head bead, as in the diagram.

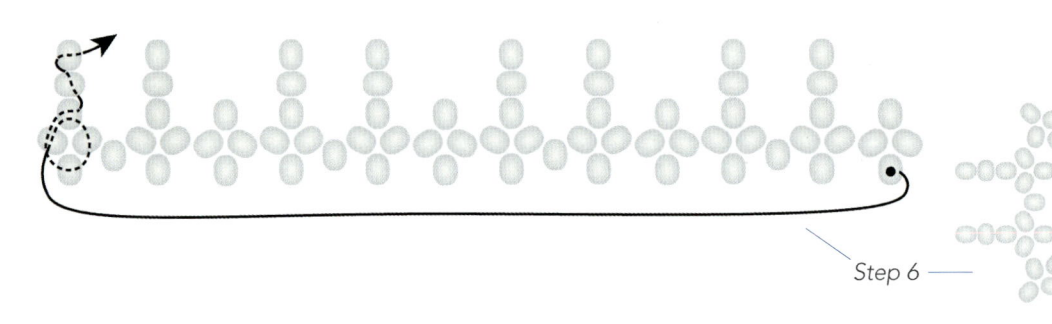

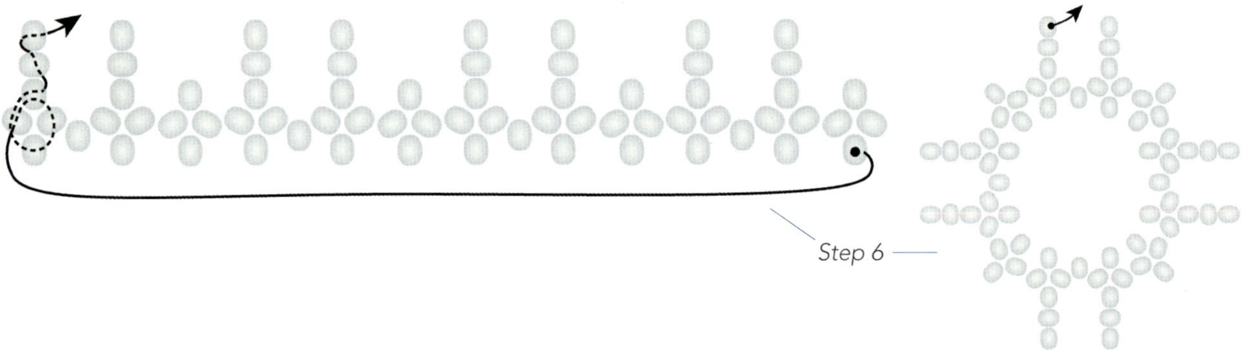

Step 6

**Row 2 (Front):**

**7** Every stitch will be inverted Hubble combined with HorSO. The future head beads are now the head beads.

a) Pick up 3A.
b) Pass through all 3A again (don't be tempted to pass through the existing beadwork – this must dangle at the side).
c) Pass through the head bead from the threadless side.
d) Pass through the awaiting arm bead to finish the stitch.

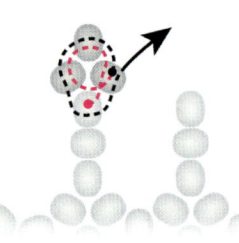

Step 7

**8** a) Pick up 4A.
b) Pass again through the 2nd A picked up, in the same direction.
c) Pass through the next head bead (carefully check which one as it's easy to turn and pass through the wrong one by accident).
d) Continue on through the awaiting arm bead.
e) Snuggle up with vigilance.

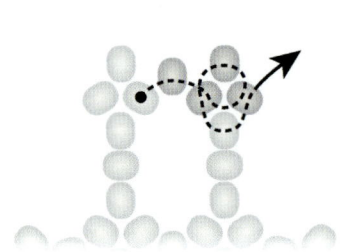

Step 8

Matins and Vespers

**9**    a) Pick up 1C, 3A.
b) Pass again through the 1st A picked up, in the same direction.
c) Work steps 8c)–e).

*Step 9*

**10**    a) Repeat steps 8–9 twice more.
b) Repeat step 8 once more.
c) Pick up 1C and pass through the arm and head beads of the 1st stitch made in this row.
d) Pass around all 4 beads of the 1st stitch for security, to exit the head bead, as in the diagram.
e) Weave on to exit the next head bead after a corner, making a few half-hitch knots along the way.
f) Finish off the tail thread but keep the working thread for connecting the elements, making dangles on the arms and foot of the cross, or making the bail.

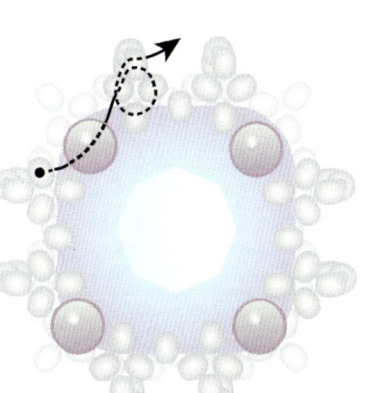

**Connecting the SRs:**

*Step 10*

**11**    The head beads on both the front and back of the trap (marked X in the diagram), are the connection points. A simple ladder stitch between corresponding head beads of 2 adjacent elements is all it takes:

a) Weave around so that the thread exits the side of a head bead facing away from C.
b) Pass through the corresponding head bead on the other element towards its C.
c) Pass through the 1st head bead again from the threadless side.
d) Weave through the arm, spacer, arm and head beads.
e) Connect the 2nd set of head beads in the same way.
f) Weave down through the spacer bead below the front head bead and on through the back head bead to emerge facing away from the corner.
g) Connect the back head beads together in the same way.
h) Snuggle up and either keep the working thread for connecting a further element, or making a dangle, or finish off by weaving around to the back.

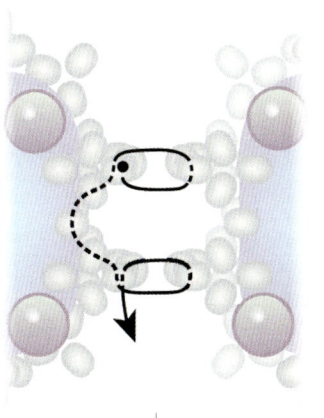

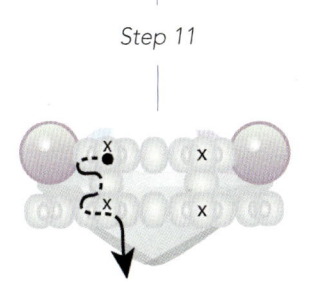

*Step 11*

## Dangles

**12**
a) Weave around to exit a front spacer bead.
b) Pick up 2E, 1F, 3E.
c) Missing out the 3E, pass back through F and 2E in the opposite direction.
d) Pass through the spacer bead from the threadless side.
e) Finish off by weaving around to the back.

*Step 12*

## Lattice rope (Make 1)

**1** **Row 1**: With a good wingspan of thread, a size 13 needle and leaving a tail thread of 40cm/16", make a foundation basic Hubble stitch thus:

a) Pick up 3A and pass again through the 1st A picked up, in the same direction.
b) Pick up 1A (head bead), and pass down through the awaiting arm bead.
c) Pass through the body bead, as in the diagram, to step up for the next stitch.

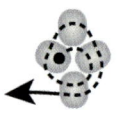

*Step 1*

**2** Pick up 4B and pass again through the 1st B picked up, in the same direction.
**Note**: Do not pass through the body bead yet.

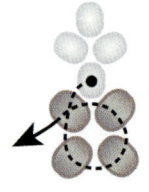

*Step 2*

**3** a) Pick up 1A and pass through the next B bead. Make sure the A bead sits tightly between the B beads.
b) Snuggle up the beads firmly to the body bead.
c) Repeat step a) twice more; this positions 3 corners.
d) Pass through the body bead from the threadless side, to use it as the 4th corner. We'll call this a B square (BSq).
e) Weave through B, A, B, A to exit the opposite corner of the BSq.

*Step 3*

Matins and Vespers

4. Make a basic Hubble on this corner bead, using it as a body bead:

   a) Pick up 2A and pass through the corner bead of the BSq.
   b) Pass again through the 1st A picked up, in the same direction.
   c) Pick up 1A and pass through the awaiting arm bead.
   d) Weave through the body, arm and head beads, as in the diagram, to step up for the next stitch.

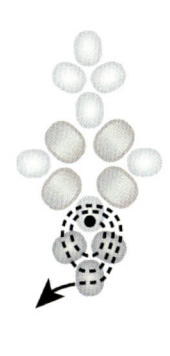

   *Step 4*

5. a) Pick up 12A and pass again through the 1st 3A picked up, in the same direction. Allow the new beads to dangle to the side.
   b) Pick up 1A and pass through 3A, positioning the 1st corner.
   c) Repeat b) twice more, to position the next 2 corners.
   d) Pass through the head bead of the Hubble stitch from the threadless side, to use it as the 4th corner. We'll call this an A Square (ASq).

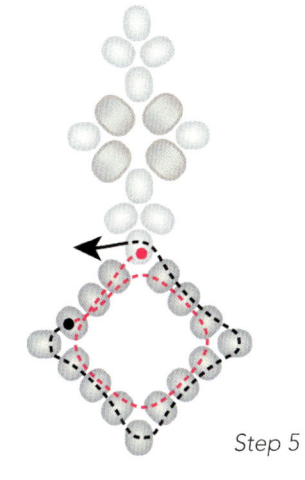

6. Weave through 8A to exit the opposite corner of the ASq.

7. a) Pick up 3A.
   b) Pass through all 3A again, in the same direction.
   c) Pass through the ASq corner bead (now the head bead).
   d) Continue on through the awaiting arm bead to complete the stitch.
   e) Pass through the body bead, as in the diagram, to step up.

   *Step 5*

8. a) Repeat steps 2–7 another 39 times.
   b) Work steps 2–4d) once more.
   c) Weave through to exit the next corner bead of the BSq.

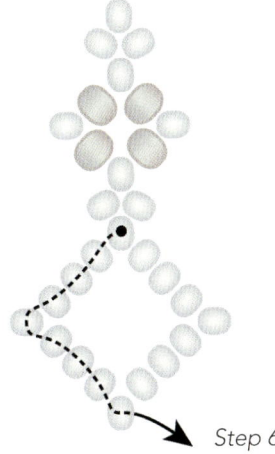

*Step 6*

*Step 7*

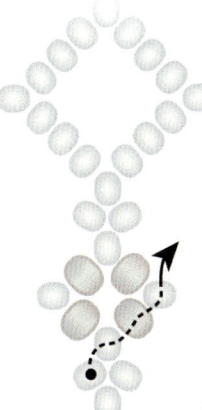

*Step 8*

> "I would not only give you my treasure, but my blood, for your honour and that of your house."
>
> Isabella D'Este.

Matins and Vespers

**9** **Row 2**: This row is identical to row 1, but the sequence is staggered. Work an ASq onto this corner bead and weave on to exit the corner bead, as in the diagram.

**10**  a) Work step 7 (on page 61) to make the inverted Hubble.
b) Work a BSq incorporating the corner of the ASq, instead of picking up an A for that corner.
c) Weave on to emerge from the end corner bead.
d) Work step 5 to make a basic Hubble stitch and step up out of the head bead.

**11** a) Working from step 6 onwards, continue repeating the sequence and incorporating the corner beads from the 1st row, until the 2nd row is complete.
b) Weave around the final ASq to exit the corner bead as in the diagram, ready to start the 3rd row.

**12** **Row 3**:

a) Work a BSq from this corner bead.
b) Weave around to the topmost corner to build the end Hubble stitch before weaving on to work step 5 (to complete the partner 'bookend' Hubble stitch) and continue with the sequence.

**13** **Row 4**: This row will be zipped onto the 1st row, while simultaneously incorporating the G beads.

a) Curl row 1 around behind to join row 4 from the right-hand side, as shown in the diagram.
b) Work an ASq from the row 3 BSq corner bead, incorporating the corner bead from the row 1 BSq.
c) With the ASq completed, the thread is exiting the shared corner between rows 4 and 3, as in the diagram.

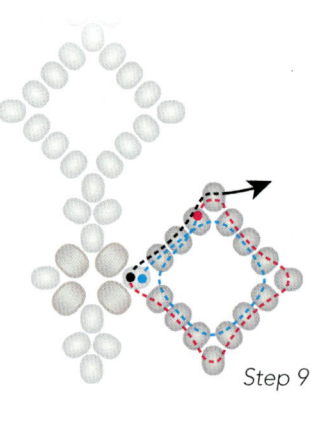

*Step 9*

*Step 10*

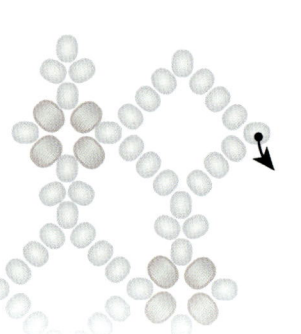

*Step 11b*

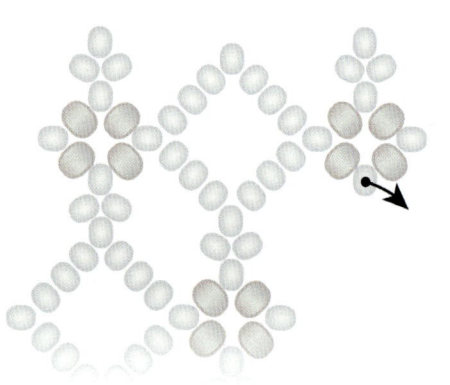

*Step 12*

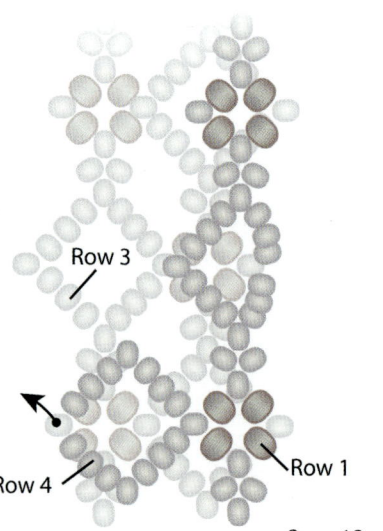

*Step 13*

14. Work this next stitch loosely so you can see all threads clearly, before snuggling everything up tightly.

    a) Pick up 1G and pass down through the corner bead shared between rows 1 and 2.
    b) Pass up inside the tube of beadwork (so no thread will be visible on the outside of the beadwork when G is in position), and back through G, in the opposite direction.
    c) Pass down inside the tube of beadwork and up through the previous corner bead, from the threadless side, to emerge exactly as in step 13.
    d) Snuggle up tightly, but if it's a bit of a struggle, it could be due to the finish on the beads affecting their size. Try squeezing the beadwork around G, like a pea in a pod, and slide G away from the junction inside the tube a fraction, while snuggling.

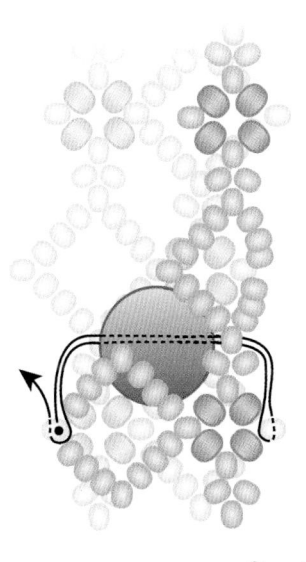

15. Weave up to exit the next corner bead to continue the sequence.

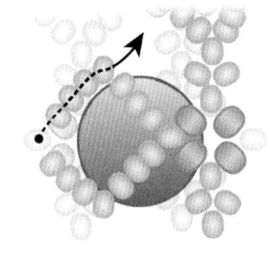

16. Work the following:

    a) Inverted Hubble.
    b) BSq, continuing to incorporate the corner beads from rows 1 and 3.
    c) Basic Hubble stitch.
    d) ASq.
    e) Step 14 (to incorporate the next G bead).
    f) Step 15.
    g) Repeat steps a)–f) until the rope is complete.
    h) Weave around to exit the corner bead at the rope end.

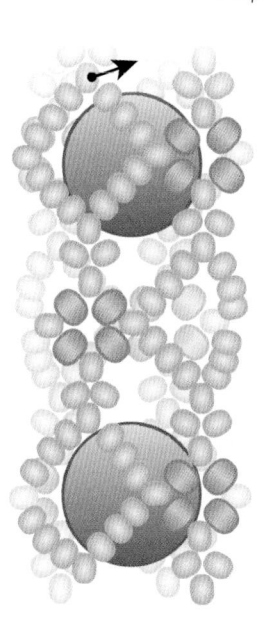

17. View the rope end on.

18. Let's tidy up the rope end:

    a) Work step 7 on page 61 (inverted Hubble stitch).
    b) Weave around to exit the corner bead of row 2, opposite.
    c) Make another inverted Hubble stitch.

19. a) With the thread emerging from a body bead, pick up 1A and pass through the adjacent head bead.
    b) Pick up 1A and pass through the adjacent body bead.
    c) Repeat steps a)–b).
    d) Weave on to emerge from the next body bead, as in the diagram.

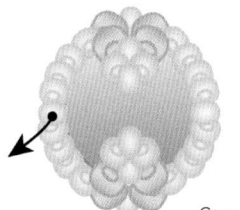

*Step 14*

*Step 15*

*Step 16*

*Step 17*

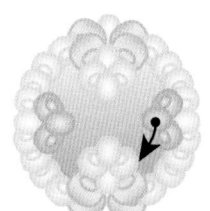

*Step 18*

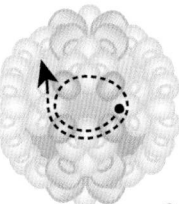

*Step 19*

Matins and Vespers

**20** Make a link thus:

    a) Pick up 7A and pass through the body bead opposite.
    b) Pass back through all 7A, in the opposite direction.
    c) Pass through the 1st body bead from the threadless side.
    d) Finish off.

*Step 20*

**21** At the other end of the rope, weave the tail thread around to exit the corner bead, as in step 18 diagram; follow steps 19–21 to tidy this end in the same way.

## Bail

**1** **Row 1 – 1st stitch**:

    a) Take your pendant and weave around to exit the left side of the left, front, head bead at the top of the cross.
    b) Pick up 2A, pass through the head bead below and on through the 1st A just picked up.
    c) Pick up 1A, 1E, 1A (arm, spacer and future head).
    d) Missing out the last A, pass down through E in the opposite direction, and on through the 1st A in the same direction as before.
    e) Pass through the awaiting arm bead.
    f) Snuggle up as described in step 2e) of the SR on page 57.

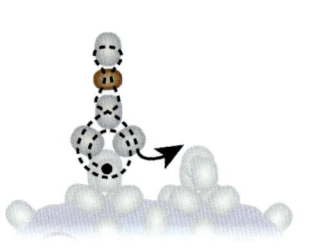

*Step 1*

**2** **2nd stitch**:

    a) Pick up 3A.
    b) Backstitch through the next head bead.
    c) Pass up through the 2nd A picked up, in the same direction as before.

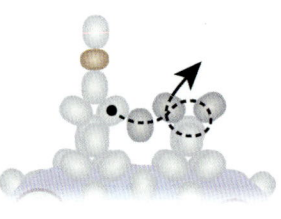

*Step 2*

**3** **2nd stitch cont.**:

    a) Work steps 1c)–f) to complete the extension of the stitch.
    b) To step up, pass through the body, arm, head, spacer and future head beads, to emerge as in the diagram.

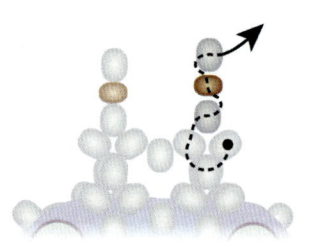

**4** a) Repeat steps 1–3 six more times (7 rows in all).

**Row 8**:

    b) Curl the bail over the rope, between where the 2 central G beads are positioned, to set the cross in place.
    c) **1st stitch**: Repeat step 1b).
    d) Pass through the corresponding back, head bead on the SR, and down through the awaiting arm bead.
    e) Snuggle up, ensuring the bail settles centrally between the 2 G beads of the rope.
    f) **2nd stitch**: Repeat step 2.
    g) Repeat step d) to complete the 2nd stitch.

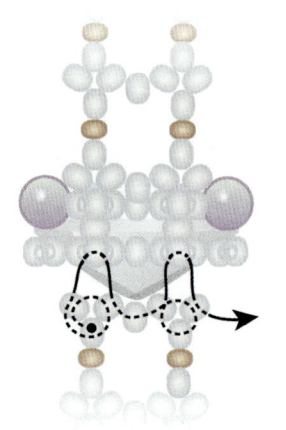

*Step 3*

*Step 4*

## 5. Bail embellishment:

a) Follow the threadpath in the diagram to emerge from the spacer bead of the 7th bail row.
b) Pick up 1C and pass through the spacer bead of the 6th row, to emerge on the right side.

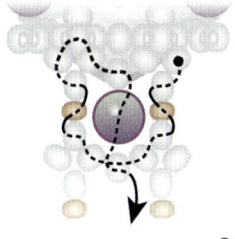

## 6.
a) Repeat step 5b) five more times, working back through the rows of the bail (6 C beads placed in all).
b) With the thread emerging from the right side of the row 1 spacer bead, pass back up the last C bead placed, in the opposite direction.
c) Pass through the next spacer bead from left to right, balancing the stitch correctly.

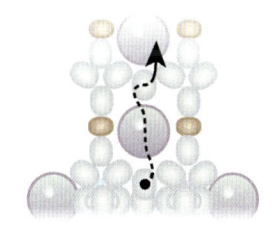

## 7.
a) Repeat the threadpath described in 6b) five more times to balance all the stitches.
b) Finish off.

*Step 5*

*Step 6*

## Toggle (bar, ring and links)

### Toggle bar (make 1)

## 1. Row 1 (foundation wave Hubble):

a) With 0.75m/30" thread and using B, work steps 1a)–b) only, of the rope, twice to make 2 basic foundation Hubble stitches, and snuggle them together tightly, so that the 2nd one flips upside down.
b) Make 3 more stitches, snuggling each one up to the last in the same way. That's 5 stitches in total – 3 upright and 2 inverted.
c) Step up to exit the head bead, as in the diagram. In reality all the stitches will be much more snuggled up than in the diagrams, with neighbours' arms fully slid over one another.

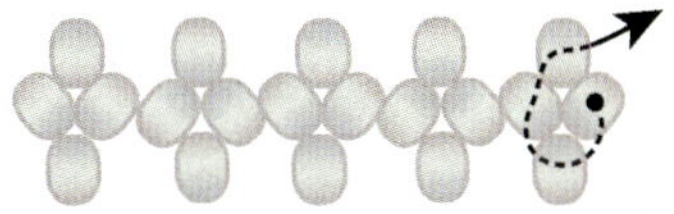

## 2. Row 2 – 1st stitch (basic Hubble stitch):

a) Pick up 2B.
b) Pass through the head bead below, making a ring, and continue on through the 1st B picked up.
c) Pick up 1B and pass through the awaiting arm bead.

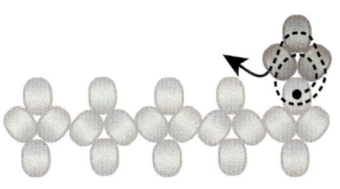

## 3. 2nd stitch (inverted Hubble stitch):

a) Pick up 3B.
b) Pass again through the 1st B picked up, in the same direction.
c) Making sure the next foundation row stitch is upside down, pass through the presenting body bead.
d) Pass through the awaiting arm bead.

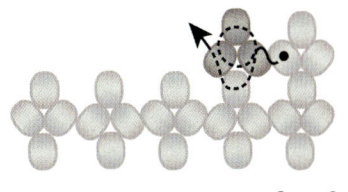

## 4. 3rd stitch (basic Hubble stitch):

Making sure the next foundation row stitch is upright, make a basic Hubble stitch.

*Step 1*

*Step 2*

*Step 3*

*Step 4*

*Matins and Vespers*

**5** **4th and 5th stitches**:

   a) Work step 3 (inverted).
   b) Work step 4 (upright).
   c) Step up to exit the head bead, as in the diagram.

**6** **Row 3**: Repeat steps 2–5 to complete the 3rd row.

   Lie the beadwork flat on your work mat. Using the head/body beads as hinges, fold the 1st and 3rd rows towards you to form a little 'gutter' shape.

**7** **Row 4 (zip up)**: This is an interesting threadpath, where stitches are worked alternately on one side, then the other.

   a) **1st stitch**: With the thread exiting the row 3 head bead, pick up 2B (arm beads) and pass through the same head bead, making a ring.
   b) Pass again through the 1st B picked up.
   c) Pass through the presenting body bead of row 1 opposite.
   d) Continue on through the awaiting arm bead.

**8** a) **2nd stitch**: Pick up 2B, backstitch through the row 1 head bead (marked 2).
   b) Pass again through the 1st B picked up, in the same direction.
   c) Pass through the presenting body bead of row 3 opposite.
   d) Continue on through the awaiting arm bead.
   e) **3rd stitch**: Pick up 2B, backstitch through the row 3 head bead (marked 3).
   f) Repeat steps b)–d)
   g) **4th and 5th stitches**: as for 2nd and 3rd stitches, respectively.

**9** Turn the beadwork to view it end on; outermost are the 4 arm beads with the thread exiting one of them.

   a) Make a basic Hubble stitch on this arm bead.
   b) Pick up 1C, 2A and backstitch through the next arm bead.
   c) Pass again through the 1st of the 2A picked up, in the same direction.
   d) Pick up 1A and pass down the awaiting arm bead.

**10** a) Repeat steps 9b)–d) twice more.
   b) Pick up 1C and pass up through the arm and head beads of the 1st stitch made in this row.
   c) Weave through the arm and body beads to emerge from the body bead (that was the end arm bead), as in the diagram.

**11** a) Pick up 1G, 1E and, missing out E, pass back through G in the opposite direction.
   b) Pass through the body (end arm) bead on the opposite side of the bar.
   c) Work back along this threadpath towards the 1st body bead.
   d) Pass through the 1st body bead from the threadless side, making a circuit.

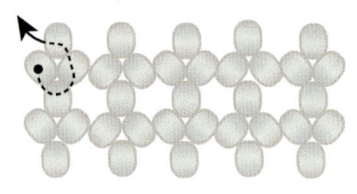

*Step 5*

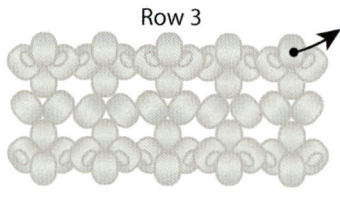

Row 3

Row 1

*Step 6*

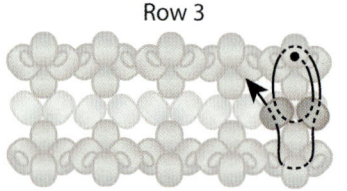

Row 3

Row 1

*Step 7*

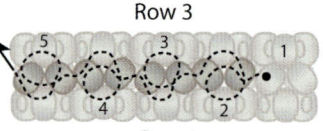

Row 3

Row 1

*Step 8*

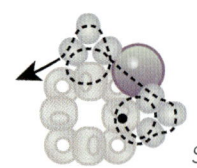

*Step 9*

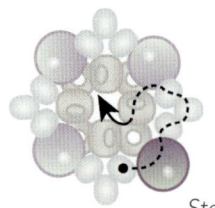

*Step 10*

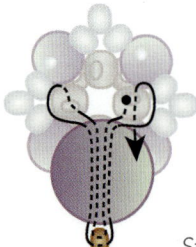

*Step 11*

*Matins and Vespers*

12. Make a loop connection:

    a) Weave through to exit the body bead marked 3.
    b) Pick up 9A and pass through the threadless side of the body bead.
    c) Weave on to exit an arm bead at the other end of the bar.

13. Work steps 9–11 to complete the bar embellishment.

*Step 12*

**Toggle ring**

14. **Row 1 (foundation circular wave Hubble):**

    a) With 1m/40" thread and using B, work 12 wave Hubble stitches as per the toggle bar. There will be 6 upright and 6 inverted stitches.
    b) Join the 12th stitch onto the 1st by passing through the arm and head beads.
    c) Pass around all 4 beads of the 1st Hubble once more for security, to exit the head bead, as in the diagram.

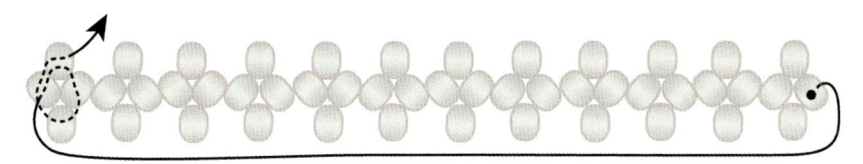

*Step 14*

15. **Row 2**: This is an increase row so it's worked in HorSO wave Hubble; we'll use A beads as the spacers.

    a) **1st stitch (upright)**: Make a Hubble stitch on this head bead.
    b) **2nd stitch (inverted)**: Pick up 1A, 3B and, ignoring A, pass again through the 1st B picked up, in the same direction.
    c) Checking that the 2nd stitch of the 1st row is upside down, pass through the presenting body bead and on through the awaiting arm bead.

16. a) **3rd stitch (upright)**: Pick up 1A, 2B and, checking that the 3rd stitch of the 1st row is upright, backstitch through the presenting head bead.
    b) Pass through the 1st B picked up, in the same direction.
    c) Pick up 1B and pass through the awaiting arm bead.

*Step 15*

17. a) Repeat steps 15b)–16c) four more times, continually checking that the row 1 stitches are correctly upright or inverted (for odd stitches they must be upright, evens – inverted).
    b) Repeat steps 15b)–c) once more.
    c) Closing the row: Pick up 1A and pass through the arm and head beads of the 1st stitch.
    d) Pass around all 4 beads of this 1st stitch again, for security, exiting the head bead, as in the diagram.

*Step 16*

*Step 17*

Matins and Vespers

**18** **Row 3:** This row is also HorSO wave Hubble, but the spacers are B beads. Work steps 15–17, substituting B beads where A beads were used. Don't forget the final B spacer bead.

**19** **Row 4 (zip up):** This row also reflects row 2. The head beads, where the 12 stitches will be made, have been numbered in the diagram.

a) Currently the beadwork is slightly conical, so, using that hinge characteristic between rows, manipulate the 1st row to turn inside the cone, making a circular gutter shape.
b) **1st stitch**: Work step 7 of the bar.
c) **2nd stitch**: Pick up 1A, 2B and, ignoring A, make the stitch on the head bead marked 2, as per steps 8a)–e) of the bar.

*Step 18*

**20** **Row 4 cont.:**

a) Repeat 19c) ten more times, working back and forth for each stitch on a numbered head bead.
b) Closing the row: Pick up 1A and pass through the arm and head beads of the 1st stitch, towards the centre of the ring. The direction of this pass is very important!
c) Pass around the 4 beads of the 1st stitch and continue on through the arm and body beads to emerge as in the diagram.

**21** a) Pick up 1A, 1C, 1A and pass through the adjacent head/body bead.
b) Repeat a) 11 more times.
c) Weave down to the underside to exit a head/body bead, ready to make the connection loop.

*Step 19*

**22** Make a connection loop as per step 12b) of the bar, and finish off.

**Links**

**23** Using A beads only, and following the links instructions as for Anne Boleyn, page 44.

a) Make 1 link between the rope and the toggle ring.
b) Make 3 links between the other end of the rope and the toggle bar.

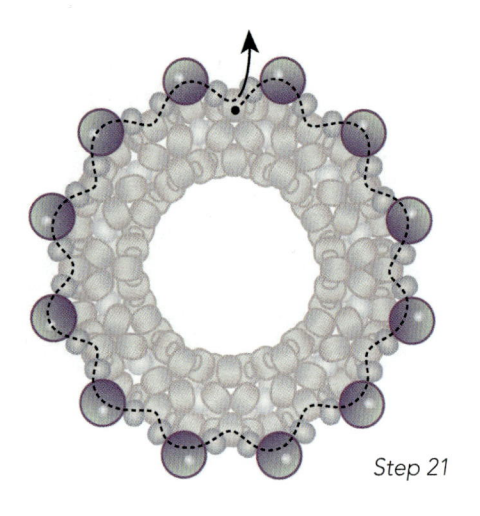

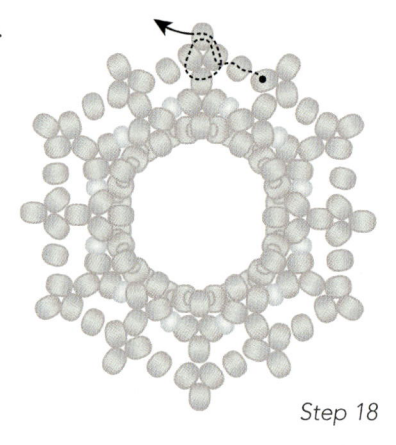

*Step 20*

*Step 21*

*Step 22*

Matins and Vespers — 68 —

MERELS TOKEN NECKLACE

# MERELS TOKEN NECKLACE

In winter, the gaming table was brought near to the hearth in the great hall. Many hours would be filled, pondering over the next move, to outwit or be outwitted; while outside the weather froze the river and closed the roads. Chess, drafts and backgammon were marked out in dark and light woods on the table top, but at one end and almost worn away, were the inlaid lines of the Merels game. On New Year's day, the day for exchanging gifts, two brothers had been given a set of gaming tokens of fine metal filigree, gold for the eldest, silver for his younger brother, each token holding a gleaming garnet. Strategy was everything in the game of Merels, and the perfect education for boys who would grow up to enter the world at court, where intrigue, spies, factions and favours meant that nothing was as it first seemed.

The Tudor period was filled with pattern – geometric pattern. Diamond patterns were stitched into garments and studded with pearls or jewels at every intersection. Fine embroidery of black thread in complex patterns on white linen was used on shirts and cuffs. On a grand scale, chequerboards were picked out in floor tiles and ceiling plaster; windows were filled with diamond panes of leaded glass. Outside, complex knot gardens were created and intricate decorative brickwork was juxtaposed with blackened timbers to better show off the limed white walls between them.

There is something reassuring about beading the repetitious lattice of netting and it had to be included for that reason. The pendants were inspired by metal and jewel billiments and ouches*, which were stitched directly on to clothing.

*Billiments and ouches were metal and jewel pieces with metal loops. Often square, they would be stitched along the edges of garments and headwear. Both could be removed and re-used, and they were frequently stitched with groups of pearls between them. Billiments were laid in rows, ouches were stitched individually, often to highlight the pattern in a fabric.

**Elements**: bezelled pendant rivoli, peyote ring, plain Albion stitch ring, cabochon bead ring, netted rope

**Techniques**: Albion stitch, right angle weave, netting

**Completed necklace length**: 54cm/21¼"

**You will need**:

16g x Miyuki seed beads size 11° 1087 (metallic dark steel) (A)
17g x Miyuki seed beads size 11° 460 (metallic plum iris) (B)
2g x Miyuki seed beads size 15° 4221 (duracoat galvanised light pewter) (C)
2g x Miyuki seed beads size 15° 460 (metallic plum iris) (D)
13 x 2-hole cabochon beads 6mm (pearl tahitian blue) (E)
2 x Miyuki seed beads size 8° (use what you have that matches) (F)
3 x Swarovski® rivolis #1122 14mm (amethyst) (G)
40–45cm 4mm diameter neoprene jewellery tube (or similar)
1 necklace clasp and 2 jump rings (antique copper)

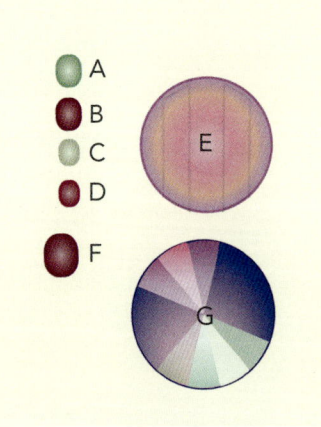

## Fascinating fact:

*Nine Men's Morris was a hugely popular game and boards have been found carved into cloister seats in several English churches including Canterbury and Salisbury Cathedrals and Westminster Abbey. Giant outdoor boards were also marked out. In Shakespeare's 'A Midsummer Nights Dream', Titania comments, 'The nine men's morris is filled with mud'.*

*Merels Token necklace*

### Pendant rivoli (Make 3)

It's always fun to find alternative ways to bezel stones and cabochons. This element uses a combination of peyote stitch and netting. The front of the bezel is worked first, then the back, then some embellishment to add detail to the sides and corners and a neat little loop in one corner.

1. Use a stop bead and pick up: 32A, pass through the beads to secure in a ring.

2. Peyote stitch one round of A, then step up at the end of the round.

3. Pick up 5C and pass through the next up bead of the peyote row. Peyote stitch 1B. Keep working round, alternating 5C, 1B. At the end of the round step up through 3C of the 1st 5C added.

4. Pick up 2B, pass through the centre C of the next 5C. Repeat all the way round. At the end of the round, circle through the 2B, 1C beads a 2nd time to secure them in a ring.

5. Weave back to the start round and exit an up bead. Place the rivoli into the bezel face down and hold it as you work the next round.

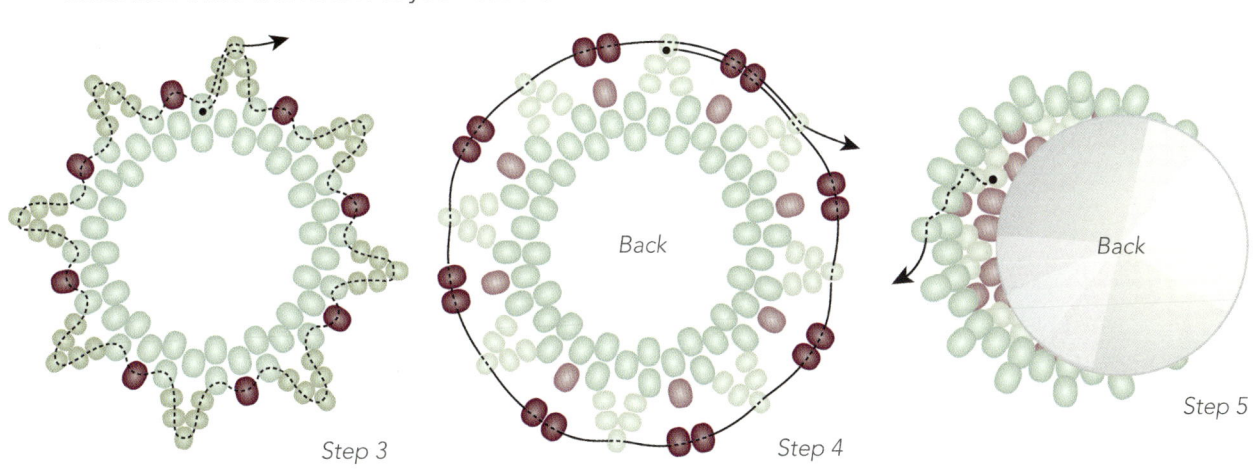

*Step 1*

*Step 2*

*Step 3*

*Step 4*

*Step 5*

Merels Token necklace

6. Peyote stitch 1 round of D, then step up.

7. Pick up 5D, skip 1D (pass over without going through) and pass into the next 1D of the peyote round. Repeat until you are back at the start, then step up through 3D of the 1st set of 5D added.

8. Place 1A between each centre D bead. At the end of the round, circle through the 1D, 1A beads a 2nd time to tighten this ring of beads. Weave back to the start round again, and exit a centre A bead.

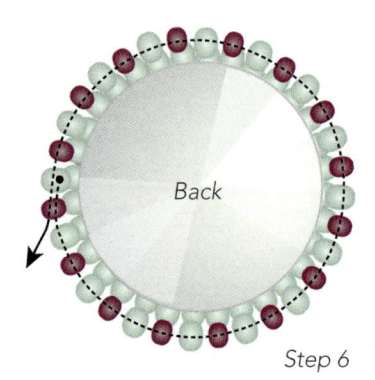

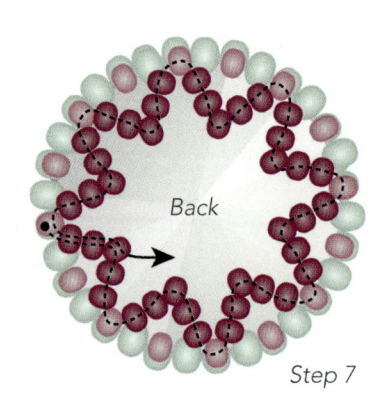

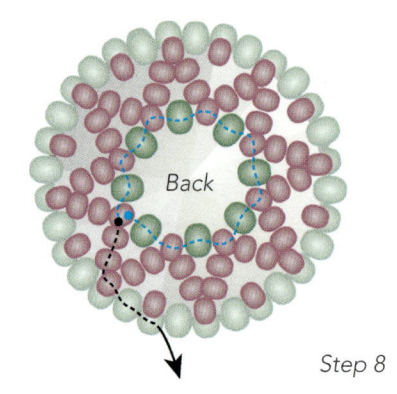

*Step 6*

*Step 7*

*Step 8*

**Edge embellishment**

The edge embellishment creates the corners. On one corner a loop will be added.

1. Peyote stitch 1A in the ditch (that is, peyote stitch through the beads of the centre round of A beads). Repeat until you are back at the start, then step up to exit the 1st 1A added.

2. Pick up 1B, 3D, 1B, skip over 1A and pass into the next 1A. This forms a side embellishment.

3. Pick up 6A, circle through the 3rd A. Pick up 2A, skip 1A and pass into the next 1A. This forms a corner embellishment.

4. Repeat steps 2 and 3 until you are back at the start.

5. Weave through the beads to exit the 1st 2A of a corner.

    Pick up 1B, pass through 3A, pick up 1B, pass through the last 2A of the corner. Repeat to embellish each corner, then weave through the beads to exit the top 1A of the next corner.

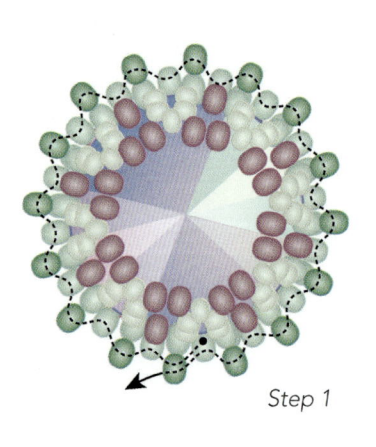

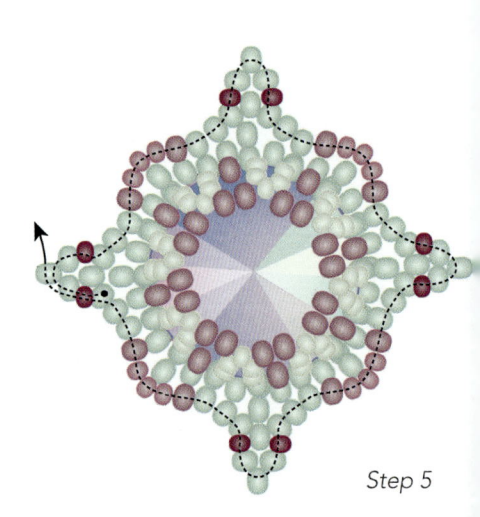

*Step 1*

*Steps 2–4*

*Step 5*

Merels Token necklace

– 72 –

## Corner loop

This is a little loop positioned so that the piece will lie facing forward, so it is important to check the threadpath as you work.

1. Exit the centre top A of a corner. Pick up 2B, 11C, 2B. Pass back through the 1A so the new beads form a ring.

2. Pick up 1B, pass through the 2nd 1B, 11C, and the 1st 1B. Pick up 1B, pass back through the 1A. Repeat the threadpath a 2nd time to strengthen the loop. Finish off the thread tails.

   Make 2 more bezelled rivolis with corner loops.

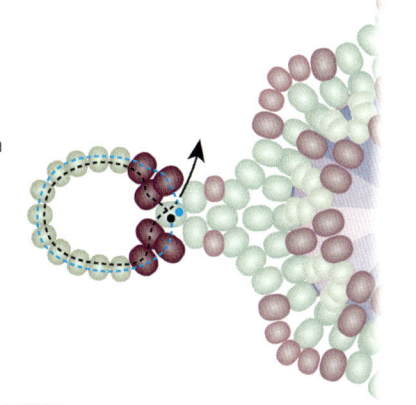

*Steps 1–2*

## Cabochon drop

This is a little pendant worked separately, then attached to the corner opposite a loop on one of the bezelled rivolis.

1. With 50cm/20" of thread, pass through 1 hole of an E. Pick up 2A, pass through the 2nd hole of the 1E.

2. Pick up 2A, pass through the 1st hole of the 1E, then pass through the 2A of step 1.

3. Pick up 1A, 1B, 4A, 1B, 1A. Pass through the 2A of step 2.

4. Pick up 1A, 1B, 4A, 1B, 1A. Pass through the 2A of step 1 and then through the next 1A.

5. Pass through all the A beads, skipping the B beads so they stick out and form little corners. Step up to exit 1B.

6. Make sure the rivoli and cabochon beads are both facing in the same direction.

   Pick up 1B, pass through the centre 1A of the rivoli corner opposite the loop.

   Pick up 1B, pass back through the 1B of the cabochon drop.

   Weave through the beads a 2nd time to strengthen the loop, then finish off the thread tails.

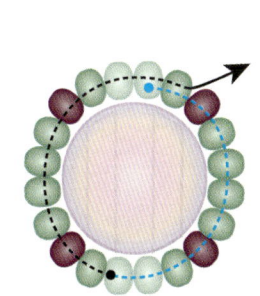

*Steps 1–2*

*Steps 3–4*

*Step 5*

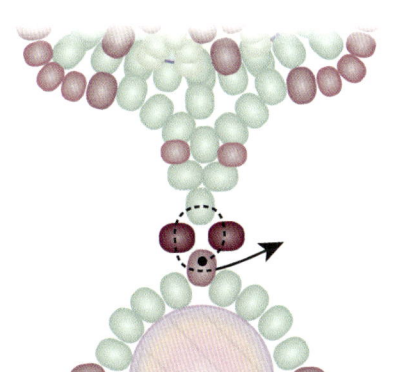

*Step 6*

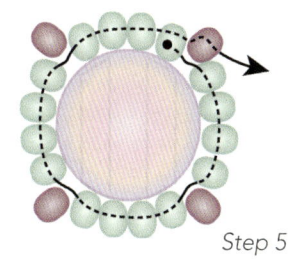

Merels Token necklace

## Peyote ring

Each bezelled rivoli has a little peyote stitch ring, which is worked through the corner loop. **You will need to swivel the ring beads through the loop as you work.** The thread does not pass through any beads of the loop.

1. With 65cm/25" of thread, pick up 24C, pass the needle through the corner loop of a bezelled rivoli, then secure the 24C in a ring.

2. One round C, one round A, one round B, stepping up at the end of each of these 3 rounds.

3. a) Weave back to the start round and exit an up bead.
   b) Peyote one round A, then zip this round to the 1B round. Finish off the thread tails.

   Repeat at the loop corners of the other 2 bezelled rivolis.

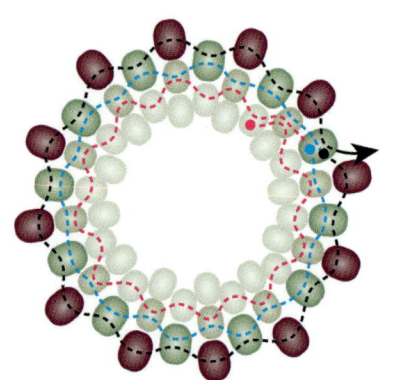

*Rivoli bezel*    *Step 1*

*Step 2* 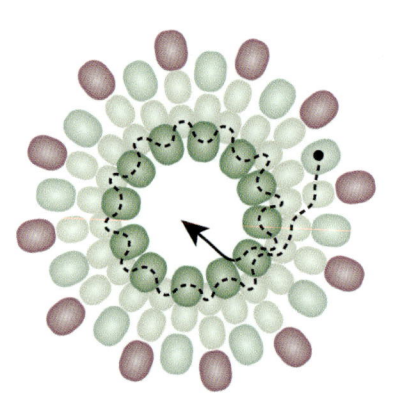    *Step 3a* 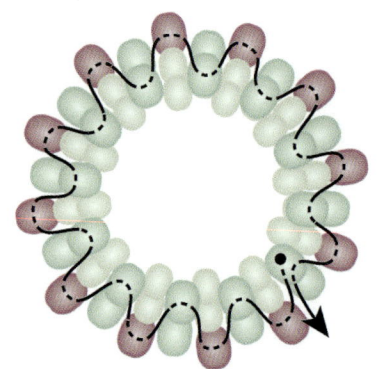    *Step 3b*

## Netted rope

A simple netted rope worked around a centre core. The centre core needs to be a soft, flexible material so that the beadwork can move during wear. Work with the core in place, it is much easier than trying to feed one in later.

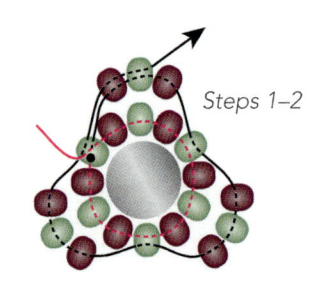

1. Start with a 1.5m/60" length of thread and leave a 20cm/8". Pick up 1A, 1B alternately until you have a total of 12 beads (6A, 6B). Secure the beads in a ring with a knot, leave a 30cm/12" tail. Exit 1A.

2. Pick up 1B, 1A, 1B, skip over 1B, 1A, 1B of the ring and pass into the next 1A. Repeat until you are back at the start, then step up through 1B, 1A of the 1st set added.

3. Pick up 1B, 1A, 1B, pass through the centre 1A of the next set of beads of the previous round. Repeat until you are back at the start, then step up through 1B, 1A of the 1st set added in this round.

   Keep repeating step 3 until the core is covered and your necklace is the right length.

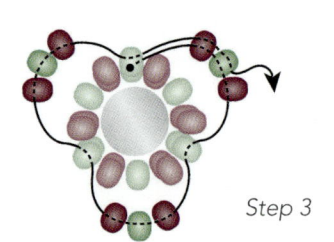

*Steps 1–2*

*Step 3*

> *Fascinating fact:*
>
> *The configuration of the board was given significance as a symbol of protection from evil. At the centre, the mill, or cauldron symbolising regeneration, from which the four cardinal directions, four winds or four elements radiate with geometric precision.*

Merels Token necklace

## Finish the ends

1. Step up as usual on the last round, then pass through the 3 centre A beads, then exit 1A. Pick up 1F, 9C. Pass back through the 1F and pass through a different 1A from which you started.

2. Repeat the threadpath to strengthen the loop, then weave back through to the end rows of netting.

   Use the remaining thread to stitch through the core and the netting beads. This secures the core in place so the netting doesn't stretch beyond the end of the core.

   Repeat the steps at the start end. Attach a jump ring through each 9C loop and a clasp to the jump rings.

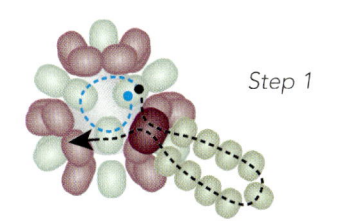

*Step 1*

## Cabochon bead rings (Make 3)

Each cabochon ring slides on to the netted rope. Each has a loop of beads worked through the peyote ring to create the bezelled rivoli pendants. The beading creates a ring with four apertures, which have a cabochon bead stitched across them as embellishment.

1. With a wingspan of thread, leave a 15cm/6" tail and then pick up 24A and secure them in a ring. Exit 1A.

2. Pick up 4B stalk, 1A tip. Pass back through 4B and the 1A started from. Then pass through 6A on the ring.

3. Repeat step 2 until you are back at the start, then step up to exit the 1A of the 1st stitch added (4 stitches in total).

4. Place 5A between each 1A stitch tip, then secure all the A beads in a ring.

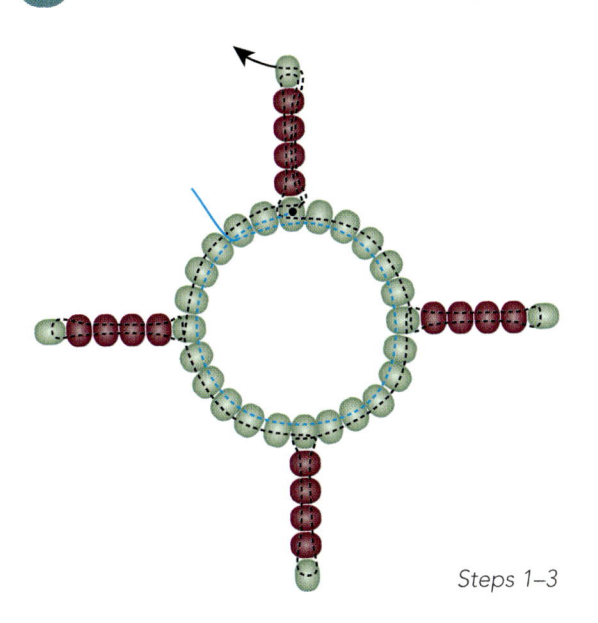

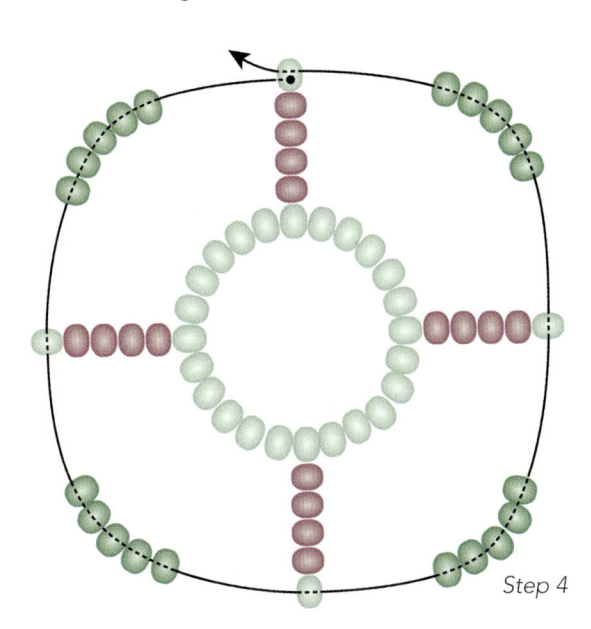

*Steps 1–3*

*Step 4*

## Fascinating fact:

*Garnets were worn around the neck to drive away childish fears, overcome sorrow and banish troublesome dreams. Garnets were also thought of as a symbol of constancy, to promote wealth and strengthen the heart; the perfect choice for a father to give to a son.*

5. Exit a tip bead and pick up 1C, 1E (so the dome faces outwards), 1C.

   Pass through the tip bead, the 5A beads of the aperture and the next tip bead.

   Pick up 1C, pass through the 2nd hole of 1E, pick up 1C, pass through the next 1A tip bead.

   Repeat to embellish each aperture, then exit a 1A tip bead.

6. Each cabochon ring has a loop of beads worked from the edges. The loop passes through the peyote ring already attached to the bezelled rivoli.

   a) Exit 1A tip bead, pick up 2B, 11C, 2B, pass the needle through the peyote ring. Pass through the 1A opposite the tip bead started from on the cabochon ring.

   b) Pick up 1B, pass through 2nd 1B, 11C, 1st 1B. Pick up 1B then pass through the 1A started from in step 1. Weave through all the beads of the loop a 2nd time to strengthen it, then finish off the thread tails. Repeat with the other two bezelled cabochons.

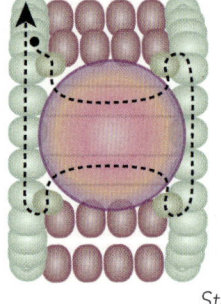

*Step 5*

## Plain Albion stitch ring (Make 8)

These are slightly smaller rings, a little tricky to slide onto the netted rope, but they will stay where you leave them, enabling you to arrange the pendants at the front of the necklace.

1. Pick up 20A and secure in a ring, then exit 1A.

2. Pick up 1B stalk, 1A tip. Pass back through 1B, back through the 1A started from, then through 2A of the ring. Repeat (10 stitches in total), then step up to exit 1A tip bead of the 1st stitch added in this round.

3. Pick up 1A, pass through the next 1A tip. Repeat all the way round, then secure this ring of 20A. Finish off the thread tails.

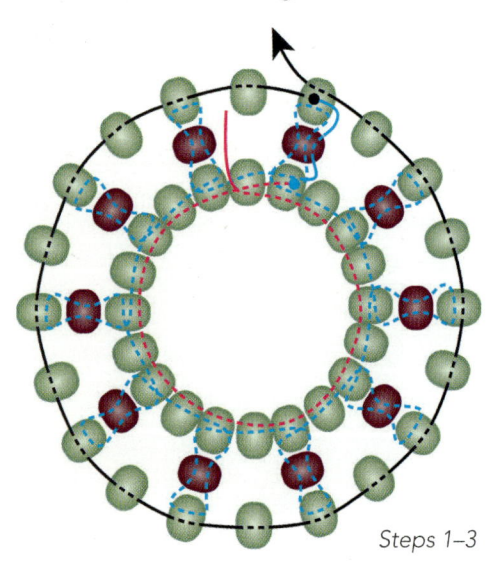

*Steps 1–3*

Merels Token necklace

– 76 –

THE NONSUCH TOUR DE COU

# THE NONSUCH TOUR DE COU

April 22nd, 1538, Hampton Court Palace. A laugh, like the deep, satisfied roar of a lion, burst forth from Henry as he remembered that glorious day six months before when his son and heir, Edward, had been born. This morning he had awoken, content and excited, as today not only marked his 30th year as regent over the whole of England, but also the plans for his magnificent new palace had come to fruition, and work was to begin immediately. The moment Henry was told of the Prince's birth, he had begun discussions with the royal architects, to celebrate the house of Tudor, and leave a great legacy for all to behold, that would rival even Francis I's elegant Château de Chambord.

After a good deal of opposition from those troublesome villagers at Cuddington, Henry's plans were finally able to proceed when the crown granted them a generous compensation for their displacement, and the village was razed to the ground in readiness for the building work. Within weeks, word had spread about the plans for the new palace. There was talk that none such building had ever been created, so the project soon became known as the Nonsuch Palace.

On that joyous day in October, Henry had also summoned the royal jewellers from London, to give them a fine commission – a beautiful jewel of equal magnificence for his dear wife, Jane, who had finally borne him the heir he had craved for so long. This jewel was to encircle her neck in the style she preferred – a 'Tour de Cou' – and it was to bear a reference to Henry, showing his great love for her and his deepest gratitude. He had planned to present it to her at the first feast held in the new palace. But that charming plan had dissolved into nothing when Jane died 12 days after giving birth, and today, as he watched the carts of provisions arriving and the groundsmen going about their business, Henry's happiness was displaced by this memory. Oh, how he missed her kind, gentle companionship. Shaken from his reverie, he opened a little drawer in his desk to reveal the lovely golden piece that the jewellers had delivered, two weeks too late. Closing the drawer with purpose, Henry rushed from his chamber to the nursery where he found his beloved son being cradled in the arms of the startled wet nurse. With a sad smile he approached them and planted the lightest of kisses on the sleeping infant's forehead.

**Elements**: bubble Hubble motifs, centrepiece, chimney toggles

**Techniques**: Hubble stitch variation – bubble Hubble (3-drop Hubble and HorSO Hubble combined), CRAW, tubular peyote, brick stitch (modified)

**Finished choker length**: 35.30cm/13¾"

Composed of 11 motifs (each 2.9cm/1¼") plus the centrepiece (3.4cm/1⅜"). Options for lengthening the choker, and adaptations for shaping into a necklace, will be discussed in the motif instructions.

**You will need**:

21g x Miyuki seed beads size 8° 4203 (duracoat galvanized yellow gold) (A)
6g x Miyuki seed beads size 11° 4203 (duracoat galvanized yellow gold) (B)
8g x Miyuki seed beads size 15° 4203 (duracoat galvanized yellow gold) (C)
27 x Swarovski® pearls #5810 3mm (cream) (D)
12 x Swarovski® rivolis #1122 ss47 10mm (pacific opal) (E)
0.5g x Czech charlotte seed beads size 15° (24Kt gold-plated) (F)
60 x Swarovski® xilion chatons #1088 ss17 4–4.2mm (scarabaeus green) (G)
2 x Swarovski® pear drops #5500 9x6mm (crystal paradise shine)
   (can substitute other crystal drop beads) (H)
1 x Swarovski® tear drop pendant #6000 15x7.5mm (crystal paradise shine)
   (can substitute other drop beads) (J)

> "*My dear friend and mistress. The bearer of these few lines from thy entirely devoted servant will deliver into thy fair hands a token of my true affection for thee, hoping you will keep it forever in your sincere love for me... H. R.*"
>
> *A letter from Henry to Jane whilst Anne Boleyn was in the Tower awaiting trial*

## Motif (Make 11)

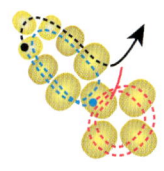

**1** With a good wingspan:

    a) Pick up 4A.
    b) Pass through all 4A again making a ring, and the 1st A once more. These will be the body beads for 3-drop Hubble stitches in the next row.

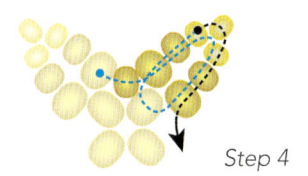

*Steps 1–3*

**2** Phase 1, making the body:

    a) Pick up 1A, 1B, 2C, 1B, 1A.
    b) Pass through the A bead of the 1st row, and continue on through the 1st A, B and C just picked up.

*Step 4*

**3** Phase 2, adding the head: pick up 1C, pass through the adjacent C, B and A. That completes one 3-drop Hubble stitch.

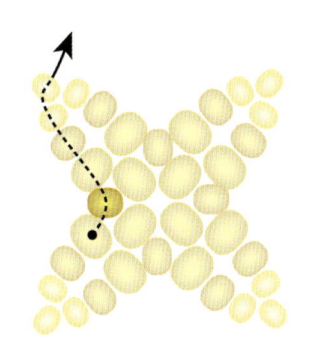

**4**   a) Pick up 1B (spacer bead), 1A, 1B, 2C, 1B, 1A.
    b) Backstitch through the next A bead of the 1st row.
    c) Continue on through the 1st A, B and C picked up, in the same direction.
    d) Repeat step 3.

**5**   a) Repeat step 4 twice more.
    b) The final spacer bead must be added before closing the row. Pick up 1B and pass up through the adjacent A, B, and 2C of the 1st stitch in this row, to exit the head bead. **Note**: This is the finished bubble Hubble unit (BHU). There are no connections between the spacer beads and the central ring of A beads. When weaving around the BHU, **do not** connect them as it will spoil the shape.

*Step 5*

The Nonsuch Tour de Cou

## 4-way connector (4W)

**6** The motif comprises 4 BHUs joined at the centre by a 4W. Pick up 4C, draw them down close to the beadwork, and pass through the 1st C bead just picked up, in the same direction, making a little ring that dangles to the side of the BHU. **Note**: Do not pass through that head bead, just let it dangle!

**7** a) Pick up 1C and pass into the next C, forming corner 1. Make sure that C bead snaps tightly into place, making a lovely corner.
b) Snuggle up so that no thread is visible now between the connector and the BHU. Try to remain aware of the side of the head bead where the thread was dangling.
c) Repeat a) twice more to place a C bead in each of positions 2 and 3. Finally complete the 4th corner by passing through the head bead of the BHU from the threadless side.

*Steps 6–7*

**8** Weave around to emerge from the position 3, C bead.

**9** This stitch has a head but no body, so we must build an inverted 3-drop Hubble here. With the thread emerging from the lower side of the 4W bead, pick up 1C, 1B, 3A, 1B, 1C, and pass through all 7 beads again. **Note**: Do not pass through the 4W bead yet.

**10** a) Pass through the 4W bead from the threadless side.
b) Continue on through the adjacent C, B, and 2A to emerge as in the diagram.

*Step 8*

**11** a) Pick up 3A and pass through the A bead from which the thread was emerging, making a ring.
b) Continue on through A, B, C, C, C, B, A of the 3-drop Hubble as in the diagram.

**12** Work steps 4–5 to complete the 2nd BHU, and weave on around the outer edge of the BHU to exit the head bead, from the side facing away from the 1st BHU, as in the diagram.

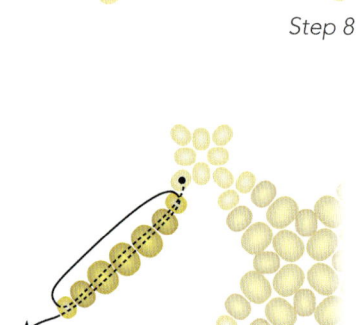

*Step 9*

*Step 10*     *Step 11*     *Step 12*

The Nonsuch Tour de Cou

- 80 -

## 3-way connector (3W)

**13** The BHUs are joined at the edges of the motif by 4 3Ws. Pick up 3C and pass through the 1st C picked up again.

**14** a) Pick up 1C and pass through the next C.
b) Pass through the head bead of the 1st BHU.
c) Pass through the next C.
d) Pass through the head bead of the 2nd BHU.

*Due to the number of threadpaths to follow around these BHUs, you might find you are exiting the head bead on the opposite side to that in step 12, ie towards the adjacent BHU. If so, simply follow steps 13 and 14 for the alternative 3W threadpath.*

*Steps 13–14*

## Alternative for 3-way connector (3W)

**13** Pick up 3C and pass through the 1st C picked up again.

**14** a) Pass through the head bead of the adjacent BHU.
b) Pass through the next C.
c) Pick up 1C and pass through the next C.
d) Pass through the head bead of the other BHU.
e) Weave on to the next place you need to be.

**15** Continuing on from step 14, weave through the 2nd BHU back to the 4W, to exit another corner, as in the diagram.

*Steps 13–14 (Alternative)*

**16** Work steps 9–15 to make the 3rd BHU and the 3W connecting it to the 1st BHU.

**17** a) Work steps 9–15 to make the 4th BHU.
b) Weave around to make the 2 remaining 3Ws, again taking care which threadpaths you follow.
c) Weave on to the specific A bead, as in the diagram.

**18** We're going to build a 3-drop Hubble structure (one stitch from each BHU) over the front of the beadwork, to trap E.

a) Work steps 2–3 on this A bead.
b) Weave along the threadpath in the diagram to exit the specified A bead.

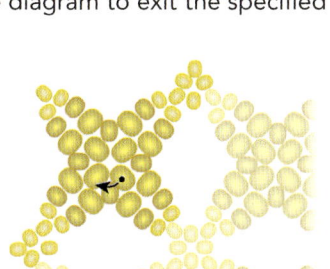

*Step 15*

*Step 16*

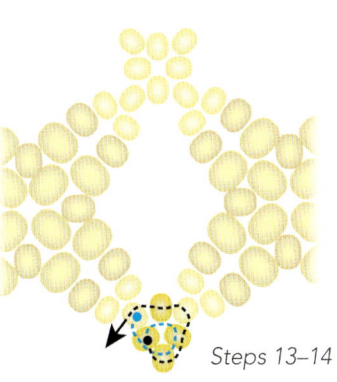

*Step 17*

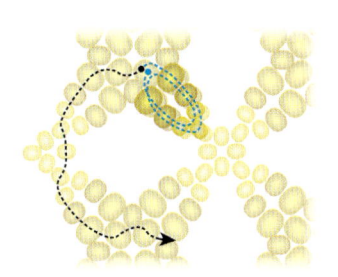

*Step 18*

– 81 –

The Nonsuch Tour de Cou

19. Make the other three 3-drop stitches and weave up to exit the head bead of the last stitch.

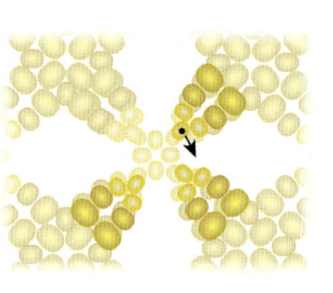

20. Now for a larger version of the 4W:
    a) Pick up 8C and pass through the 1st 2C picked up once more (let it dangle).
    b) Place an E in the centre of the beadwork.
    c) Pass through the next head bead.
    d) Pass through 2C.
    e) Work c)–d) twice more.
    f) Pass through the 1st head bead, from the threadless side, to complete the square.
    g) Weave on to exit the body bead of this stitch, as in the diagram.

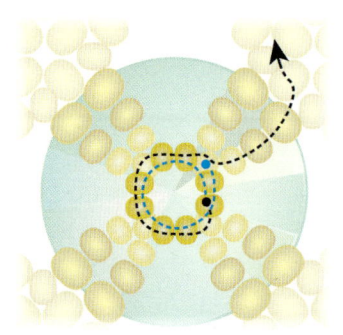

*Step 19*

21. **Tiny chaton trap (TCT)**: Make a basic Hubble stitch onto the A bead thus:
    a) Pick up 2C (arm beads).
    b) Pass through the A bead from which the thread was emerging.
    c) Continue on through the 1st of the 2C just picked up.
    d) Pick up 1C (the head bead).
    e) Pass through the 2nd of the 2C picked up and on through the A bead below.
    f) Continue on to exit the next adjacent A, as in the diagram.

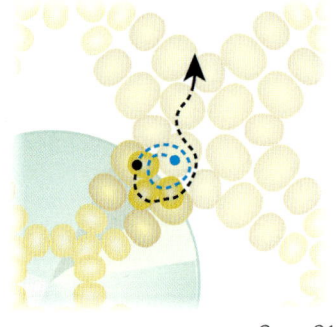

*Step 20*

22. Repeat step 21 three more times to complete the 4 basic Hubble stitches, snuggling up each one tightly, and weave on to exit the head bead.

    **Hot tip!** Sometimes the 4A at the centre of a BHU doesn't settle perfectly, so gently push an awl into the central space between them, twirling it as you do, until the A beads are equally spaced apart. This will help to seat the chaton nicely in the next step.

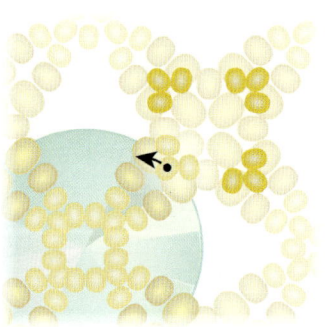

23. Switch to a size 15 needle.
    a) Pick up 2F and pass through the next head bead.
    b) Repeat a) 3 more times.
    c) Keep it loose, and place a G into the trap, ensuring the point at the back is seated in the space at the centre of the A beads.
    d) Holding G exactly in place, draw up the slack thread.
    e) Run around the entire top circuit one or more times, for security.
    f) Weave on to the next TCT location, making 2 half-hitch knots on the way.

*Step 21*

24. Make the other 3 TCTs and weave on to exit a head bead, as in the diagram.

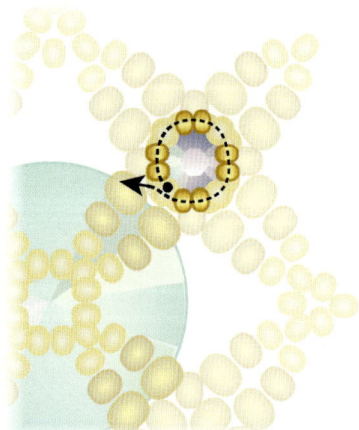

*Step 22*

*Step 23*

*Step 24*

The Nonsuch Tour de Cou — 82 —

**25** **Pearl connection:**
  a) Pick up 1D, 1C and, missing out the C, pass back down through the D in the opposite direction.
  b) Pass through the head bead from the threadless side.
  c) Weave over to the other corner.
  d) Make a 2nd pearl connection.
  e) Pass through D and C again. That's a completed motif.

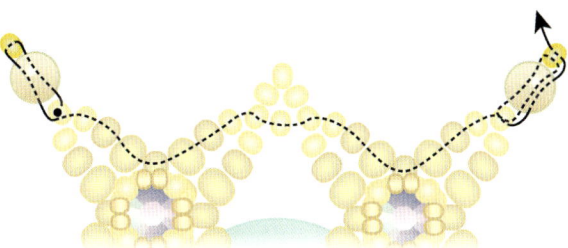

*Step 25*

**26** Work from step 9 onwards, because we must start with an inverted stitch.
**Note**: The bead marked X, is always shared between the 3Ws of adjacent motifs.

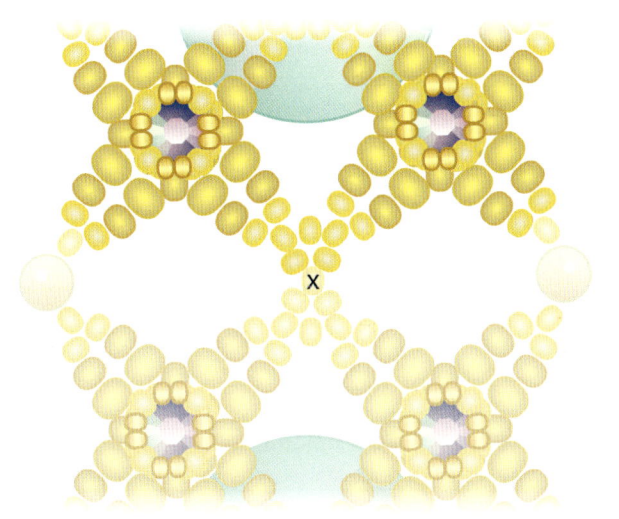

*Step 26*

### Necklace variation

To adapt the choker into a necklace, ie turn it from being linear as a choker, to curving around the neck, here are a couple of modifications that you could try:

  a) Use a larger D bead at the junction between motifs along one edge of the necklace. The curve will be determined by the size of the D bead you choose – the larger the bead, the greater the curve.
  b) Simply don't make a junction between motifs along one edge of the necklace; leave them free moving.

You may wish to increase the length of the choker. This could be by a small distance (millimetres), in which case the simplest solution would be to use larger D beads at the motif junctions or to add an extra C bead at either side of the D.

To increase by larger amounts, you can add another motif as well as modifying the D beads.

Decreases work in the same way – reduce the D bead to a 2mm pearl; work one less motif.

Combine both these sets of adaptations to achieve the length you require.

*The Nonsuch Tour de Cou*

## Centrepiece (CP) (composed of frame and trap) (Make 1)

### Frame

**1** With a good wingspan and using A:

   a) Work a square frame in CRAW, 7 units long x 7 units wide.
   b) Weave around to exit an edge bead (either outer or inner).

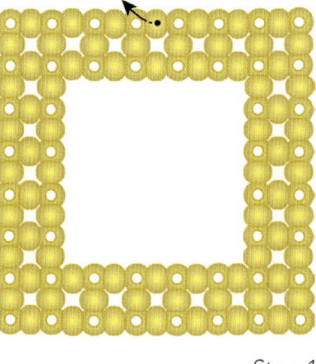

**2** a) Pick up 2C and pass into the next A bead along the edge.
   b) Put 2C into the space between every A bead around both the outside and inside edges, for both the front and the back of the CRAW square, including all external and internal corners.

**3** a) Follow motif steps 21–23 to make a TCT on the 4A of the corner CRAW unit.
   b) Weave on to exit the west A bead of the 2nd stitch along.
   c) Make a 2nd TCT on the 3rd stitch of the front.
   d) Weave on to exit the north bead of the 4th CRAW stitch, as in the diagram.

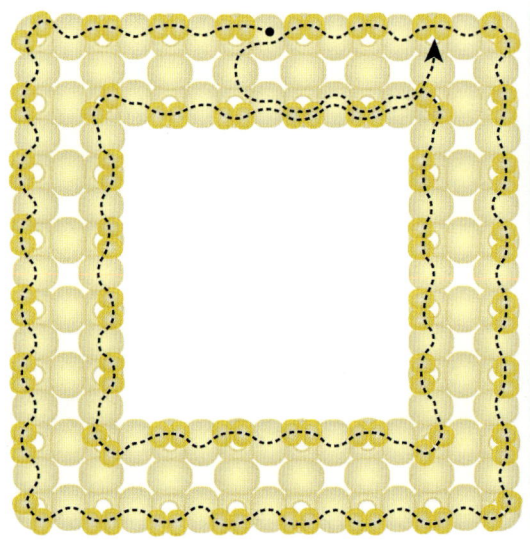

**4** a) Work motif step 21 another 3 times to make 3 basic Hubble stitches.
   b) We won't need to make the 4th Hubble stitch because we're going to share the existing one of the TCT next door. So simply pass up through the arm and head beads of the shared stitch, as in the diagram.

**5** a) Work motif step 23 to complete the 3rd TCT.
   b) Weave on to exit the north A bead of the 5th CRAW stitch.
   c) Work a 4th TCT, sharing the Hubble stitch of the 3rd TCT, as before.
   d) Weave on to exit an A bead of the corner CRAW.
   e) Starting again at step 3, continue until you have completed 16 TCTs.
   f) Finish off.

### Trap

**6** With a new 0.75m/30" length of thread:

   a) Pick up 4C.
   b) Pass through all 4C again making a ring, and the 1st C once more.
   c) Place 1C between each of the 4C – effectively making a lone 4W.
   d) Step up to exit the 1st corner bead.
   e) Work motif steps 9–10 of the motif to make an inverted 3-drop Hubble stitch.
   f) Pass through the body bead, to step up.

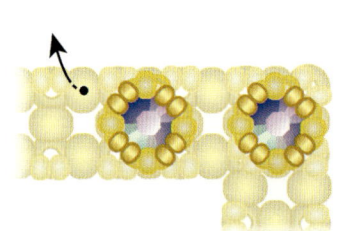

*Step 1*

*Step 2*

*Step 3*

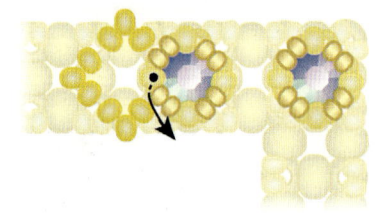

*Step 4*

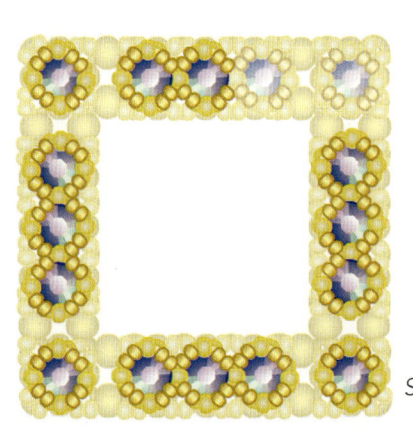

*Step 5*

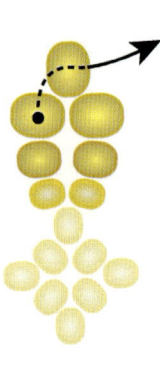

*Step 6*

*The Nonsuch Tour de Cou*

**7**  a) Work motif steps 2–3 to make a 3-drop Hubble onto the body bead of the inverted Hubble.
b) Weave down through the shared body bead, the A, B and C of the arm, the head C bead and finally 2C of the 4W, to emerge as in the diagram.

**8**  a) Work steps 6–7 another 3 times, making 4 branches.
b) Weave up to exit the head bead of the 1st 'branch' we made.

**9**  Here comes another larger 4W again. Pick up 8C, draw them down close to the beadwork, and pass through the 1st 2C beads just picked up, in the same direction, making a little ring that dangles to the side of the head bead.

*Step 7*

**10**  Now we're going to pick up each branch head bead in turn to make the corners. Lay out the beadwork exactly as in the diagram to help with pass directions. The shared body beads of the 3-drop Hubbles are pivot points, allowing the outer stitch to fold over the front of the beadwork.

Pass through the head bead of the next branch, as in the diagram, and on through the next 2C of the larger 4W.

**11**  a) One by one, add the head beads at the corners of the large 4W, keeping it loose so that you can slip E into the little trap before snuggling everything up.
b) Weave on to exit the 1st body bead.

**12**  a) Pick up 1C, 1D, 1C and pass down through the A bead in the centre of the inner wall of the corner, the hole of which is vertically orientated.
b) Pass back through the CDC and on through the threadless side of the A body bead on the E trap.
c) Weave on to exit the next trap body bead on the edge of E.

*Step 8*

**13**  a) Repeat step 12 for the remaining 3 corners.
b) Weave into the frame to exit an A bead at any edge.

*You will notice that the E trap wiggles a little. This is important as the centrepiece is also the clasp. The toggle bars must be able to pass through the gap between the E trap and the frame, so some movement is required.*

**Note**: *If you choose to make this element as a pendant, you can set the trap more solidly in the frame thus: For steps 12–13, omit the two C beads flanking D at each corner, and continue to attach the trap as directed.*

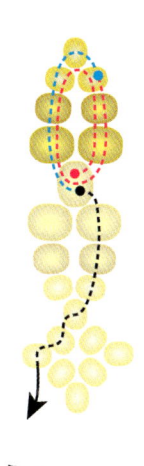

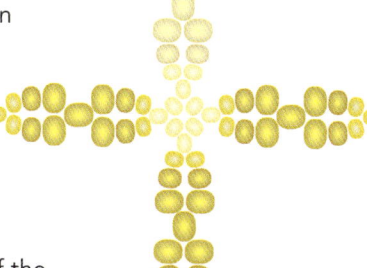

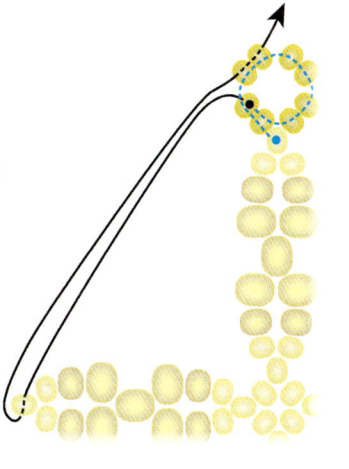

*Steps 9–10*

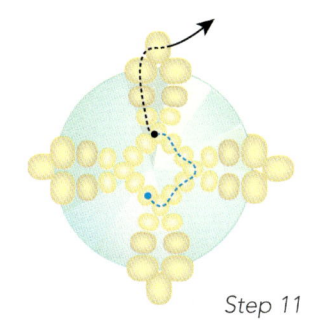

*Step 11*

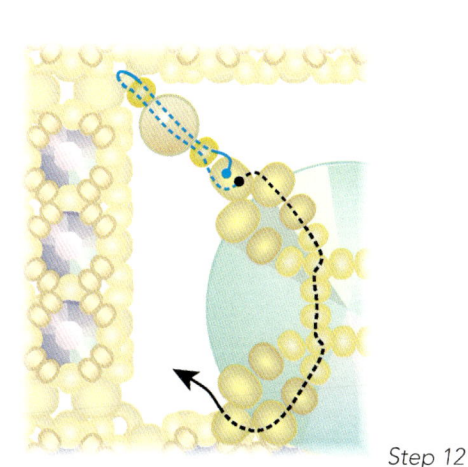

*Step 12*

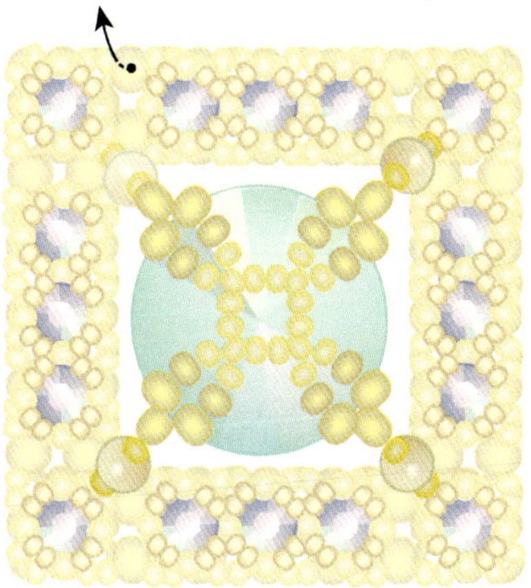

*Step 13*

– 85 –

The Nonsuch Tour de Cou

**14** Turn the beadwork onto its side and weave on to exit the east A bead of the 2nd RAW stitch, marked 1 in the diagram, and make a dangle thus:

a) Pick up 5C, 1D, 1C, 1H, 3C.
b) Missing out the last 3C picked up, pass back through H, C, D, 3C in the opposite direction.
c) Pick up 2C.
d) Pass through A2 from lower to upper side, as in the diagram.
e) Work back along the threadpath of this dangle, in the opposite direction, towards bead A1, and pass through it from the threadless side (upper to lower), to exit as at the beginning of this step, making a complete circuit.
f) Weave on to exit A3 from its lower side, ready to make the central dangle.

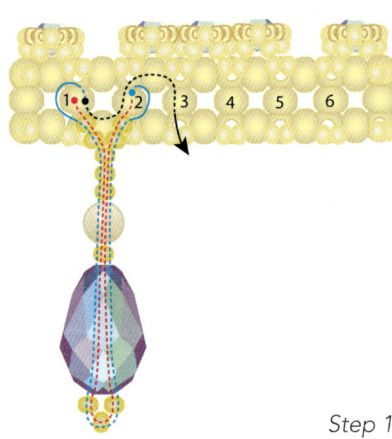

*Step 14*

**15** a) Pick up 6C, 1D, 5C, 1J, 4C.
b) Pass back through the 1st of the 5C picked up before J, then on through D and 3C, all in the opposite direction.
c) Pick up 3C and pass through A4 from lower to upper side.
d) Following the threadpath of this dangle in the opposite direction, work back towards bead A3 and pass through it from the threadless side (upper to lower), to exit as at the beginning of this step, making a complete circuit.
e) Weave on to exit A5 from its lower side, ready for the last dangle.

**16** a) Work step 14 on beads A5 and A6 to make the last dangle.
b) Finish off both working and tail threads.

### Toggle bar (Make 2)

**1** a) Pick up 27C and work a total of 8 rows in odd count peyote.
b) Zip the last row onto the 1st, remembering to complete the zip up by joining together the 2 end beads – pass through the end bead of row 8, away from the tube end.
c) Turn and pass through the next end bead to exit the end of the tube, as in the diagram.
d) Snuggle up both the working and tail threads, and finish off the tail thread only.

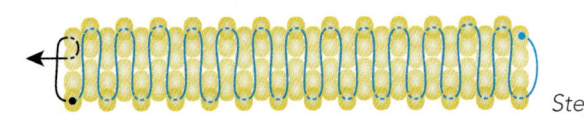

*Step 15*

*Step 1*

**2** Turn the tube to look at it end on.

a) Pick up 1C and pass back down the tube end bead, from the threadside, settling the new extension bead with its hole horizontally orientated.
b) Pass up the next tube end bead.
c) Repeat steps a)–b) 3 more times.
d) To step up, pass through the 1st C picked up in this step.

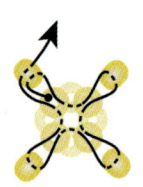

*Step 16*

*Step 2*

### Fascinating fact:
*It was a common occurrence to have jewellery reworked into more fashionable pieces. Henry VIII was renowned for taking back jewels to be remade for his next bride.*

The Nonsuch Tour de Cou

**3**    a) Pick up 1C and pass through the next extension bead.
b) Repeat step a) 3 more times.
c) Step up through the 1st C placed in this step.

**4**    a) Make a basic Hubble stitch on the body bead (for a reminder see motif step 21).
b) Weave on through 2C as in the diagram, ready to make the next Hubble stitch.

*Steps 3–4*

**5**    a) Repeat step 4 another 3 times.
b) Step up to exit the head bead of the 1st Hubble stitch.

*Step 5*

**6**    Change to a size 15 needle if necessary.

a) Pick up 2F and pass through the next head bead.
b) Repeat step a) 3 more times.
c) Lightly take up the slack and run around the circuit once more.
d) Loosen the thread to place G into the centre space.
e) Hold G in place with your thumb as you draw up the thread tightly.
f) You may wish to run around the circuit again to get a good tight grip over G.

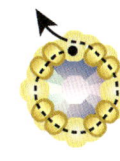

*Step 6*

**7**    Toggle bar attachment:

a) Weave through the arm and body beads, the adjacent extension bead, and continue down through 8 beads of the tube itself, to exit bead X, as in the diagram.
b) Pick up 13C.
c) Pass through the head bead of a 3W on the end motif of the choker.
d) Pick up 13C.
e) Pass through bead Y of the tube.
f) Follow the threadpath in reverse back to bead X.
g) Pass through bead X from the threadless side.
h) Weave back through the toggle bar attachment to bead Y, and continue on to exit a bead at the other end of the tube.

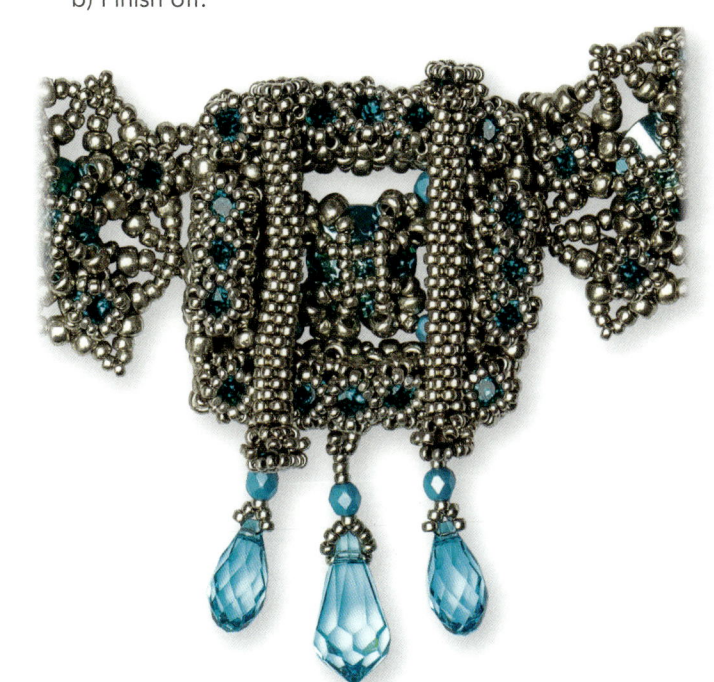

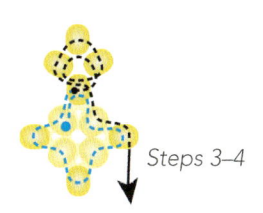

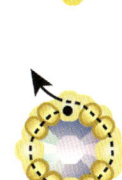

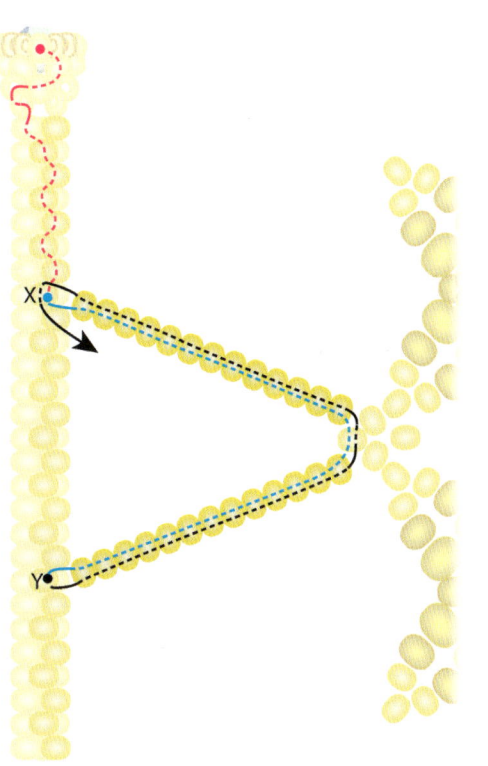

**8**    a) Work steps 2–6 to embellish this end of the tube.
b) Finish off.

*Steps 7–8*

The Nonsuch Tour de Cou

> "I will have here but one mistress and no master."
> Elizabeth to Robert Dudley

---

**Fascinating fact:**

Cheapside was an area in London controlled by the Guild of Goldsmiths. It comprised a row of open fronted shops with workshops above and behind. The shopkeepers would buy raw and uncut stones, make jewellery and undertake commissions and repairs.

DOTIS NOMINE NECKLACE

# DOTIS NOMINE NECKLACE

It was no longer safe to openly count the paternoster, Mary and mystery beads, so Grandmother's ornate rosary, rich with gold and jewels, was to be broken up. Her father had already removed the crucifix and hidden it about the lintel of the manor house door, where its presence might continue to give comfort to all who knew it was there. The rest would be taken to the jeweller's shop in Cheapside, to be re-fashioned into a necklace. It would be her dowry piece, a gift sealed in the marriage agreement as hers alone, to be worn on high days and holidays, an insurance of wealth should she ever need to purchase safety.

I was fascinated by the detailed chains in a number of portraits of the period we looked at. Many of the sitters wore ornate gold chains set with precious stones, or with decorated links. Several of the chains found in the Cheapside Hoard include enamelled links and links carved from semi-precious stones. Chains were held in place with jewelled brooches. Others are used to suspend ornate filigree pendants, for use as a pomander to ward off noxious smells.

Dotis Nomine is Latin for dowry. A dowry could be one of two things: land, property or money given by the bride's family, which then belonged exclusively to the husband; or gifts of jewellery and money given specifically to the bride, which remained hers. Arranged marriages were expected between wealthy families, in a time when political or social alliances of great houses, or the expansion of estates, took precedence over love.

**Elements**: beaded bead, chaton beaded bead, centre pane, bezelled Swarovski® stone, baroque bead drop, right angle weave chain

Each of these is a variation on the elements created for the Walsingham Cypher necklace and bracelet (refer to page 47 for the steps to make the panes), but this time the flat elements are worked as 3D shapes.

**Techniques**: Albion stitch, right angle weave, netting

**Completed length**: necklace 54cm/21¼", pendant section 7cm/2¾"

**You will need**:

- 4g x Miyuki seed beads size 11° 2010 (matte metallic charcoal grey) (A)
- 8g x Miyuki seed beads size 15° 4203 (duracoat galvanised gold) (B)
- 4g x Miyuki seed beads size 15° 1087 (gunmetal iris) (C)
- 5g x Miyuki cube beads size 1.8mm 457 (metallic bronze) (this changes from 1E in Walsingham Cypher) (D)
- 22 x Swarovski® xilion chatons #1088 ss39 8mm (indicolite) (E)
- 1 x Swarovski® oval stone #4120 18x13mm (amethyst) (F)
- 8 x Swarovski® pearls #5810 10mm (scarabaeous green) (G)
- 12 x Czech glass rings 9mm (metallic bronze) (H)
- 1 x Swarovski® baroque bead #5058 14mm (amethyst) (J)
- 1 x lobster clasp 10mm (antique bronze)
- 2 x jump rings 6mm

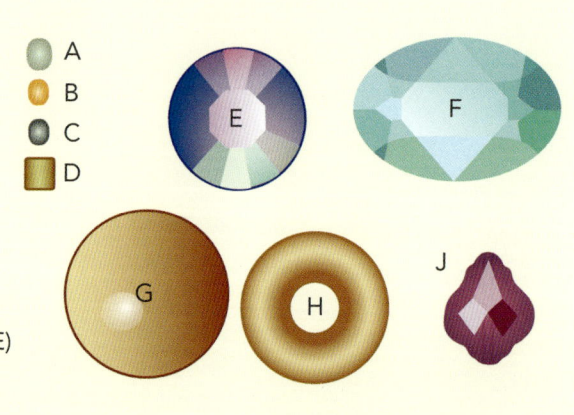

*Fascinating fact:*

*When Queen Elizabeth banned the use of rosaries it was a serious offence to be found in possession of one, leading to confiscation of lands, wealth and imprisonment. Catholics found a way to continue their prayers, using a discreet rosary ring, which had ten raised prayer studs.*

Dotis Nomine necklace

> *"And wilt thou leave me thus,*
> *That hath loved thee so long*
> *In wealth and woe among?*
> *And is thy heart so strong*
> *As for to leave me thus?*
> *Say nay, say nay!"*
>
> *Sir Thomas Wyatt*
> *And Wilt Thou Leave*
> *Me Thus?*

## Beaded bead (Make 4)

10mm pearls are covered with a lattice of beadwork. The technique is the same as for the Walsingham Cypher project on page 47.

1. With a very long wingspan of thread, leave a 15cm/6" tail. Make a centre pane, then add a pane to each side of this centre pane. Add 1 more pane to the end of 1 of the 4. This makes the classic cross formation used to make a cube.

2. Join each of the 4 side panes to its neighbour, through the side D beads using D beads. This recreates the way the original panes are joined, but now the piece is folding into a cube shape.

3. Put the 1G into the cube. The hole of the 1G will not be used. Fold the last pane over and join its 3 sides to the top D beads of the other panes.

   **Note**: depending on your thread tension this will either be a squeeze or a breeze. If your tension is tight you will need to pull hard on the thread to make the joins close. The cube will take on the rounded shape of the bead. Once the beadwork is secure, weave the thread and tail back into the beadwork to finish off.

*Step 2*

*Step 3*

### Glass ring loops

Each beaded bead has two loops and each passes through a glass ring.

The loops are worked from the centre D beads of two panes and will lie opposite to each other. Start with the thread exiting from a centre D bead.

1. Pick up 1C, 1A, 9B, 1A, 1C. Pass the needle through a glass ring, then through the 1D opposite the 1 started from on the same pane.

2. Pick up 1C, pass through 1A, 9B, 1A, pick up 1C pass back through the 1D started from. Retrace the threadpath to strengthen the loop. Repeat on the opposite pane of the beaded bead. Once the loops are secure, weave the thread and tail back into the beadwork to finish off.

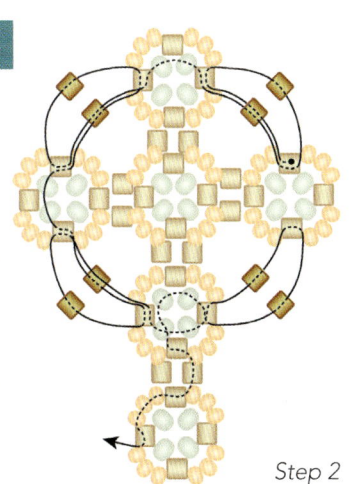

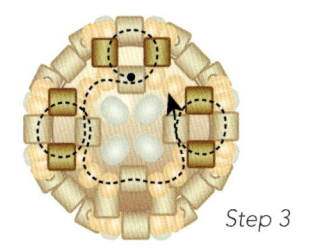

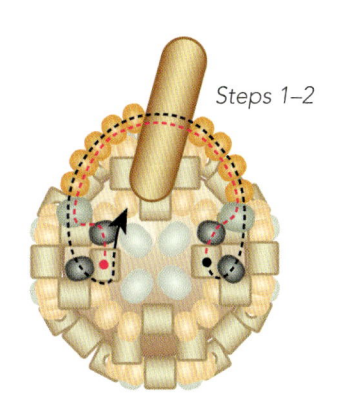

*Steps 1–2*

*Dotis Nomine necklace*

## Chaton beaded beads (Make 4)

The chaton beaded bead is a beaded bead with chatons added to four panes to create four sides, leaving two panes (front and back) unembellished. The chatons are added in exactly the same way as for the Walsingham Cypher project on page 47. There are just more of them – four per bead.

Start by making 4 beaded beads following steps 1–3.

1. Start 1.5m/60" of thread and attach it to a beaded bead. Exit 1D of a pane. place a stitch over each of the centre 4 D beads: 3B stalk, 3B tip. At the end of the round, step up to exit a centre B at the tip of a stitch.

*Step 1*

2. Join each centre B bead with 4C, put the chaton in face up and tighten the ring of beads. When the ring is secure, exit a 3B stitch tip.

3. The following beads are attached by passing through the 3B stitch tips, and the centre C beads of the 3C on the pane edge. They will sit around the sides of the chaton. The diagram shows the back view of a bezelled chaton.

   Pick up 3C, pass through the centre C on the pane edge. Pick up 3C, pass through the next 3B stitch tip. Repeat all the way round.

   Weave through to the next adjacent pane and repeat. Keep going until you have 4 sides embellished with chatons.

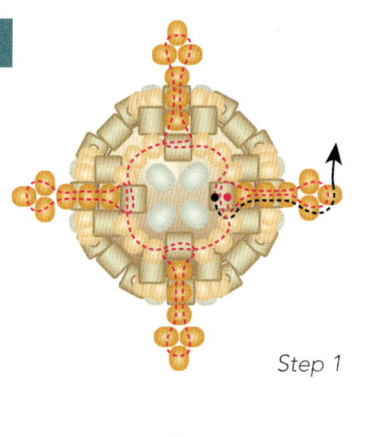

*Step 2*

### Connecting loops

Two chaton beaded beads will link to each other, and at the other end they will link to a beaded bead glass ring (already in place). So, one loop will pass through a ring on a beaded bead, the other loop will have a ring attached for the 1st chaton beaded bead... or pass through a glass ring already in place on a chaton beaded bead.

1. Exit a centre B stitch tip bead on 1 chaton edge. Pick up 1C, 1A, 9B, 1A, 1C. Pass the needle through a new glass ring, then through the centre B stitch tip bead on the next chaton edge. The loop will span between 2 chatons.

2. Pick up 1C, pass through 1A, 9B, 1A, pick up 1C and pass back through the centre B started from. Retrace the threadpath to strengthen the loop.

*Step 3*

3. Repeat steps 1 and 2 to make a loop between the opposite pair of chatons. If it is the 1st chaton beaded bead, pass the needle through a glass loop. If it is a 2nd chaton beaded bead, pass the needle through the glass loop already in place on the 1st chaton beaded bead.

   Weave thread and tail back into the beadwork and finish off.

   Keep working to create 2 separate pieces with the sequence of elements: 1 beaded bead, 2 chaton beaded beads, 1 beaded bead.

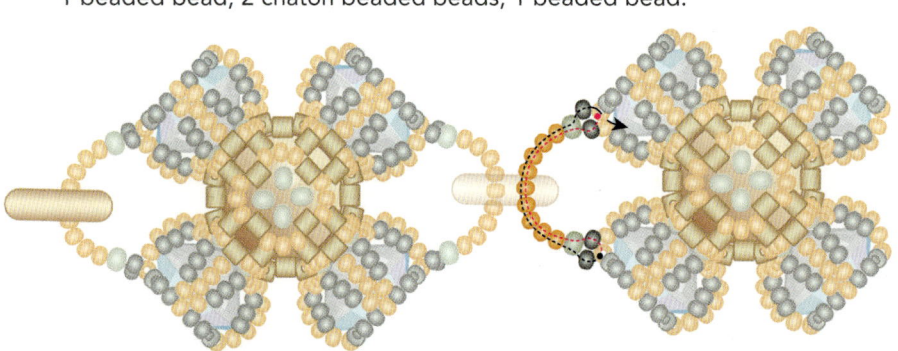

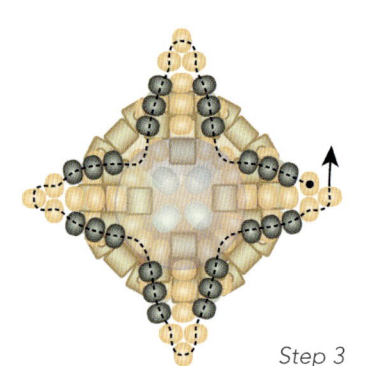

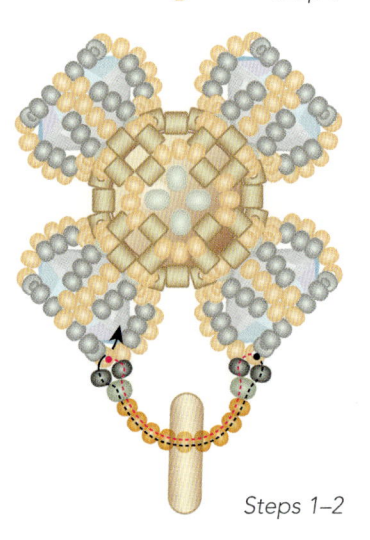

*Steps 1–2*

*Step 3*

Dotis Nomine necklace

## The centre pane

A single pane with three loops: two are worked from D beads and link through the glass rings on the ends of the beaded beads. The third is worked from a centre B bead and has a glass ring added to it. This glass ring will link to the oval stone pendant element.

1. With a 50cm/20" length of thread, make a single pane, then exit 1D.

2. Pick up 1C, 1A, 9B, 1A, 1C. Pass the needle through a glass ring attached to a beaded bead, then pass back through the 1D.

3. Pick up 1C, pass through 1A, 9B, 1A. Pick up 1C, pass back through the 1D started from. Retrace the threadpath to strengthen the loop.

4. Repeat to make a 2nd loop working from the next 1D round on the single pane. Attach it through the glass ring of the beaded bead at the end of the 2nd section.

5. Weave through the edge beads of the single pane to exit the centre 1B below the 2 existing loops.

6. Make a loop as before, this time passing the needle through a new glass ring. Weave thread and tail back into the beadwork and finish off.

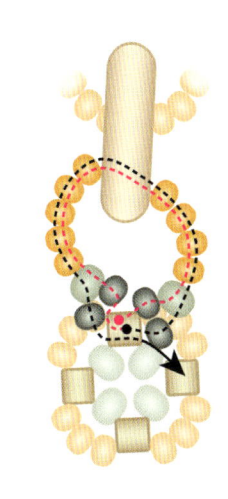

*Steps 2–3*

*Step 5*

## Bezelled Swarovski® stone

The oval stone has a bezel of chaton embellished panes and a neat edge of 3-bead tip Albion stitches joined to hold the stone in place. The stitches that hold the stone are the same front and back, so can be worked in pairs as you work around the bezel edges.

1. Make a row of 6 single panes, then bring the 1st and last edges together and join them through the D beads with a right angle weave stitch using D beads (just as you did for the beaded beads).

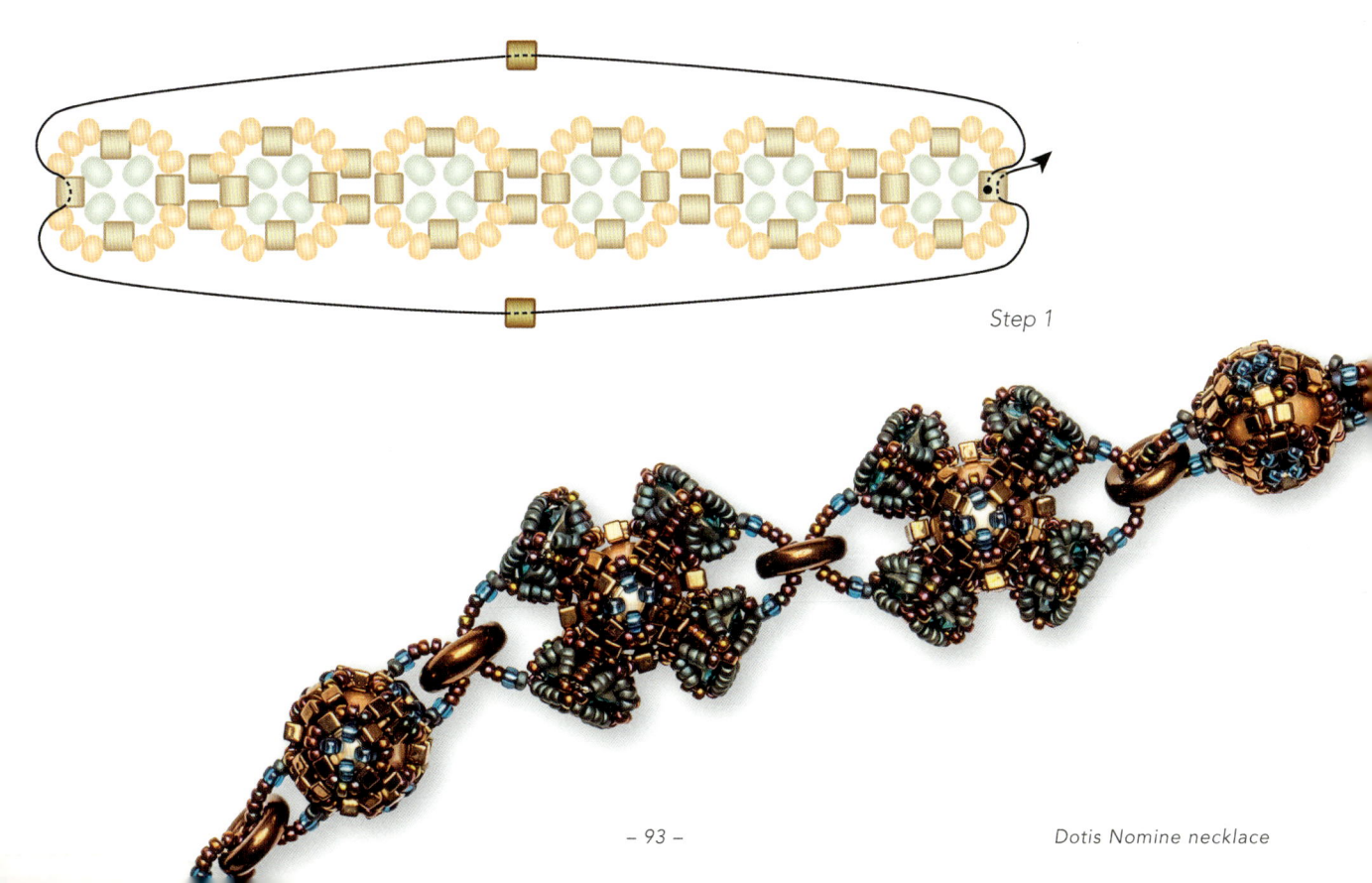

*Step 1*

*Dotis Nomine necklace*

2. Exit 1D side bead. Make a stitch: 1B stalk, 3B tip. Pass back through the 1B stalk, then through the D beads to exit the D bead opposite the one started from. Make the same stitch over this D bead.

3. Weave through to exit the next set of D beads joining 2 panes together and add stitches over the outside 2 D beads. Keep working until you have 6 pairs of stitches.

4. Step up to exit a centre B stitch tip bead. Place 4C between each centre B tip bead. Each side has 6 stitch tips which are joined to create the bezel to hold the stone. Weave through the beads a 2nd time to secure this ring.

5. Pass through the beads to the other side and exit a centre B stitch tip to be in place to repeat step 4. Place F into the bezel before tightening and securing this ring of beads.

Align the stone so that a stitch lies centre top and centre bottom of the stone. There will be 1 pane either side of these stitches. This is important, so that when the chatons are added, they will be in the right place to add a centre top and centre bottom loop between the top 2 and bottom 2 chaton edges.

6. Weave through the beads to exit a centre 1D of a pane. Embellish each pane with a chaton as before (in the same way as for the chaton beaded bead).

When the last chaton is in place, weave through the beads to exit a centre B stitch tip bead, on the edge of a chaton at the top of the oval, on the centre top side.

7. Add a loop just as you did for the chaton beaded beads, but this time, pass the needle through the glass ring at the bottom of the single pane.

8. Add a loop directly opposite and between the 2 bottom chatons as before and this time add a new glass ring. Weave thread and tail back into the beadwork and finish off.

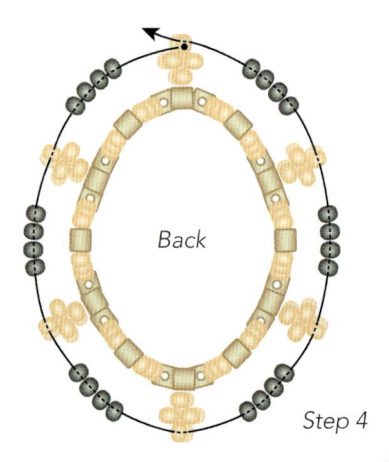

*Step 2*

*Back*

*Step 2*

*Back* — *Step 3*

*Back* — *Step 4*

*Step 5*

*Step 7*

Dotis Nomine necklace

## Baroque bead drop

The baroque bead drop is attached to the glass ring at the bottom of the bezelled F. Change thread to use Fireline or similar for this if you have been working with a softer thread up to this point.

1. Pick up 1A, 1B, pass back through the 1A, then through the 1J from bottom to top.

2. Pick up 1A, 1D, 1C, 1A, 9B, 1A, 1C. Pass the needle through the glass ring at the bottom of the bezelled Swarovski® oval stone. Pass through 1D, 1A and 1J from top to bottom, 1A, 1C.

3. Pull the thread up firmly so all the beads settle into place, then weave back up through 1A, 1J, 1A, 1D. Pick up 1C, pass through 1A, 9B, 1A. Pick up 1C, then weave back to the starting point. Finish off the thread tails.

*Steps 1–2*

## Right angle weave chain (Make 2)

The right angle weave chain is worked separately, then linked with a loop at one end to attach through the end glass ring of a necklace side. At the other end a smaller loop is worked to hold the jump ring and clasp.

1. With a long wingspan of thread, leave a 30cm/12" tail to make a loop of beads to attach to a glass ring later. Pick up 4A and secure in a ring.

2. Work a row of right angle weave: 1st stitch A (already in place), 2nd stitch C, 3rd stitch B. Repeat the sequence A, B, C until the chain is the right length to complete one side of the necklace.

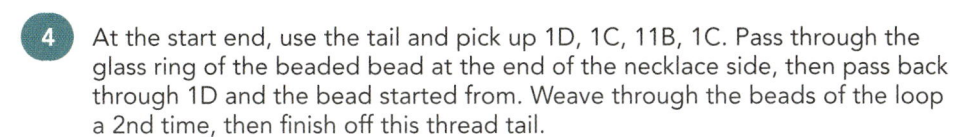

3. Pick up 1D, 1C, 7B, 1C. Pass back through 1D and the bead started from. Weave through the beads of the loop a 2nd time, then finish off this thread tail.

4. At the start end, use the tail and pick up 1D, 1C, 11B, 1C. Pass through the glass ring of the beaded bead at the end of the necklace side, then pass back through 1D and the bead started from. Weave through the beads of the loop a 2nd time, then finish off this thread tail.

Repeat all the steps to make a 2nd chain, then attach jump rings through the end loops and a clasp to the jump rings.

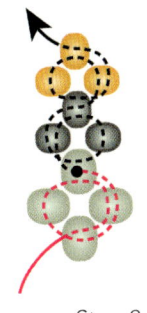

*Step 3*

*Step 2*

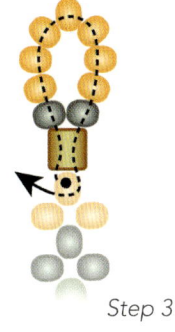

*Step 3*

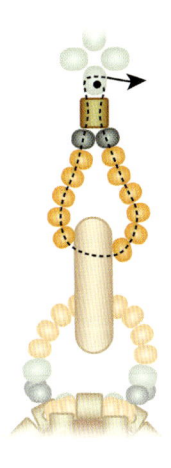

*Step 4*

Dotis Nomine necklace

> "I will be as good unto ye as ever a queen was unto her people. No will in me can lack, neither do I trust shall there lack any power. And persuade yourselves, that for the safety and quietness of you all, I will not spare, if need be, to spend my blood."
>
> Elizabeth's speech to the Lord Mayor and people of London, on the eve of her coronation (15 January, 1559)

---

**Fascinating fact:**

Elaborate chains were also simple fashion accessories, many were delicate and enamelled and there is a contemporary account complaining that the enamel flaked off too easily. Fake jewellery was common and sometimes called Martin's gold. Unscrupulous jewellers were protected from prosecution by the Goldsmith's Guild by a quirk in the law, for the duration they worked within the protection of the parish of St Martin's in the Field.

PEASE POD CHAIN OF OFFICE

# PEASE POD CHAIN OF OFFICE

September 8th, 1560, Windsor Castle. A rosy twilight defined the bare silhouettes of the trees to the west of the castle as the hoof beats slowed to a sudden stop. Two grooms ran forward to grab the reins of the steaming, foam-flecked horse, allowing the exhausted rider to dismount. Escorted by guards, he stumbled through the portico, and gasped a few words to Walsingham, who, white-faced, hastened him into the great chamber for an audience with her majesty. On bended knee and too afraid to look her in the eye, he delivered the news to the ground before her – Amy Dudley had been found dead at the foot of the stairs in the family home at Cumnor. The shock pierced Elizabeth's heart like an icy dagger and it took determination of steel to resist glancing towards the corner of the room where her 'Sweet Robin', Robert Dudley, stood. In a single heartbeat, the two of them were silently reeling with the myriad consequences that this sickening news heralded for them.

Murmuring thanks to the messenger, Elizabeth rose and retreated into her chambers. She was shaking with, well, could it be fear, rage or even a strange triumph? She had no idea. Weeks ago, Robert had told Elizabeth of his wife's painful malady of the breast, and that her health was failing rapidly. So was it possible that the poor wretch could have thrown herself upon God's mercy and taken her own life? But few at court had known of her condition, and Elizabeth had begun to hear dangerous whispers about Robert and his Queen. She had to steady herself as the thought grew that her subjects might conclude she or Robert may have somehow engineered the death.

Taking up the locked casket from her bedside and cradling it to her breast, Elizabeth slowly sank into the chair at the desk by the window. The little box contained her most treasured possessions – his letters – and now she unlocked it with the silver key that remained with her at all times, on her Chain of Office. Taking out the last of the letters, she let her eyes wander over the contents, not reading them but simply absorbing the sweeping motion of the marks his pen had made. Folding it again and tenderly replacing it, Elizabeth drew out a small sheet of vellum from her desk. She dipped her quill in the tiny bottle of ink and, wiping away the excess with a practised stroke, made two distinct marks – ÔÔ followed by the number 8. This was their code; the marks were her own device, meaning his eyes, which made her smile every time she drew them, and the number was the time at which they must urgently meet. He knew the secret meeting place, so there was no need to say anything more. Counting 10 drops of blood-red wax to form a little puddle over the folded edges of the message, Elizabeth sighed heavily as she pressed the thistle seal onto it. If a message bearing the royal Scottish symbol were to be intercepted, it would not be traced to her.

One by one, Elizabeth's ladies-in-waiting had quietly entered the bedchamber, feeling their mistress's anguish, and now she turned to them with tears in her eyes. She called to Lettice and handed her the message without saying a word. Lettice curtsied deftly and hurried away, knowing exactly what to do.

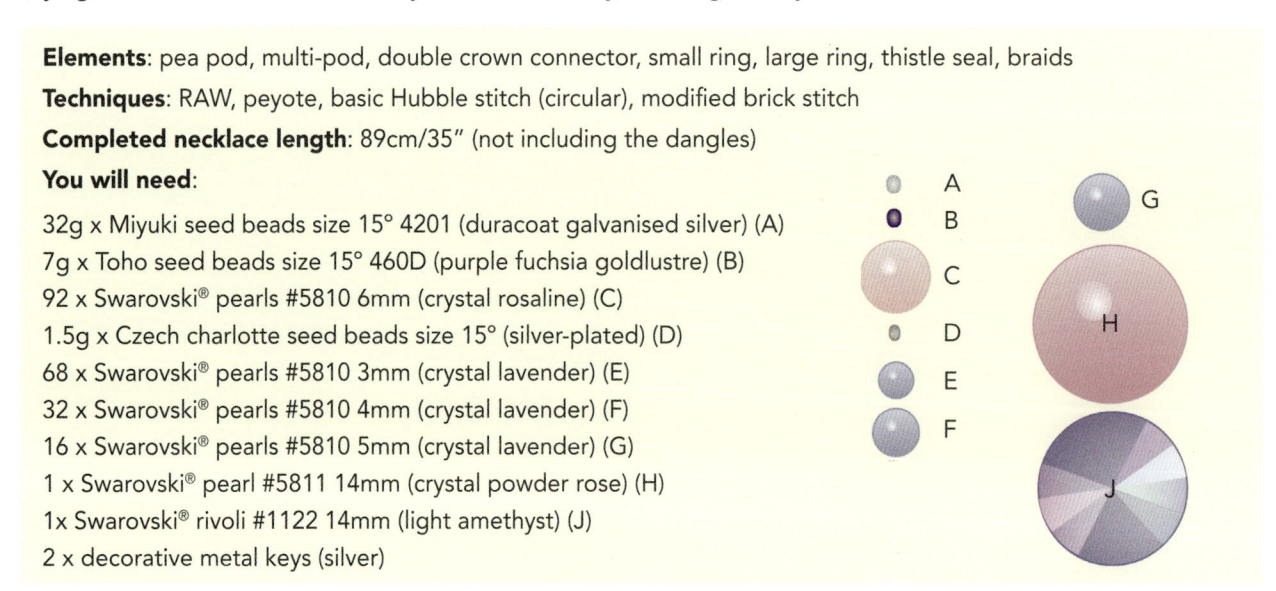

**Elements**: pea pod, multi-pod, double crown connector, small ring, large ring, thistle seal, braids
**Techniques**: RAW, peyote, basic Hubble stitch (circular), modified brick stitch
**Completed necklace length**: 89cm/35" (not including the dangles)
**You will need**:

32g x Miyuki seed beads size 15° 4201 (duracoat galvanised silver) (A)
7g x Toho seed beads size 15° 460D (purple fuchsia goldlustre) (B)
92 x Swarovski® pearls #5810 6mm (crystal rosaline) (C)
1.5g x Czech charlotte seed beads size 15° (silver-plated) (D)
68 x Swarovski® pearls #5810 3mm (crystal lavender) (E)
32 x Swarovski® pearls #5810 4mm (crystal lavender) (F)
16 x Swarovski® pearls #5810 5mm (crystal lavender) (G)
1 x Swarovski® pearl #5811 14mm (crystal powder rose) (H)
1x Swarovski® rivoli #1122 14mm (light amethyst) (J)
2 x decorative metal keys (silver)

*Pease Pod Chain of Office*

> *"Vouchsafe, O comely Queene, yet longer to remaine, Or still to dwell amongst us here! O Queene commaunde againe This Castle and the Knight, which keepes the same for you; ... Live here, good Queene, live here; ..."*
>
> *Robert Dudley's speech, delivered at Elizabeth's departure from Kenilworth, July, 1575*

## Pea pod (PP) (Make 16)

*The pod is worked in four rows, where the fourth row zips onto the first making a closed pod and entrapping a pearl. Each row consists of a series of five connected squares of three different sizes.*

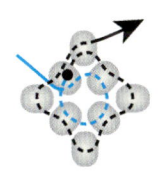

**1** **Row 1** – With 0.9m/35" thread and a size 13 needle:

   a) Pick up 4A and pass again through the 1st A picked up, making a ring.
   b) Pick up 1A and pass through the next A, making a corner.
   c) Repeat b) 3 more times. This positions another 3 corners.
   d) Step up into the 1st corner. **We'll call this a 1Sq.**

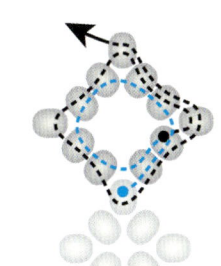

*Step 1*

**2** a) Pick up 8A and pass through the 1st 2A just picked up, in the same direction. Do not pass through any of the previous square's beads – this must hang to the side of the beadwork. The same scenario occurs in subsequent squares.
   b) Pick up 1A and pass through the next 2A.
   c) Repeat b) twice more. We now have 3 corners.
   d) Pass through the 1Sq corner bead from the threadless side and continue through the next 2A. **This is a 2Sq.**
   e) Weave on to exit the north corner bead, as in the diagram.

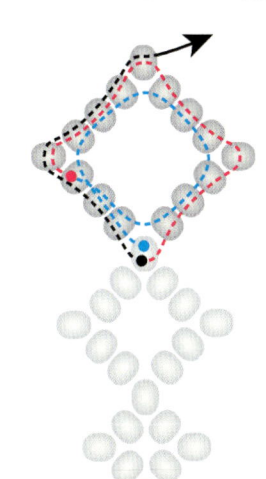

*Step 2*

**3** a) Pick up 12A and pass through the 1st 3A just picked up, in the same direction.
   b) Pick up 1A and pass through the next 3A.
   c) Repeat b) twice more. That's 3 corners.
   d) Pass through the 2Sq corner bead from the threadless side, continue through the next 3A. **This is a 3Sq.**
   e) Weave on to exit the north corner bead, as in the diagram.

*Step 3*

Pease Pod Chain of Office

**4**
a) Repeat step 2 to make a 2Sq.
b) Make a 1Sq. This completes the 1st row.
c) Weave on to exit an east corner of the 1Sq, as in the diagram.

**5** **Row 2**: Build a 1Sq onto the 1st row 1Sq and weave on to emerge from the south corner bead, as in the diagram.

**6**
a) Continue working row 2, sharing a row 1 corner bead as you build each square.
b) Weave around to exit the east bead of the last 1Sq.

**7** **Row 3**: Work as for row 2.

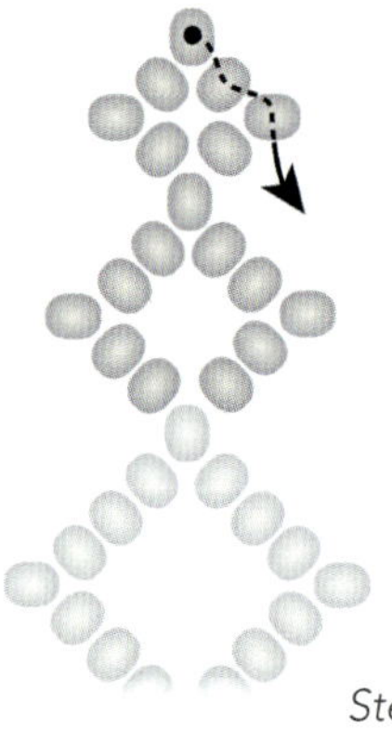

*Step 4*

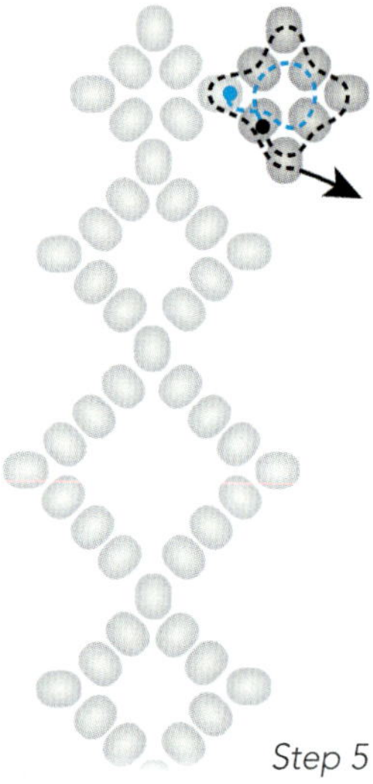

*Step 5*

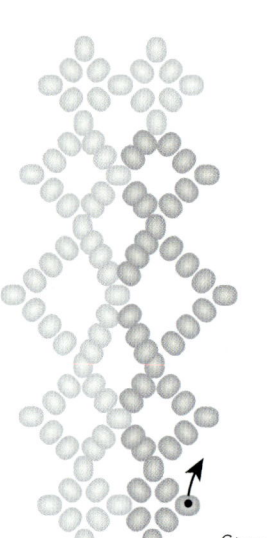

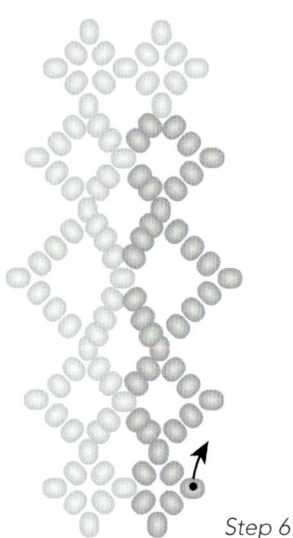

*Step 6*

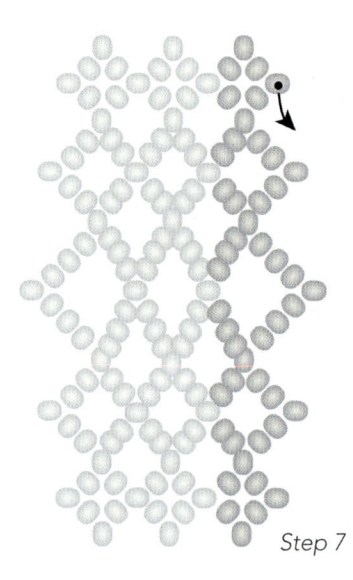

*Step 7*

**8** **Row 4**: This is a zip-up row where both east and west corner beads are shared. Build a 1Sq onto both rows 3 and 1, and weave around to exit the north corner bead, as in the diagram.

**9**
a) Turn the beadwork to view it end on.
b) Using B, build a 1Sq incorporating all 4 presenting corner beads.
c) Pass once more through the 1st B bead picked up.

**10** Add a connector bead:

a) Pick up 1B (connector).
b) Pass through the opposite B of the 1Sq.
c) Pass back through the connector B, in the opposite direction.
d) Pass again through the original 1Sq B from the threadless side, making a circuit.
e) Weave around the 1Sq to exit the south corner bead.

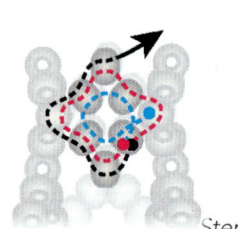

*Step 8*

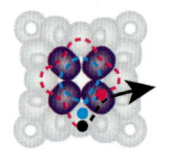

*Step 9*

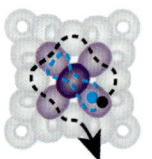

*Step 10*

Pease Pod Chain of Office

**11**
   a) With the thread emerging again from the north bead of the row 4 1Sq, weave down to its south bead.
   b) Build a 2Sq, and then a 3Sq.
   c) Weave around to exit the east corner bead.

*Now we're ready to incorporate the pea!*

**12** For this next stitch, all passes through corner beads must be made via the inside of the pod, **never the outside**, as threads would be visible.

   a) Pick up 1C and pass up through the corner bead opposite (outlined in pink – shared between rows 1 and 2).
   b) Pass back through C in the opposite direction.
   c) Pass down through the 1st corner bead from the threadless side.
   d) Weave on to exit the south corner bead of the 3Sq.

**13**
   a) Build a 2Sq and a 1Sq.
   b) Work steps 9–10 to close this end of the pod, and add a connector bead.
   c) Finish off both the tail and working threads.

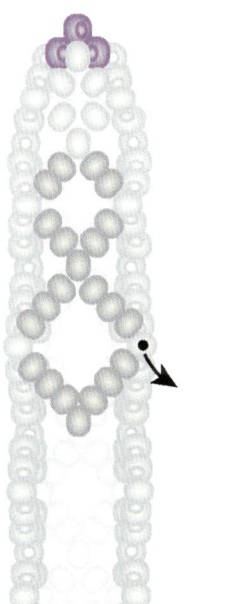

*Step 11*

*Step 12*

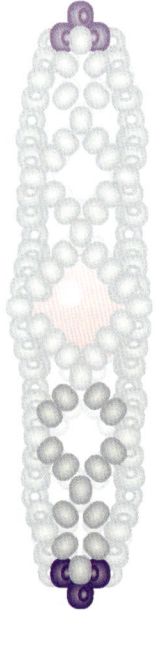

*Step 13*

### Multi-pod (MP) (Make 4)

**1**
   a) With a wingspan of thread, make a PP; weave on to exit the west corner bead of the 1Sq.
   b) Make a 1Sq onto this corner bead; weave on to exit the south corner bead.

**2** Build the rest of the squares onto the pod corner beads down the row, and weave around to exit the east bead of the pod 1Sq, emerging as in the diagram.

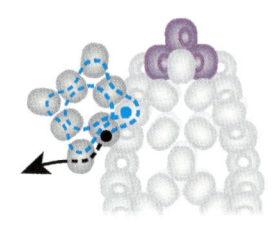

*Step 1*

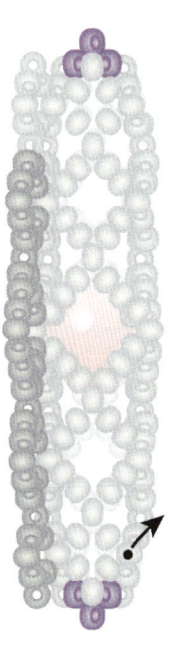

*Step 2*

Pease Pod Chain of Office

**3** Repeat steps 1–2 to make a 2nd row at the next line of shared corner beads, and weave on to exit the north bead of the PP 1Sq.

**4** a) Pick up 1E, 1D, 1F, 1D, 1G, 1D, 1F, 1D, 1E and pass through the south bead of the PP 1Sq at the other end.
b) Pass back through all the beads picked up, in the opposite direction.
c) Pass through the north corner bead of the 1Sq again, from the threadless side.

**5** a) Using B, build a 1Sq onto the north corner bead, incorporating the north corner beads of the embellishment rows.
b) Weave around to exit the PP north corner bead again.
c) Pass down through E, D, F, D, G, D, F, D, E and on through the PP south corner bead (an A bead).

**6** a) Using B, build a 1Sq here to mirror the other end of the pod. This completes the 1st of 4 burst pods around the outside of the central pea pod.
b) Weave on to exit the west corner bead of the PP 1Sq, marked X in the diagram. Rotate the beadwork to view the next location for a burst pod.

**7** a) Here's the rotated view. Work steps 1b)–6 to make the 2nd burst pod. The 2nd row of the previous burst pod and the 1st row of the new burst pod are worked on the same corner beads of the PP.
b) Weave on to exit the west corner bead of the PP 1Sq, ready for the 3rd burst pod.

**8** Make the remaining 2 burst pod embellishments and finish off.

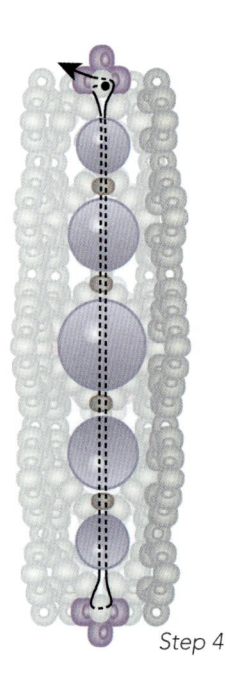

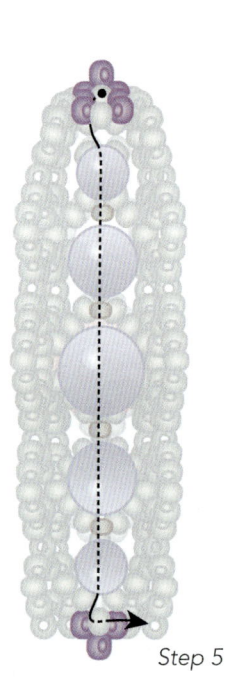

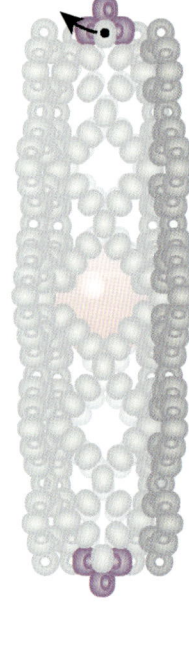

*Step 3*

*Step 4*

*Step 5*

*Step 6*

*Step 7*

Pease Pod Chain of Office

## Double crown connector (DCC) (Make 21)

1. With 0.5m/20" thread:

   a) **Row 1**: Pick up 6B and pass again through the 1st B picked up, making a ring.
   b) **Row 2**: Pick up 1B and pass through the next B. Make sure the new bead clicks firmly into place between the 2 beads of the ring.
   c) Repeat step b) 5 more times.
   d) To step up, pass through the 1st B placed in row 2.

2. **Row 3 (circular Hubble stitch)**:

   a) **1st stitch**: Pick up 2B, pass through the row 2 bead below (from which the thread is emerging) and up through the 1st B picked up, in the same direction.
   b) Pick up 1B and pass down through the awaiting arm bead.
   c) **2nd stitch**: Pick up 2B, backstitch through the next row 2 bead, and pass up through the 1st B just picked up.
   d) Repeat step b).
   e) Snuggle the stitches together so that they just touch, and no thread is showing.

3. **Row 3 (cont.)**:

   a) Repeat steps 2c)–e) 4 more times.
   b) Close the row by passing up the arm and head bead of the 1st stitch in the row.
   c) Pass around all 4 beads of the stitch for security, emerging from the head bead, as in the diagram. This forms a little cup-shaped frill or crown.

4. Turn the beadwork to view it from the back, and weave down to exit the body bead, as in the diagram.

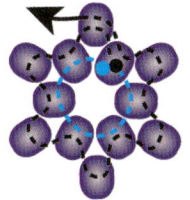

*Step 1*

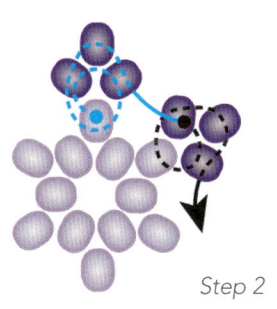

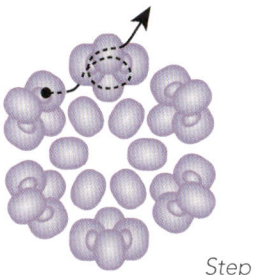

*Step 2*

*Step 3*

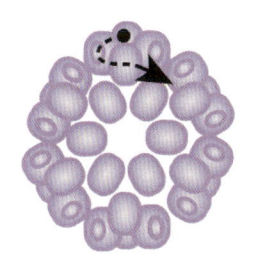

*Step 4*

– 103 –

Pease Pod Chain of Office

5 **Row 4**: Repeat steps 2–3 to make another row of Hubble, forming the 2nd crown, facing in the opposite direction.

6 Weave through to emerge from the body bead (row 2 bead) between the 2 crowns.

7 Now we're going to embellish the groove around the centre, between the 2 crowns. The front crown has been made invisible in the diagram.

   a) **Row 5**: Pick up 2D and pass through the next row 2 bead.
   b) Repeat a) 5 more times.
   c) Pass up into the 1st of the 2D placed in this row, to step up.

*Step 5*

8 **Row 6**:

   a) Pick up 1D; pass down through the adjacent D, the row 2 bead and the 1st D of the next pair.
   b) Repeat a) 4 more times.
   c) Repeat a) once more but this time do not pass into the 1st D of the next pair.
   d) Pass through the arm and head beads of the adjacent Hubble stitch in either of the crowns.
   e) Finish off.

*Step 6*

9 Connecting PPs, MPs, SR and LR with the DCC: In the worked piece, the sequence is 4 PPs and one MP, all linked by DCCs; this sequence is repeated 4 times, so there will be a PP at one end of the chain and an MP at the other. The chain ends with the SR at the PP end and the LR at the MP end (for respective connection methods, see step 4 for the SR and step 4 for the LR).

   a) With 50cm/20" thread and leaving a tail thread of 20cm/8", keep hold of the tail thread, pick up 1C, pass through the DCC, pick up 1C and pass through the connector bead of a 1st element.
   b) Pass back through C, the DCC, C in the opposite direction, and continue through the connector bead of a 2nd element.
   c) Make a square knot using the working and tail threads, snuggling up everything firmly.
   d) Weave back through C, the DCC, C and the 1st element connector bead again, as in b).
   e) Weave into the 1st element and finish off.
   f) With the tail thread, weave through the adjacent connector bead of the 2nd element and finish off.

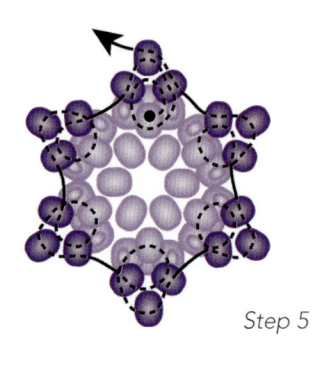

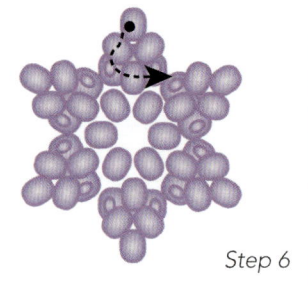

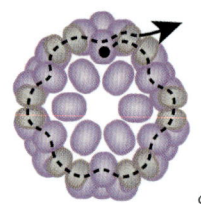

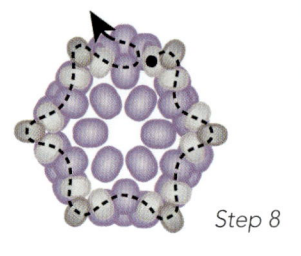

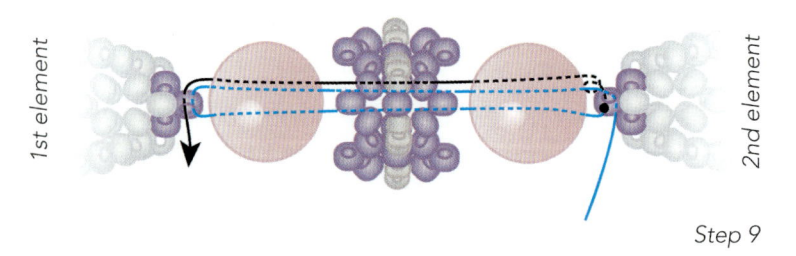

*Step 7*

*Step 8*

*Step 9*

1st element

2nd element

Pease Pod Chain of Office

– 104 –

## Small ring (SR) (Make 1)

**1** Core:

   a) With 0.5m/20" thread, pick up 13C, pass again through all 13C, and the 1st C once more, making a ring.
   b) Make a half-hitch knot and pass through 2C.
   c) Repeat b) 5 more times.
   d) Finish off the working thread.
   e) Check from which bead the tail thread is exiting so that you head away from the working thread direction, and pass through 1C.
   f) Repeat d) and finish off the tail thread.

*Step 1*

**2** a) With a wingspan of thread, make a row as for the PP (don't make the final 1Sq yet).
   b) Wrap the 2 ends of the beadwork over the core.
   c) Make the final 1Sq, sharing the south corner bead of the 1st 1Sq with the final 1Sq.
   d) Complete the east corner of the final 1Sq and weave on to exit the west corner bead, as in the diagram.

**3** a) Build a further 17 closed rows onto the 1st row.
   b) Build the 18th row, zipping it onto the 1st row, to close up the ring.
   c) Finish off.

**4** Connecting the SR:

The SR is connected to the PP at the end of the chain by a DCC, via one of its 3Sq east/west corner beads (marked X in the diagram).

*Step 2*

## Large ring (LR) (Make 1)

**1** Core: with 1m/40" thread, make a core as for the small ring, using 17C.

**2** a) With a wingspan of thread, make a row as for the PP, **but** use 1B for each of the 1st 1Sq south corner bead and last 1Sq north corner bead.
   b) Weave around to exit B of the last 1Sq.
   c) Wrap the beadwork over the core.
   d) Pick up 1E and pass through the other B.
   e) Pass back through E in the opposite direction.
   f) Pass through the 1st B from the threadless side.
   g) Weave on to exit the west corner bead. **Note**: The beadwork will not feel as tight around the core as it was for the SR, but this is not an issue.

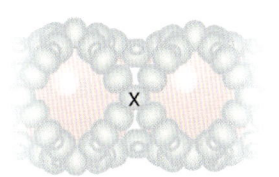

*Step 4*

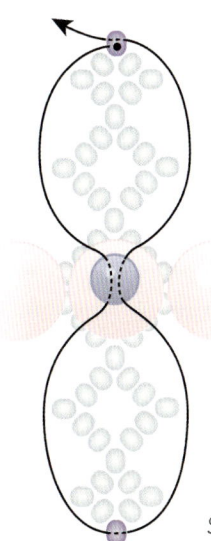

**3** a) Build a further 21 of these rows onto the 1st, simultaneously enclosing the C beads.
   b) Build the 23rd row, zipping it onto the 1st, to close the ring.
   c) Finish off.

**4** Connecting the large ring:

**Before making this connection**, pass the end MP through the SR.

The LR can then be connected to the MP by a DCC, via an east/west corner bead of one of its 3Sqs (as for the SR).

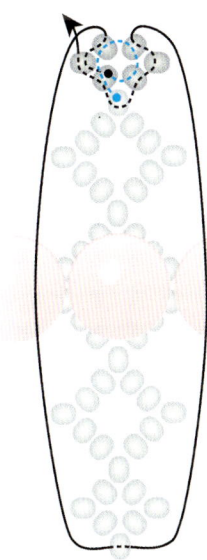

*Step 2*

– 105 –

Pease Pod Chain of Office

### Thistle seal (TS) (Make 1)

**1** Threadpaths are not shown due to the amount of weaving around needed, and the variety of directions which can be taken.

   a) **Row 1**: With a wingspan of thread, make 1Sq, 2Sq, 3Sq, using A.
   b) Make a 2Sq using A, but use 1B for the north corner bead.
   c) Make a 1Sq using B.
   d) Weave down to exit the west bead of the 2Sq.
   e) **Row 2**: Repeat b).
   f) Weave up to exit the B corner bead.
   g) Repeat c). **Note**: The B 1Sqs are not connected to each other.
   h) Weave down to exit the south bead of the 2Sq.
   i) Make 3Sq, 2Sq, using A.
   j) Weave around to exit the west bead of the 2Sq.

*Step 1*

**2** **Rows 3–6**:

   a) Repeat the pattern of rows 1 and 2, twice more.
   b) **Row 7**: Work as for the row 1 pattern.
   c) **Row 8**: This is the zip-up row and is worked as for the row 2 pattern. All the row 1 east corner beads (marked X in the diagram) are shared with row 8. Wrapping the beadwork around a narrow core object may help.
   d) Draw up the slack thread, but don't snuggle up yet.
   e) Finish off the tail thread.

*Step 2*

**3** a) Place H inside the structure and snuggle up tightly.
   b) Weave around to exit the north corner bead of the nearest 1Sq.

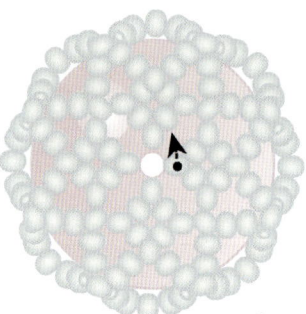

**4** a) To tidy up this end, work step 9b) as for the PP, to make a 1Sq in B.
   b) Weave through to exit an east corner bead of a 1Sq.
   c) Close by is the west bead of the adjacent 1Sq, the north bead of a 2Sq and the east bead of another 1Sq. Pass around these 3 corner beads, and the 1st one again.
   d) Weave on to where the next 3 corner beads are close neighbours.
   e) Repeat c)–d) 3 more times.
   f) Weave away from the tidy up zone, as in the diagram, and continue on to the other end of the TS, to exit the north B bead of a 1Sq.

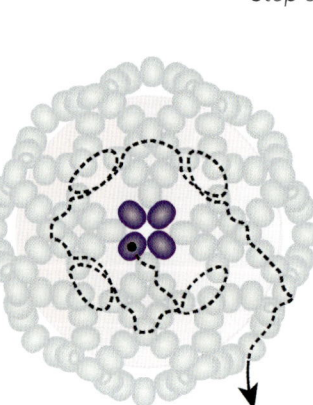

*Step 3*

**5** Stabilising H and positioning the TS connector bead.

   a) Set the working thread aside for use in step 7.
   b) With a new 25cm/10" thread, pass through the centre of the B 1Sq and H.
   c) Pick up 1B, pass back through H, in the opposite direction and on through the centre of the B 1Sq.
   d) Pick up 1B and make a square knot with the tail and working threads.
   e) Snuggle up.
   f) Pass through the entire circuit once more.
   g) Finish off both the working and tail threads.

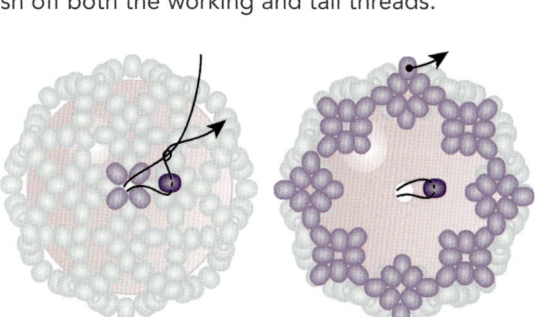

*Step 4*

*Top*     *Bottom*     *Step 5*

Pease Pod Chain of Office — 106 —

6. Using 40cm/15" thread, make a core of 9E, as for the SR and LR, and lie it against H, as in the diagram. The core will be sandwiched between H and the rivoli, distancing the pointed back of the rivoli from H.

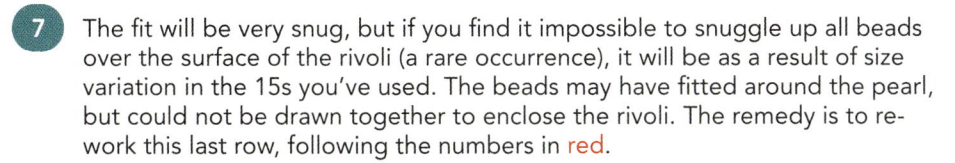

7. The fit will be very snug, but if you find it impossible to snuggle up all beads over the surface of the rivoli (a rare occurrence), it will be as a result of size variation in the 15s you've used. The beads may have fitted around the pearl, but could not be drawn together to enclose the rivoli. The remedy is to re-work this last row, following the numbers in red.

   a) Set J inside the rim of unconnected 1Sqs, against the core. Secure it in place with your thumb while you bead.
   b) With the thread exiting the north corner bead on the right-hand side, pick up 5D (7D) and (heading left) backstitch through the next north corner bead.
   c) Pass back through the last D (2D) bead picked up in the opposite direction.
   d) Pick up 4D (5D) and backstitch through the next north corner bead.
   e) Repeat c).
   f) Repeat d)–e) 5 more times.
   g) Pick up 3D, pass down through the 1st D (1st 2D) picked up in this row, towards the B corner bead.
   h) Backstitch through the corner bead and pass back up 1D (2D).
   i) For security, follow the threadpath of the 1st stitch made to the left.
   j) Weave into the beadwork around H and finish off.

*Step 6*

*Step 7*

## Braid 1 (for the thistle)

1. With 1m/40" thread, using A and leaving a tail thread of 20cm/8":

   a) Make a single row as per row 1 of the PP.
   b) Weave around to exit the end corner bead, as in the diagram.
   c) Pick up 1B, 1E, 1B, 1A for a pearl bridge.
   d) Missing out A, pass back through B, E, B, in the opposite direction.
   e) Pass through the corner bead from the threadless side.
   f) To step up, pass back through B, E, B, and A again, to emerge as in the diagram.

2. a) Work another single row from the last A bead plus a pearl bridge.
   b) Repeat step a).
   c) Work another single row only.
   d) **Connecting the TS**: Pick up 1B, 1E and pass through the connector bead at the back end of the TS.
   e) Pass back through E, B, in the opposite direction.
   f) Pass through the corner bead from the threadless side.
   g) Finish off.

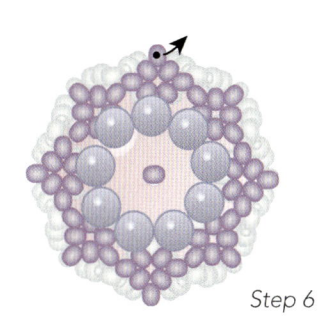

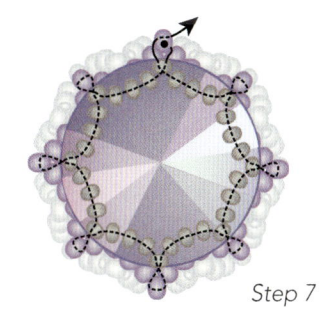

*Step 1*

*Step 2*

– 107 –

Pease Pod Chain of Office

**3**  a) Pass the tail thread end of the braid through the LR.
b) Ensuring the braid is not twisted, pass through the B and E beads at the other end of the braid, towards the TS.
c) Pass through the TS connector bead.
d) Pass back through E and B in the opposite direction and on through the tail thread end corner bead, from the threadless side.
e) Finish off.

## Braid 2

With 1m/40" thread and using A, leave a tail thread of 15cm/6":

a) Work a chain of 35 1Sqs.
b) Weave around to exit the end corner bead.
c) Pass the tail thread end through the large ring.
d) Pick up 3B, pass through the top space/loop of a key.
e) Ensuring the braid is not twisted, pass through the end corner bead of the tail thread end.
f) Pass back through the 3B and the key loop.
g) Pass through the end corner bead of the 1Sq on the working thread end, from the threadless side.
h) Weave into the braid and finish off.

*Step 3*

## Braid 3

With 1m/40" thread and using A, leave a tail thread of 15cm/6":

a) Work a 1Sq.
b) Pick up 1B, 1A.
c) Missing out A, pass back through B in the opposite direction.
d) Pass through the corner bead of the 1Sq from the threadless side.
e) Pass once more through B and A.
f) Repeat steps a)–e) 23 more times.
g) Repeat a).
h) Post the tail thread end of the braid through the LR, and smooth out the chain ready for connection to the working end.
i) Pick up 1B, pass through the top space/loop of a key and the end corner bead of the last 1Sq on the tail end.
j) Pass back through B, the key loop and the end corner bead of the last 1Sq on the working end, from the threadless side.
k) Weave into the braid and finish off.

> *"You are like my little dog; when people see you they know I am nearby."*
>
> Elizabeth to Robert Dudley

Pease Pod Chain of Office

GLORIANA REGNAT
NECKLACE AND BRACELET

# GLORIANA REGNAT NECKLACE AND BRACELET

The rigging creaked as the Golden Hind finally lay at anchor in Plymouth. Sailors eyed the dock and longed for shore leave, but had to wait. Drake, their captain, was delivering their plunder to a delighted Queen. Each of the 56 men that remained of the 80-strong crew that had set sail so many months ago, had a small pouch of treasure. Some had chosen gold and silver pieces they could use to buy a better life, while others chose jewelled ornaments to buy love. None could quite believe that the voyage of a lifetime with such a prize bounty had come to an end, and each wondered in his own way how life ashore would ever match it.

Under Elizabeth's rule, English ships plied the oceans, mapping and exploring. These were the glory days of privateering, of Francis Drake and Walter Raleigh, of expedition ships and trading vessels. Sir Francis Drake was unofficially commissioned by the Queen to act as a privateer against the Spanish. It is recorded that she said, 'Drake, so it is that I would gladly be revenged on the King of Spain, for diverse injuries that I have received.'

In 1579, off the coast of Ecuador, Drake captured the Spanish galleon Nuestra Señora de la Concepćion. He relieved the ship of treasure worth £480 million in today's terms, which included half a ton of gold, many tons of silver, jewellery, coins, loose jewels and porcelain. The Queen's share paid off her entire government debt for a year, and the rest she invested in a trading company to voyage to the Levant. It was this classic vision of pirated treasure that inspired the Gloriana Regnat necklace and bracelet; it just had to have jewels and pearls laid out together in satisfyingly traditional formations.

These elements are so enticing that they grew into a set of jewels fit for a queen, with three more elements added to create an alternative pendant formation and a bracelet. The first project is the Queen's Pendant.

---

**The first pendant has four elements**: framed stone, quatrefoil framed stone, pearl drop pendant, peyote rope

**Techniques**: Albion stitch, netting, square stitch, peyote stitch

**Completed necklace length**: 61cm/24"

**You will need**:

10g x Miyuki seed beads size 11° 457 (dark bronze) (A)
6g x Miyuki seed beads size 11° 4469 (duracoat jujube) (B)
10g x Miyuki seed beads size 15° 457 (dark bronze) (C)
27 x Swarovski® pearls 3mm (crystal bronze) (D)
17 x Swarovski® bicones #5328 3mm (astral pink) (E)
4 x Swarovski® pearls #5810 8mm (crystal bronze) (F)
2 x Swarovski® cushion square fancy stones #4470 12mm (siam) (G)
3 x Swarovski® pear drop pearls #5821 (crystal bronze) (H)
2 x 2-hole metal prong settings for #4470 (antique copper)
1 necklace clasp and 2 jump rings (antique copper)

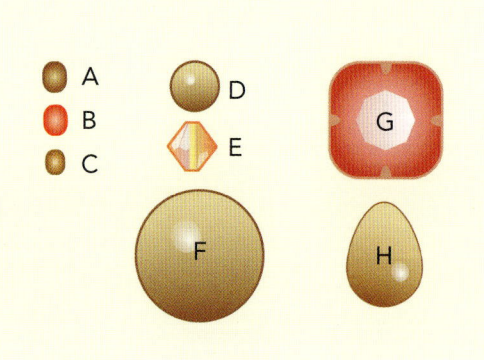

---

*Fascinating fact:*

*Queen Elizabeth prized pearls, purchasing Mary Queen of Scot's six stranded necklace of large black pearls from her. It is said these can be seen in the 'Ermine' portrait; others believe they are displayed in the Armada portrait. Throughout her reign, Elizabeth 1 refused to marry, and used portraiture as a powerful political message, showing the world that she would remain the Virgin Queen. Pearls were an enduring symbol of virginity and purity. Horace Walpole commented that she wore 'bushels of pearls'.*

*Gloriana Regnat necklace and bracelet*

– 110 –

> "...love is not love, Which alters when it alteration finds,
> Or bends with the remover to remove:
> O no! it is an ever-fixed mark, That looks on tempests and is never shaken..."
>
> Shakespeare's Sonnet 116

## Quatrefoil framed stone (Make 2)

The stone is held in place by the metal frame, then layered beadwork is worked through the holes in the frame to create a pearl and crystal encrusted square of beadwork. Stones and frames are usually supplied separately. To insert the stone, pop it into the frame, face up. Then, with flat nose pliers, or the flat of your scissor blades, gently ease each prong a little way over in turn. Rotate the setting and press the prongs a little at a time, until the stone is held firmly.

The metal frames have two holes on two sides and no holes on the other two sides. When the instructions say 'Pass through hole 1', this means pass through the frame via the holes from one side to the other.

1. Pass through hole 1 of the frame and pick up 4A. Pass through the 2nd hole of the frame.

2. Pick up 4A, pass back through the 1st hole of the frame and the 4A of step 1. Repeat the journey through the beads and 2 holes a 2nd time, then exit the 4A of step 1 again.

3. Pick up 12A and pass through the 4A of step 2. Pick up 12A and pass through the 4A of step 1.

4. Square stitch a round of beads to sit above the round in place. Exit a bead, pick up 2A, fold them back so they lie next to the bead started from and the one before it. Pass through that bead, then through the 2nd bead of the 2A.

   Pass through one more bead of the 1st round, pick up 1A, pass through the top A bead, then turn and pass through 3A of the 1st round.

   Repeat until there are 32 A beads adjacent to and behind the 32A of the original round.

*Steps 1–2*

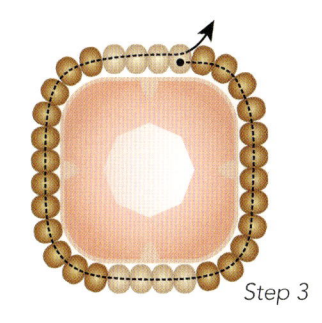

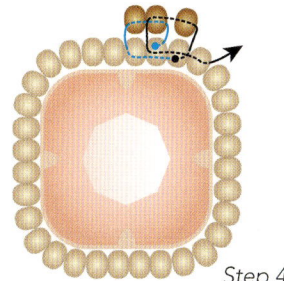

*Step 3*

*Step 4*

*Gloriana Regnat necklace and bracelet*

5. The following square stitches should have the centre bead in line with a prong on the metal frame.

   Find the bead nearest to a prong, square stitch 3A, with the centre A of the 3A over this bead.

   Weave through the beads of the round in order to square stitch 3A to sit one before, one over and one after the 8th, 16th and 24th bead, which should line up with the remaining 3 prongs.

   Now there are sets of 3A square stitched to the lower round sitting equal distances apart with the centre bead lined up with a prong. Bring the needle through to exit the end of a set of 3A.

6. Pick up 1D, 5A, 1D and pass through the next set of 3A. Repeat until you are back at the start.

7. Pass through this round of beads a 2nd time, but skip the centre bead of the sets of 5A. They need to stick outwards to shape the corners.

8. Square stitch one round of A beads to lie adjacent to and behind this round. When you reach a pearl, 2A will sit below it: exit the square-stitched bead before a pearl, pick up 3A and square stitch the last A to the A after the pearl on the previous round.

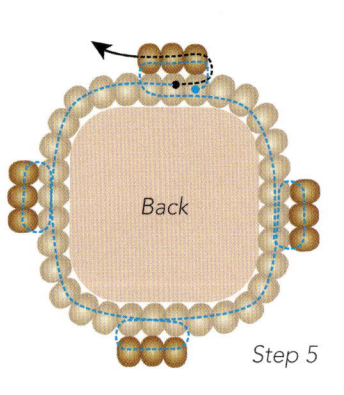

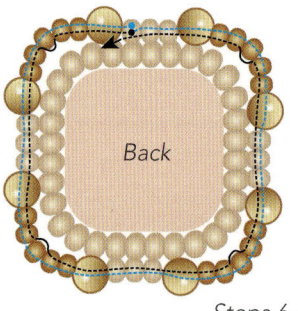

*Step 5*

*Steps 6–7*

*Step 8*

**The back of the framed stone**

1. Exit 2nd A after a corner, pick up 3A, 1B, 3A, then pass through the 2nd A bead before the corner, so that this loop of beads spans across the corner. Position 3 more sets of 3A, 1B, 3A over the 3 remaining corners. Step up to exit 1B.

2. Pick up 1A, 1B, 1A and pass through the 1B centre bead of the next loop. Repeat all the way round, then step up through 1A, 1B.

3. a) Pick up 1A and pass through the 1B centre bead of the next set added in step 2. Repeat all the way round.
   b) At the end of the round, step up and pass through the 4A just added.

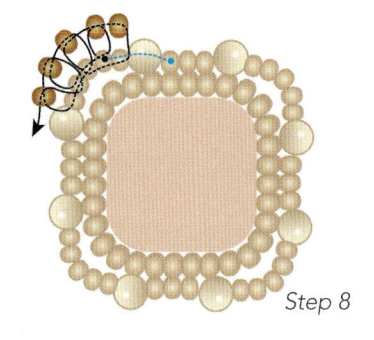

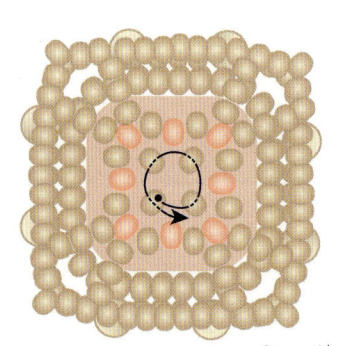

*Step 1*

*Steps 2–3a shown from the back*

*Step 3b shown from the back*

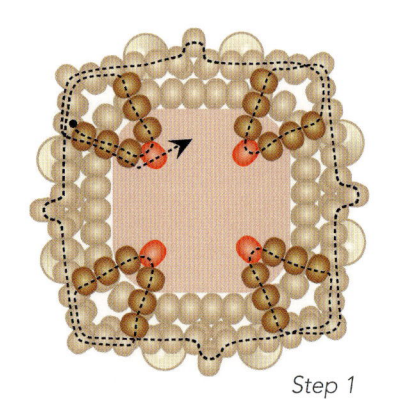

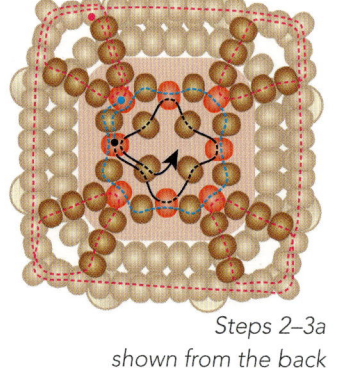

**Embellish the front**

4. Weave through the beads to exit a corner bead on the top round (the round with the pearls).

   Pick up 1E and pass through the bead directly opposite on the top round of the inner bezel. Pass back through the 1E and the 1A started from. Embellish the 3 remaining corners in the same way.

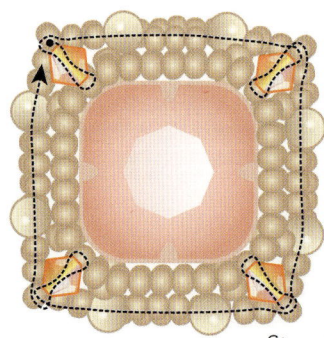

*Step 4*

Gloriana Regnat necklace and bracelet

## Beaded pendant loops

There are three loops. Two are worked on the top edge of the framed stone to create a channel for the rope, and one is worked from the centre bottom, to hold a loop for the quatrefoil framed stone.

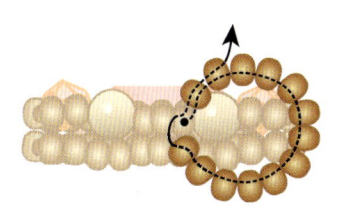

1. Exit 1A before a pearl on one edge of the frame. Pick up 13A, then pass through the 1A adjacent to the 1A started from (lower row of beads).

   Continue on through 2A of the 13A.

2. Pick up 1D stalk, 1A tip, pass back through 1D, the 1A started from and the next 2A of the 13A.

3. Pick up 1E stalk, 1A tip, pass back through 1E, the 1A started from and the next 2A of the 13A.

4. Repeat step 2, step 3, step 2, step 3. Exit the final A of the 13A, then pass through the beads of the base to exit the 1A adjacent to the 1A on the other side of the pearl.

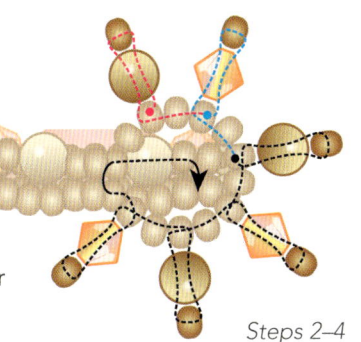

5. Pick up 1A and pass through the nearest 1A tip bead. Joint the tip beads in turn with 1A between each. Exit the last tip bead, pick up 1A and pass through the 1A next to the pearl.

   Repeat to make a 2nd loop on the same edge.

6. Weave through the beads to the bottom edge and exit the 1st 1A of the 3A between the pearls. Make the loop as before and link the tip beads starting from the last 1A of the 3A between the pearls.

   This completes the element. Finish off the thread tails.

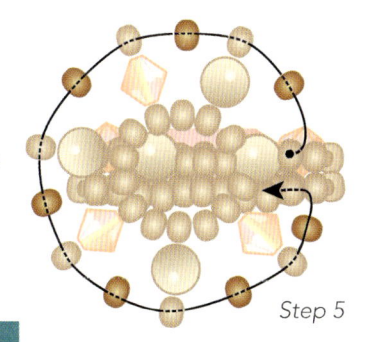

## Quatrefoil framed stone

Instead of adding beaded loops, the second framed stone has Swarovski® pearls and square-stitched pairs added to the edges. First frame the stone as before, then...

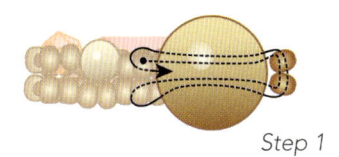

1. Exit the centre 1A of a set of 3A between the pearls on the frame edge top round. Pick up 1F, 2A. Pass back through the 1F and through the 1A adjacent to the 1A started from. Repeat the journey back through the beads a 2nd time.

2. Weave through the beads to exit 1A after a pearl. Pick up 2A, pass through the 1A adjacent to the 1A started from, then back through 1A of the 2A just added.

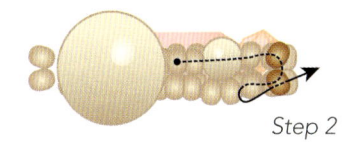

3. Square stitch 7 more pairs of A beads. (Pick up 2A, pass down through 1A of the previous pair, up through the 2nd of that pair and 1A of the new pair just added.)

4. Square stitch through the 2A at the top of the 1F. Square stitch 8 more pairs, then secure them to the A beads next to the 2nd pearl of the edge; if desired, reinforce the loops with a 2nd threadpath for a tighter frame.

   Repeat steps 1 through 4 to add pearls and square-stitched loops to the remaining 3 sides of the framed stone.

## Loops

There are four beaded loops, the first is added centre top and passed through the single beaded loop centre bottom of the framed stone. One is added centre bottom, and two to the lower sides of the square-stitched loops. These will hold the pearl drop pendants.

### Top loop

1. Exit a bead of the 7th pair from the edge on a square-stitched loop. Pick up 1A, 1B, 1A, 17C, 1A, 1B, 1A.

   Pass through the beaded loop at the bottom of the 1st framed stone. Pass through a bead of the 4th pair round from the start point (the loop will sit over the centre top 3 beads of the square-stitched loop).

2. Pass back through the 2nd bead of the pair, and 1A of the loop. Pick up 1B and pass through 1A, 17C, 1A. Pick up 1B, pass through 1A and the 2nd bead of the square-stitched pair started from in step 1.

   Repeat the threadpath to strengthen the loop.

*Steps 1–2*

### Bottom loop

1. Exit a bead of the centre pair of the bottom square-stitched loop. Pick up 1B, 1A, 10C, 1A, 1B.

   Pass through the 2nd bead of the pair started from.

2. Pick up 1B and pass through 1A, 10C, 1A. Pick up 1B, pass through 1A and the bead of the square-stitched pair started from in step 1.

   Repeat the threadpath to strengthen the loop.

*Steps 1–2*

### Side loops loop

The side loops are worked in the same way as the bottom loop, but start from the fourth pair from the frame edge on the bottom of each side loop.

### Pearl drop loop (Make 3)

Three pearl drop loops are each worked to hang from one of the three loops on the lower edges of the quatrefoil framed stone.

1. Pick up 1C, 1A and pass through 1H from bottom to top. Pick up 1A and pass back down through the 1H, 1A and 1C.

2. Pass through 1A, 1H, 1A. Pick up 1B, 1A, 9C, 1A, 1B. Pass the needle through a loop on the quatrefoil framed stone, then pass back through the 1A started from.

3. Pick up 1B and pass through 1A, 9C, 1A. Pick up 1B and pass through the 1A started from. Repeat the threadpath to strengthen the loop, then finish off the thread tails.

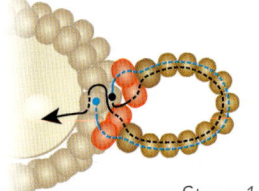

*Steps 1–3*

> *Fascinating fact:*
>
> *It is recorded that Elizabeth wasn't averse to a bit of fakery, she is known to have purchased several hundred imitation pearls at one penny each for use on a gown. At the end of her reign she owned 2000 elaborate gowns. Very few survive as they were recycled, some to pay debts, others as gifts and many to simply recover the fabric and jewels for re-use.*

Gloriana Regnat necklace and bracelet

## Peyote stitch rope (Make 1)

This is a simple spiral rope in peyote stitch; it has minimal diameter, so getting started can be a fiddle. Start by sliding the ring onto a cocktail stick or fine tapestry needle until you have worked enough length to have something to hold.

1. Pick up 4C, 2A, 2B and secure in a ring. Exit the last C before the 1st A picked up.

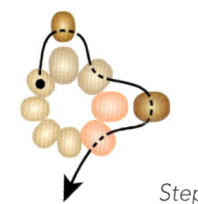

2. Pick up 1C, skip 1A and pass through the 2nd A. Pick up 1A, skip 1B and pass through the 2nd B.

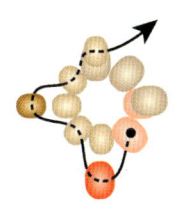

3. Pick up 1B, skip 1C and pass through the 2nd C. Pick up 1C, skip 1C and pass through the C from which this row began. Step up to exit the 1st C placed in this row.

    Repeat steps 2 and 3 until the spiral is the necklace length required.

    To finish, make a loop of 1A, 9C, passing back through the 1A and beads of the last peyote round. Do the same at the start end.

*Step 1*

*Step 2*

*Step 3*

## Peyote stitch 2-drop spiral rope

An alternative peyote stitch rope which works up quickly once you get started. You will need an additional colour of size 15° seed bead (D). Try it with two colours of size 15° beads first, then you can work all the 15s in one colour once you've got the technique. For this rope, A and B are size 11° seed beads. C and D are size 15° seed beads in the steps below. It is a continuous spiral so there is no step up, you just keep working round and round.

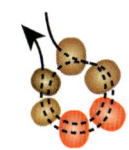

1. Pick up 2A, 2B, 1C, 1D and secure in a ring. Exit 1D before 2A.

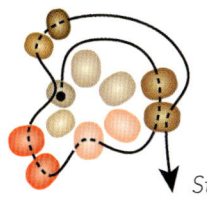

2. Pick up 2A and pass through 2nd of 2B. Pick up 2B and pass through 1D. Pick up 1C, 1D and pass through 2nd of 2A.

    Continue repeating step 2 until the rope is the desired length.

*Step 1*

*Step 2*

*Gloriana Regnat necklace and bracelet*

## The Queen's Bracelet

A queen wouldn't stop at one necklace; the additional elements of this royal suite enable you to make a bracelet.

**The bracelet elements**: framed chaton, framed pearl, framed stone

**Techniques**: Albion stitch, netting, square stitch, peyote stitch

**Completed bracelet length**: without clasp 19cm/7½", with clasp 19.5cm/7¾"

**You will need**:

10g x Miyuki seed beads size 11° 4222 (pewter) (A)
1g x Miyuki seed beads size 11° 4488 (duracoat columbine) (B)
1g x Miyuki seed beads size 15° 4222 (pewter) (C)
48 x Swarovski® pearls #5810 3mm (crystal dove grey) (D)
24 x Swarovski® bicones #5328 3mm (indicolite) (E)
5 x Miyuki cotton pearls 8mm (pale lilac) (F)
3 x Swarovski® cushion square fancy stones #4470 12mm (tanzanite)
3 x 2-hole metal prong settings for 4470 (antique bronze)
3 x Swarovski® xilion chatons #1088 ss39 8mm (purple velvet)
3 x 2-hole metal prong settings for #1088 ss39 8mm (antique bronze)
bar end bracelet clasp 2cm (antique bronze)

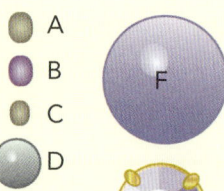

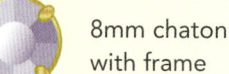

8mm chaton with frame

### Framed chaton (Make 3)

The framed chaton is worked in the same way as the framed stone, but on a smaller scale.

1. Pass through the 1st hole of the frame and pick up 2A. Pass through the 2nd hole of the frame.

2. Pick up 2A, pass back through the 1st hole of the frame and the 2A of step 1. Repeat the journey through the beads and 2 holes a 2nd time, then exit the 2A of step 1 again.

3. Pick up 10A and pass through the 2A of step 2. Pick up 10A and pass through the 2A of step 1.

4. Pass through this round a 2nd time; skip the bead that lies next to the prong. This will pull the ring into a square with the corners in line with the prongs.

5. Square stitch a round of beads to sit **below** the round in place (because the metal frame is not as deep as the one for the bigger stone). Exit a bead, pick up 2A, fold them back so they lie adjacent to the bead started from and the one before it. Pass through those 2 beads, then through the next bead on the original row. Add 1A, pass through the 1st 1A added in the previous step, then through 3A of the original row. Repeat.

   Repeat until there are 24A beads below the 24A of the original round. At the end of the round, step down to exit 1A on the **new** round.

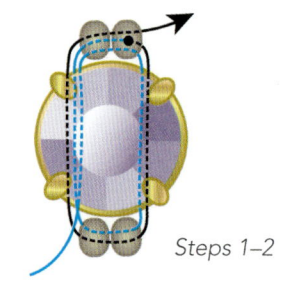

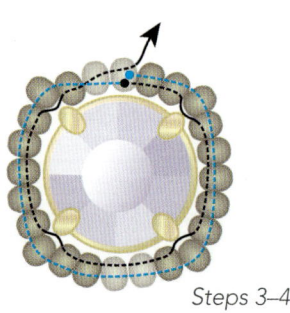

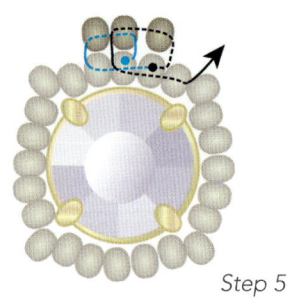

*Steps 1–2*

*Steps 3–4*

*Step 5*

Gloriana Regnat necklace and bracelet

6. The following square stitches should have the centre bead on one side between the corners. Find the centre bead of a side, square stitch 3A, with the centre A of the 3A over this bead.

   Weave through the beads of the round in order to square stitch 3A to sit one before, one over and one after the 6th, 12th and 18th beads, which should line up with the remaining side centres.

   Now there are sets of 3A square-stitched to the lower round sitting equal distances apart, with the centre bead lined up with a prong.

   Bring the needle through to exit the end of a set of 3A.

*Step 6*

7. Pick up 1D, 3A, 1D and pass through the next set of 3A. Repeat until you are back at the start.

8. Pass through this round of beads a 2nd time, but skip the centre bead of the sets of 3A; they need to stick outwards to shape the corners.

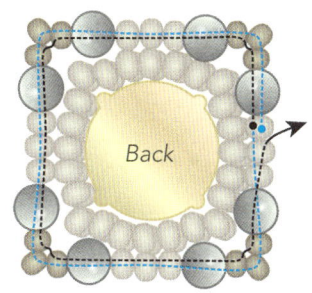

*Steps 7–8*

9. Square stitch one round of A beads to lie below this round. When you reach a pearl, 2A will sit below it: exit the A bead before a pearl, pick up 3A and square stitch the 3rd A bead to the A after the pearl on the previous round.

   At the end of the round, weave through the beads to exit the 2nd A after a corner of the bottom row.

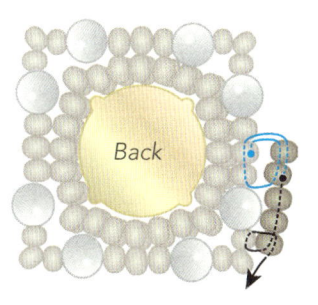

**Back of the framed chaton**

1. Exit the 2nd A before a corner, pick up 2A, 2B, 2A, then pass through the 2nd A bead after the corner, so that this loop of beads spans across the corner. Repeat to add 2A, 1B, 2A over the remaining corners. Step up to exit 1B.

*Step 9*

2. Pick up 1A, 1B, 1A and pass through the 1B centre bead of the next loop. Repeat all the way round, then step up through 1A, 1B.

3. Pick up 1A and pass through the 1B centre bead of the next set added in step 2. Repeat all the way round. At the end of the round step up and pass through the 4A just added.

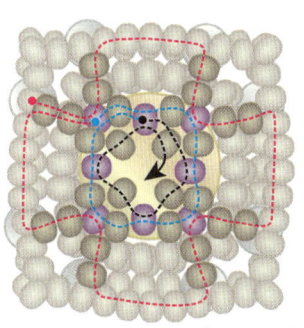

**Embellish the front**

4. Weave through the beads to exit a corner bead on the top round (the round with the pearls).

   Pick up 1E and pass through the corner bead on the top round of the inner bezel. Pass back through the 1E and the 1A started from. Embellish the 3 remaining corners in the same way.

*Steps 1–3*

*Step 4*

### Framed pearl (Make 5)

**1** Pick up 22A and secure in a ring.

**2** Square stitch one round of A to the ring. Have the beads stack so that the rings have the same circumference.

**3** Stitch an F into the centre of the ring through opposite pairs of beads.

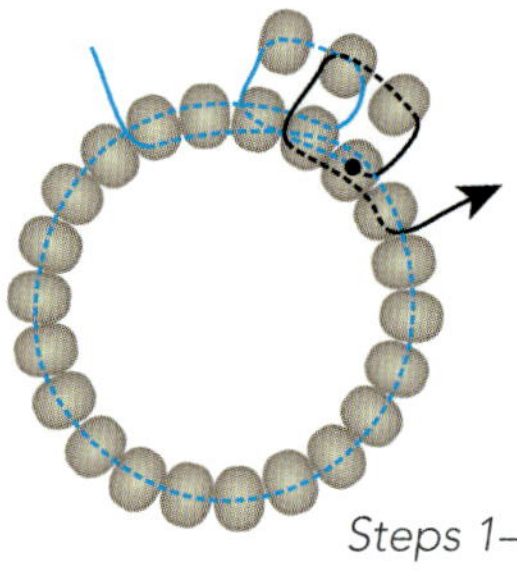

*Steps 1–2*

### Bracelet construction

The elements are joined through the square-stitched edges, linking the bottom rows directly and adding beads between the edges of the top rows. This enables the bracelet to curve around the wrist.

**1** Exit the centre 3A on the bottom edge of a framed chaton. Pass through 3A on the bottom edge of a framed pearl, then weave through the beads to exit the 3A adjacent on the top edge of the framed pearl.

**2** Pick up 1C, 1B, 1C and pass through the 3A on the framed chaton edge. Pick up 1C, 1B, 1C and pass back through the 3A on the framed pearl edge.

**3** Weave through the beads of the framed pearl top edge to exit the 3A opposite the 3A started from.

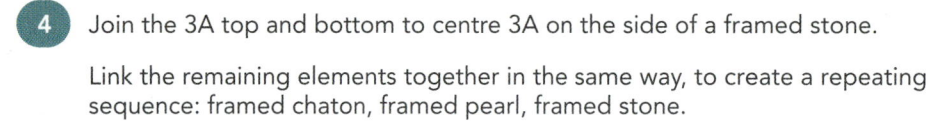

*Step 1*

**4** Join the 3A top and bottom to centre 3A on the side of a framed stone.

Link the remaining elements together in the same way, to create a repeating sequence: framed chaton, framed pearl, framed stone.

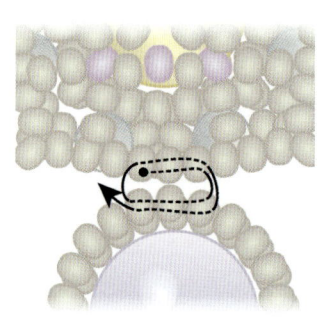

### Add a clasp

**5** Using A beads, square stitch 4 rows, 9 beads wide to the bottom edge of the 1st and last elements of the bracelet. (Check that this measurement will fit your bar clasp; if it is too wide, work fewer beads, making sure they are centred.)

Pass the tab of square stitch through the bracelet bar, then stitch it to the top row.

*Step 2*

To work around the pearls on the top edge, zip 2 seed beads through one pearl.

Alternatively, use the clasp of your choice and one of the other techniques (as shown on pages 30 and 54) for attaching clasps shown in this book.

*Step 5*

*Gloriana Regnat necklace and bracelet*

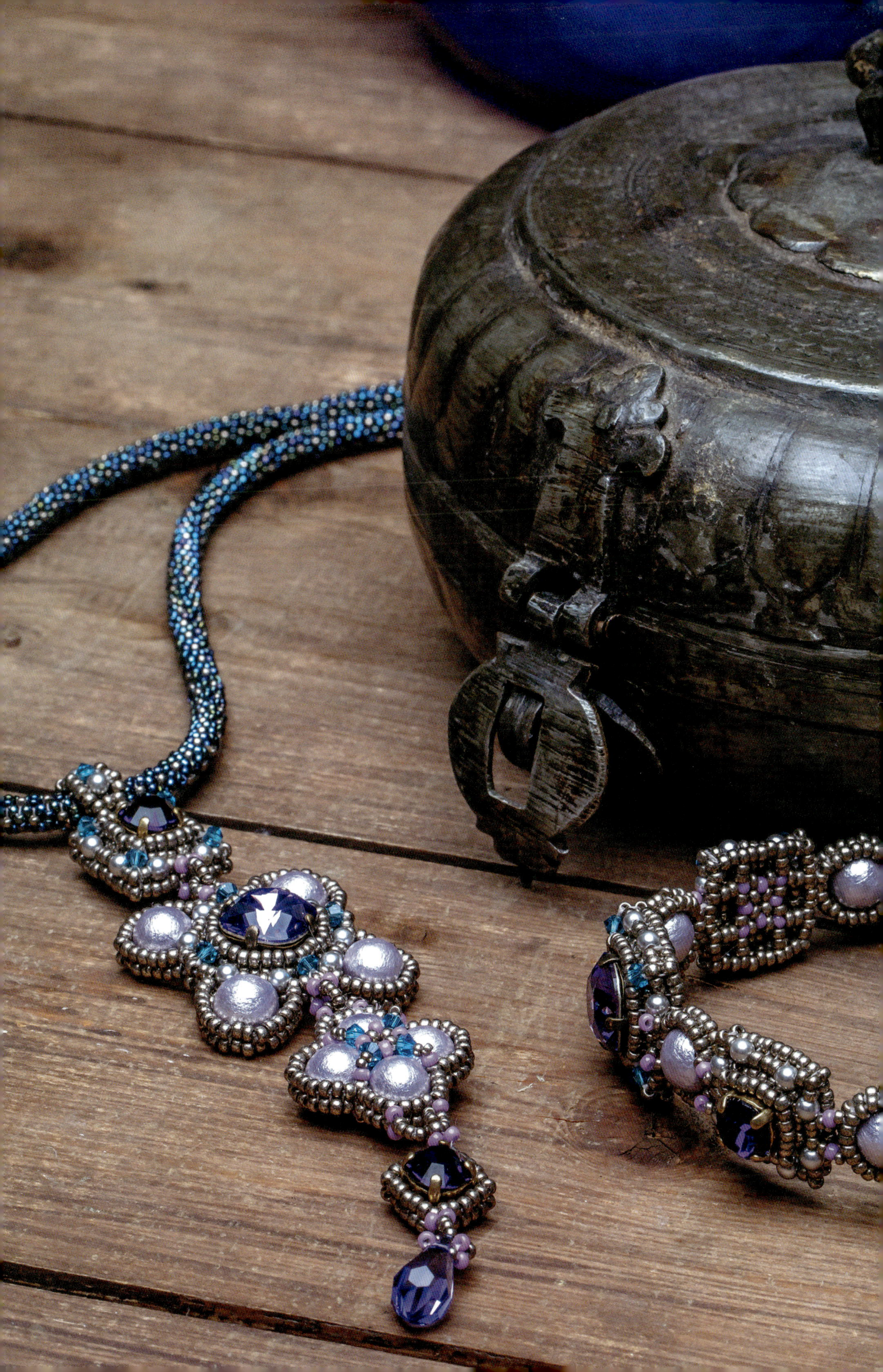

## Quatrepearl element

**The second pendant has four elements**: two framed chatons, one with and one without a second square-stitched edging; a quatrefoil stone element; and a drop using a 15mm Swarovski® crystal drop with a loop stitched through the horizontal hole. The necklace cord is worked in honeycomb stitch in size 15° seed beads.

**Finished quatrepearl element length**: 2.5 x 2.5cm (1 x 1") without loops

**Finished pendant length**: 14cm/5½" including top loop and crystal drop

**You will need**:
10g x Miyuki seed beads size 11° 4222 (duracoat galvanised pewter) (A)
6g x Miyuki seed beads size 11° 4488 (duracoat colombine) (B)
10g x Miyuki seed beads size 15° 4222 (duracoat galvanised pewter) (C)
8 x Swarovski® bicones #5328 3mm (indicolite) (E)
4 x Miyuki cotton pearls 8mm (or any 8mm pearls) (pale lilac) (F)
1 x Swarovski® crystal pendant #6000 11x5.5mm (tanzanite) (H)

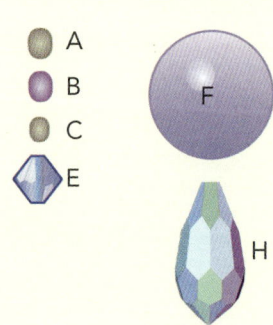

1. Pick up 4A and secure in a ring.

2. Peyote stitch one round in B. Then exit an A bead.

3. Working over A beads place an Albion stitch over each 1A: 1E, 2C, 1B stalk; 1A tip. At the end of the round, step up to exit 1A tip bead.

4. Link each tip bead with 1F. Then pass through 1F, add 1A, pass through next 1G, and so on, there will be 2A, side by side, between each 1F.

5. Place an Albion stitch over each of the new A beads added in step 4: 1B 1E stalk; 1A tip. At the end of the round exit a 1A tip bead.

6. Link each 1A tip bead with 1B. At the end of the round, pass through just the 1A tip beads to pull them inwards into a ring.

7. Weave back to a 1A which sits between the F pearls. Treat the 2A between F pearls as a pair. Square stitch 11 pairs, then join through the 2A, the other side of the F bead. Repeat for each F bead.

Add connection loops to opposite sides of this element in the same way as before on page 114.

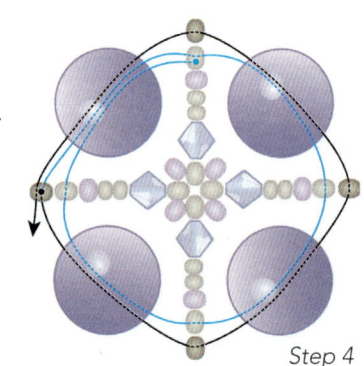

*Steps 1–3*

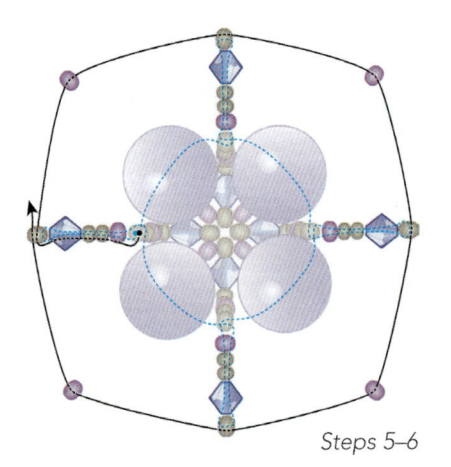

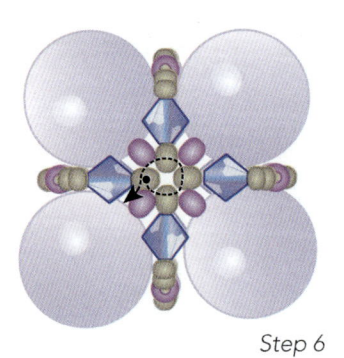

*Step 4*

*Steps 5–6*

*Step 6*

*Step 7*

*Gloriana Regnat necklace and bracelet*

## Pendant construction

On the framed chaton, and working from an edge bead either side of the centre bead of that edge, make a beaded pendant loop as shown on page 113. (Same as the bottom loop of the quatrefoil element.) This will hold the beaded rope and can be adjusted in diameter to fit a rope of your choosing by adding beads in multiples of two.

On the opposite side of the framed chaton, make a seed bead loop (see page 114) worked from the centre bead of that side.

On the quatrefoil framed stone, make seed bead loops through opposite corner beads of the bezel edge, passing one through the seed bead loop at the bottom of the framed chaton.

On the quatrepearl element, make seed bead loops over the centre three pairs of beads on the pearls, on opposite sides of the element, passing one through the loop already in place at the bottom of the quatrefoil framed stone.

On the single chaton bezel (which is made with the first square-stitched round only of a chaton bezel), make loops from opposite corner beads, passing one through the second loop on the quatrepearl element.

The crystal drop has a hole across the top. To make a loop:

Pick up 1B, 1A, 9C, 1A, 1B. Pass the needle through the loop on the quatrepearl element, then back through the crystal.

Pick up 1B and pass through 1A, 9C, 1A. Pick up 1B and pass through the 1A started from. Repeat the thread path to strengthen the loop, then finish off the thread tails.

> *Fascinating fact:*
>
> *Robert Dudley, 1st Earl of Leicester was close to the Queen for 30 years. Dudley arranged for Elizabeth I to visit Tilbury where her troops were amassed after the victory over the Spanish Armada. She gave a legendary speech, which included, 'I know I have the body of a weak and feeble woman; but I have the heart and stomach of a king, and of a king of England too'. The troops replied with a resounding 'Gloriana, Gloriana, Gloriana'. On his death, Dudley left the Queen a diamond and emerald pendant and a rope of 600 pearls, leaving his wife Lettice Knollys, with £50,000 of debts.*

## Honeycomb stitch rope

**Completed rope length**: 41cm/16"

**You will need**:
15g x Miyuki seed beads size 15° 456 (gunmetal iris) (A)
6g x Miyuki seed beads size 11° 4222 (duracoat galvanised pewter) (B)
Jewellery tube 2mm diameter
Jump rings and necklace clasp

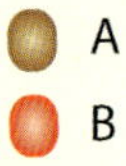

● A
● B

The beading is worked with the 2mm jewellery tube in place. The jewellery tube is a very flexible plastic tube, which will allow the beadwork around it to move and drape easily. Start with a ring of 12A and slide it onto one end of the tube, about 2.5cm/1" from the end of the tube. Work the honeycomb netting around the tube so that it covers the length of the tube as you work.

*Steps 1–3*

1. Pick up 12A and secure them in a ring. Exit a bead on the ring. Leave a 20cm/8" tail, which can be used to secure the jewellery tube and add a loop of beads for the clasp.

2. Pick up 4A and pass through the 5th and 6th bead on the ring from the one you started from (that is, bypass 4 beads on the ring).

3. Pick up 4A, pass through the 11th and 12th beads of the ring and step up through 3A of the 1st set, which was added in step 2.

*Steps 4–5*

4. Pick up 1B and pass through the centre 2A of the 2nd set (added in step 3).

5. Pick up 1B and pass through the centre 2A of the 1st set again.

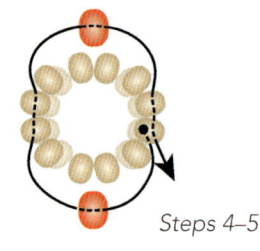

6. Add 2 sets of 4A, passing through the pairs of centre beads used to add the B beads, then step up through 3A of the 1st 4A added in the round.

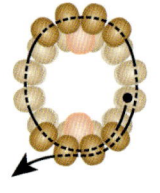

7. Add the next 1B beads, working through the centre beads of the new sets of 4A just added.

*Step 6*

8. Repeat steps 6 and 7 until the necklace is the right length. End with a step 7.

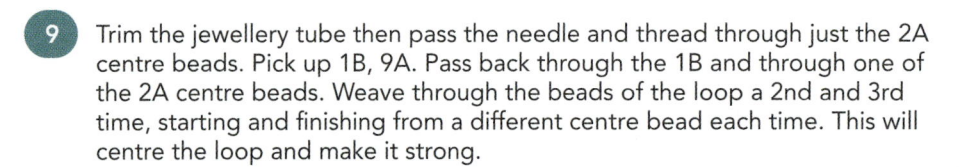

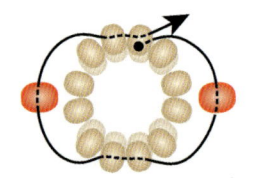

9. Trim the jewellery tube then pass the needle and thread through just the 2A centre beads. Pick up 1B, 9A. Pass back through the 1B and through one of the 2A centre beads. Weave through the beads of the loop a 2nd and 3rd time, starting and finishing from a different centre bead each time. This will centre the loop and make it strong.

*Step 7*

Finish off the thread by stitching through the beads and the jewellery tube, this will stop the beadwork from sliding beyond the tube end.

Repeat to add a loop to the start.

Attach jump rings through the loops, and a clasp to the jump rings.

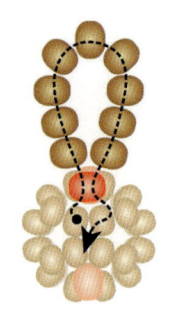

*Step 9*

*Gloriana Regnat necklace and bracelet*

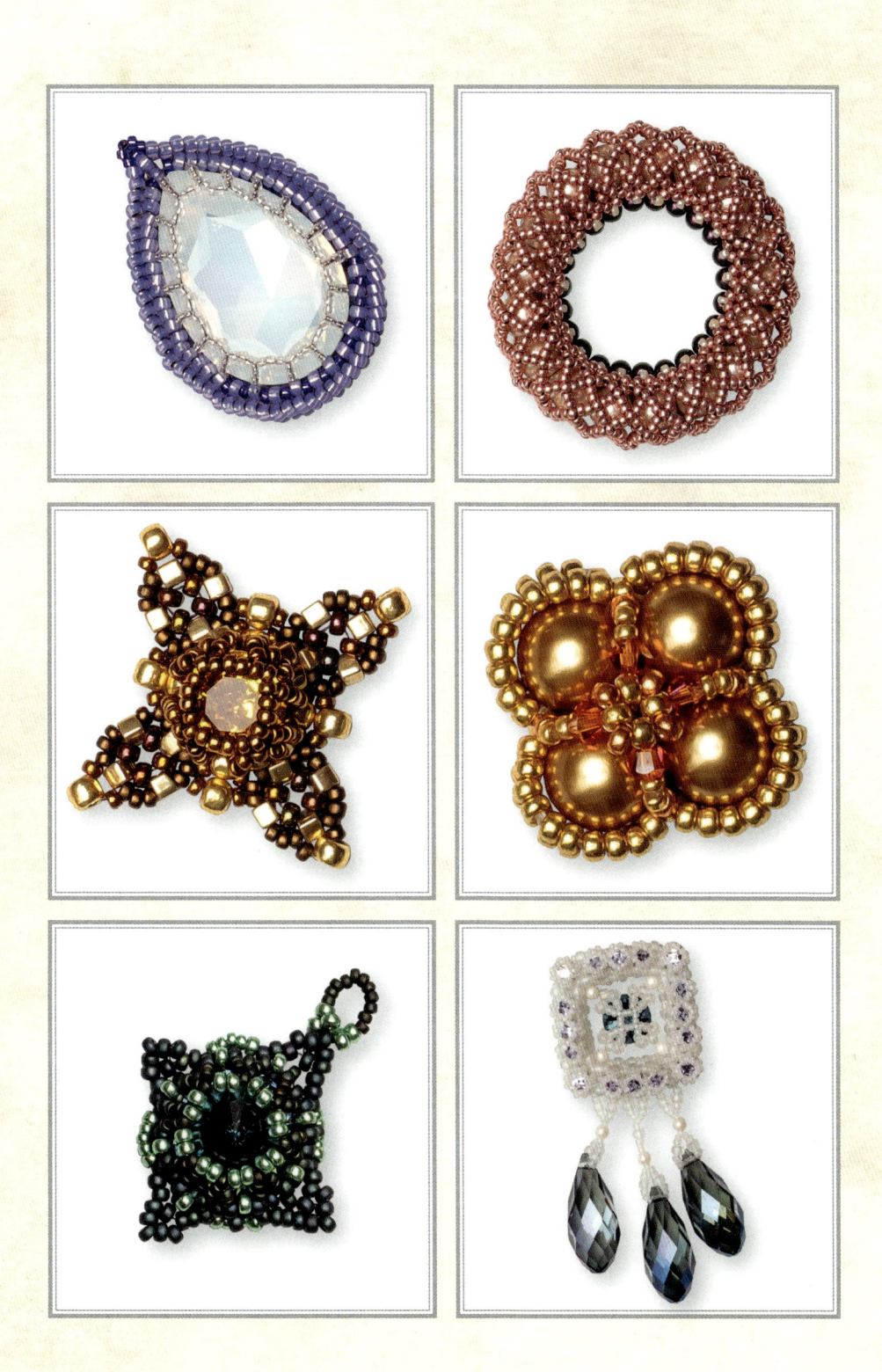

ELEMENTS LIBRARY

# ELEMENTS LIBRARY

**Note**: to calculate bead quantities by gram (g) weight use this guide as an average for Miyuki seed beads, then add 10% to your total to be sure you have enough, as some coatings and finishes can make a slight difference to the number of beads per gram.

Size 8° seed beads: 39 beads = 1g

Size 11° seed beads: 110 beads = 1g

Size 15° seed beads: 250 beads = 1g

**Examples**: An element uses 130 size 11° seed beads. You want to make 10 of these elements: 130 x 10 = 1300. 1300 divided by 110 is 11.81, so to be on the safe side you will need 13g.

An element uses 158 size 15° seed beads. You want to make 6 of these elements: 158 x 6 = 948. 948 divided by 250 is 3.79, so to be on the safe side you will need 4g.

Elements Library

## Beaded beads

**Beaded bead with glass links 3.5cm (page 91)**
28 x Miyuki seed beads size 11° (A)
72 x Miyuki seed beads size 15° (B)
8 x Miyuki seed beads size 15° (C)
48 x Miyuki cube beads 1.8mm (D)
1 x Swarovski® pearl #5810 10mm (G)
2 x Czech glass rings 9mm (H)
   (check how many you need if elements are to share glass rings)

**Caged drop bead 3.8cm (page 22)**
142 x Miyuki seed beads size 11° (A)
68 x Miyuki seed beads size 11° (B)
16 x Miyuki seed beads size 11° (C)
134 x Miyuki seed beads size 11° (D)
16 x Miyuki seed beads size 8° (E)
18 x Miyuki seed beads size 15° (F)
10 x Swarovski® pearls #5810 3mm (J)
1 x tear drop pearl 14x27mm (K)

**Caged pearls 3.5cm (page 24)**
96 x Miyuki seed beads size 11° (A)
16 x Miyuki seed beads size 11° (B)
28 x Miyuki seed beads size 11° 4201F (C)
40 x Miyuki seed beads size 11° (D)
16 x Miyuki seed beads size 8° (E)
18 x Miyuki seed beads size 15° (F)
2 x Swarovski® pearls #5810 3mm (J)
1 x Swarovski® pearl #5810 10mm (L)

**Chaton beaded bead 3cm (page 92)**
32 x Miyuki seed beads size 11° (A)
61 x Miyuki seed beads size 15° (B)
176 x Miyuki seed beads size 15° (C)
4 x Swarovski® xilion chatons #1088 ss39 8mm (E)
1 x Swarovski® pearl #5810 10mm (G)
2 x Czech glass rings 9mm (H)
   (check how many you need if elements are to share glass rings)

**Multi-pod 2.5cm (page 101)**
564 x Miyuki seed beads size 15° (A)
42 x Toho seed beads size 15° (B)
1 x Swarovski® pearl #5810 6mm (C)
16 x Czech charlotte seed beads size 15° (D)
8 x Swarovski® pearls #5810 3mm (E)
8 x Swarovski® pearls #5810 4mm (F)
4 x Swarovski® pearls #5810 5mm (G)

– 125 –

Elements Library

**Pea pod 2.5cm (page 99)**
188 x Miyuki seed beads size 15° (A)
10 x Toho seed beads size 15° (B)
1 x Swarovski® pearl #5810 6mm (C)

## Focal elements

**Baroque bead drop (page 95)**
3 x Miyuki seed beads size 11° (A)
10 x Miyuki seed beads size 11° (B)
4 x Miyuki seed beads size 15° (C)
1 x Miyuki cube bead 1.8mm (D)
1 x Swarovski® baroque drop bead #5058 14mm (J)

**Bezelled stone with glass rings 6cm (page 93)**
32 x Miyuki seed beads size 11° (A)
258 x Miyuki seed beads size 15° (B)
196 x Miyuki seed beads size 15° (C)
36 x Miyuki cube beads 1.8mm (D)
2 x Czech glass rings 9mm (H)
   (check how many you need if elements are to share glass rings)

**Cabochon drop 1cm square (page 73)**
16 x Miyuki seed beads size 11° (A)
4 x Miyuki seed beads size 11° (B)
1 x 2-hole cabochon bead 6mm (E)
You will need additional B x 2 to attach this element to another.

**Centrepiece 3.4x3.4cm (page 84)**
208 x Miyuki seed beads size 8° (A)
16 x Miyuki seed beads size 11° (B)
188 x Miyuki seed beads size 15° (C)
4 x Swarovski® pearls #5810 3mm (D)
1 x Swarovski® rivoli #1122 ss47 10mm (E)
128 x Czech charlotte seed beads size 15° (F)

**Chaton unit 1.3cm (page 10)**
64 x Miyuki seed beads size 15° (A)
48 x Miyuki seed beads size 11° (B)
24 x Czech charlotte seed beads size 15° (D)
1 x Swarovski® xilion chaton #1088 ss39 8mm (F)

Elements Library

**Framed pearl 11mm (page 118)**
44 x Miyuki seed beads size 11° (A)
1 x cotton pearl 8mm
You will also need size 11° B x 2 per join to link this element

---

**Framed stone (including loops) 4x2cm (page 111)**
239 x Miyuki seed beads size 11° (A)
8 x Miyuki seed beads size 11° (B)
17 x Swarovski® pearls #5810 3mm (D)
13 x Swarovski® bicones #5328 3mm (E)
1 x Swarovski® cushion square fancy stone #4470 12mm (G) (plus metal setting)

---

**Locket 2.5cm (page 33)**
564 x Miyuki seed beads size 11° (A)
216 x Miyuki Delica beads size 11° (B)
4 x Miyuki drop beads DP28-421D (C)
24 x Swarovski® crystal rounds #5000 2mm (can substitute firepolish 2mm) (D)
16 x Czech charlotte seed beads size 15° (E)
35 x Miyuki seed beads size 15° (F)
1 x Swarovski® bicone #5328 4mm (G)

---

**Pearl drop pendant 2cm (including loop) (page 114)**
4 x Miyuki seed beads size 11° (A)
4 x Miyuki seed beads size 11° (B)
10 x Miyuki seed beads size 15° (C)
1 x Swarovski® pear drop pearl #5821 (H)

---

**Pear drop unit 3.8cm (page 3)**
121 x Miyuki seed beads size 15° (A)
224 x Miyuki seed beads size 11° (B)
1 x Swarovski® pear drop fancy stone #4327 30x20mm (C)
109 x Czech charlotte seed beads size 15° (D)

---

**Pendant crystal drop (page 121)**
4 x Miyuki seed beads size 11° (A)
4 x Miyuki seed beads size 11° (B)
7 x Miyuki seed beads size 15° (C)
1 x Swarovski® crystal pendant #6000 11x5.5mm

---

**Pendant rivoli 2.5cm per side (page 71)**
96 x Miyuki seed beads size 11° (A)
46 x Miyuki seed beads size 11° (B)
51 x Miyuki seed beads size 15° (C)
68 x Miyuki seed beads size 15° (D)
1 x Swarovski® rivoli #1122 14mm (G)
Quantities allow for one corner loop. To add a 2nd corner loop
    you will need additional B x 16, C x 11

Elements Library

**Quatrefoil framed stone 4x4cm (including 4 x loops) (page 113)**
381 x Miyuki seed beads size 11° (A)
24 x Miyuki seed beads size 11° (B)
44 x Miyuki seed beads size 15° (C)
8 x Swarovski® pearls #5810 3mm (D)
4 x Swarovski® bicones #5328 3mm (E)
4 x Swarovski® pearls #5810 8mm (F)
1 x Swarovski® cushion square fancy stone #4470 12mm (G) (plus metal setting)

**Quatrepearl element 2.5x2.5cm (including 2 loops) (page 120)**
64 x Miyuki seed beads size 11° (A)
24 x Miyuki seed beads size 11° (B)
34 x Miyuki seed beads size 15° (C)
8 x Swarovski® bicones #5328 3mm (E)
4 x cotton pearls 8mm (F)

**Rivoli unit 2cm (page 8)**
108 x Miyuki seed beads size 15° (A)
72 x Miyuki seed beads size 11° (B)
48 x Czech charlotte seed beads size 15° (D)
1 x Swarovski® rivoli #1122 14mm (E)

**Ruffle bead 6cm (page 17)**
272 x Miyuki seed beads size 11° (A)
208 x Miyuki seed beads size 11° (B)
20 x Miyuki seed beads size 11° (C)
240 x Miyuki seed beads size 11° (D)
16 x Miyuki seed beads size 8° (E)
158 x Miyuki seed beads size 15° (F)
360 x Miyuki seed beads size 15° (G)
32 x CzechMate half tile 2-hole (H)
50 x Swarovski® pearls #5810 3mm (J)

**Single framed chaton 1.5cm (page 121)**
100 x Miyuki seed beads size 11° (A)
8 x Miyuki seed beads size 11° (B)
8 x Swarovski® pearls #5810 3mm (D)
4 x Swarovski® bicones #5328 3mm (E)
1 x Swarovski® xilion chaton #1088 ss39 8mm
1 x 2-hole setting for #1088 ss39
You will also need size 11° B x 2 per join to link this element

Elements Library

**Square chaton motif 2.3x2.3cm per side (3cm diagonal) (page 47)**
20 x Miyuki seed beads size 11° (A)
113 x Miyuki seed beads size 15° (B)
28 x Miyuki seed beads size 15° (C)
12 x Miyuki seed beads size 8° (D)
28 x Miyuki cube beads 1.8mm (E)
1 x Swarovski® xilion chaton #1088 ss39 8mm (F)

**Square rivoli 1.4x1.4cm (page 57)**
96 x Miyuki seed beads size 15° (A)
4 x Swarovski® pearls #5810 3mm (C)
1 x Swarovski® cushion square fancy stone #4470 12mm (D)

**Thistle seal (page 106)**
312 x Miyuki seed beads size 15° (A)
70 x Toho seed beads size 15° (B)
9 x Swarovski® pearls #5810 3mm (E)
1 x Swarovski® pearl #5811 14mm (H)
1 x Swarovski® rivoli #1122 14mm (J)

## Clasps

**Toggle bar 1.8cm (page 42)**
13 x Czech charlotte seed beads size 15° (E)
40 x Miyuki seed beads size 15° (F)
2 x Swarovski® pearls #5810 3mm (R)

**Toggle bar 1.9cm (page 14)**
35 x Miyuki seed beads size 15° (A)
26 x Miyuki seed beads size 11° (B)
26 x Czech charlotte seed beads size 15° (D)
2 x Swarovski® pearls #5810 3mm (G)

**Toggle bar 3cm (page 86)**
154 x Miyuki seed beads size 15° (C)
16 x Czech charlotte seed beads size 15° (F)
2 x Swarovski® xilion chatons #1088 ss17 4mm (G)

Elements Library

**Toggle bar including links 1.7cm (page 65)**
66 x Miyuki seed beads size 15° (A)
60 x Miyuki seed beads size 11° (B)
12 x Swarovski® pearls #5810 3mm (C)
2 x Czech charlotte seed beads size 15° (E)
2 x Swarovski® pearls #5810 6mm (G)

**Toggle ring 1.7cm (page 42)**
9 x Swarovski® crystal rounds #5000 2mm (can substitute firepolish 2mm) (D)
45 x Czech charlotte seed beads size 15° (E)
90 x Miyuki seed beads size 15° (F)
9 x Swarovski® pearls #5810 3mm (R)

**Toggle ring including links 2.5cm (page 65)**
68 x Miyuki seed beads size 15° (A)
156 x Miyuki seed beads size 11° (B)
12 x Swarovski® pearls #5810 3mm (C)

**Toggle ring including loop 1.7cm (page 10)**
57 x Miyuki seed beads size 15° (A)
48 x Miyuki seed beads size 11° (B)

## Connectors

**Bail 1.1cm (when connected) (page 64)**
59 x Miyuki seed beads size 15° (A)
6 x Swarovski® pearls #5810 3mm (C)
12 x Czech charlotte seed beads size 15° (E)

**Bracelet glass ring connector (page 54)**
24 x Miyuki seed beads size 15° (B)
16 x Miyuki seed beads size 15° (C)
3 x Miyuki seed beads size 8° (D)
1 x Czech glass ring 9mm (G)

Elements Library

**Cabochon bead ring 1.5cm diameter (with 1 loop) (page 75)**
48 x Miyuki seed beads size 11° (A)
22 x Miyuki seed beads size 11° (B)
11 x Miyuki seed beads size 15° (C)
4 x 2-hole cabochon beads 6mm (E)

**Centre chain section 3.5cm (page 25)**
6 x Miyuki seed beads size 11° (A)
6 x Miyuki seed beads size 11° (B)
4 x Miyuki seed beads size 11° (C)
4 x Miyuki seed beads size 11° (D)
2 x Miyuki seed beads size 8° (E)
30 x Miyuki seed beads size 15° (F)

**Centre pane 2cm (page 93)**
10 x Miyuki seed beads size 11° (A)
27 x Miyuki seed beads size 15° (B)
48 x Miyuki seed beads size 15° (C)
16 x Miyuki cube beads 1.8mm (D)
3 x Czech glass rings 9mm (H)
   (check how many you need if elements are to share glass rings)

**Crystal unit 1.3cm (page 41)**
4 x Swarovski® crystal rounds #5000 2mm (can substitute firepolish 2mm) (D)
16 x Czech charlotte seed beads size 15° (E)
76 x Miyuki seed beads size 15° (F)
4 x Swarovski® pearls #5810 3mm (R)
1 x Swarovski® xilion chaton #1088 ss39 8mm (S)

**Double crown connector (page 103)**
48 x Toho or Miyuki seed beads size 15° (B)
2 x Swarovski® pearls #5810 6mm (C)
18 x Czech charlotte seed beads size 15° (D)

**Framed chaton (page 116)**
52 x Miyuki seed beads size 11° (A)
4 x Miyuki seed beads size 11° (B)
14 x Miyuki seed beads size 15° (C)
1 x Swarovski® xilion chaton #1088 ss39 8mm (plus metal setting)

Elements Library

**Glass ring link 2.8cm (page 50)**
23 x Miyuki seed beads size 15° (B)
30 x Miyuki seed beads size 15° (C)
9 x Miyuki seed beads size 8° (D)
1 x Czech glass ring 9mm (G)

**Large ring 4.1cm (page 105)**
1035 x Miyuki seed beads size 15° (A)
46 x Toho seed beads size 15° (B)
17 x Swarovski® pearls #5810 6mm (C)
23 x Swarovski® pearls #5810 3mm (E)

**Motif 2.5cm (with pearls) (page 79)**
56 x Miyuki seed beads size 8° (A)
56 x Miyuki seed beads size 11° (B)
136 x Miyuki seed beads size 15° (C)
2 x Swarovski® pearls #5810 3mm (D)
1 x Swarovski® rivoli #1122 ss47 10mm (E)
32 x Czech charlotte seed beads size 15° (F)
4 x Swarovski® xilion chatons #1088 ss17 4mm (G)

**Pearl unit 1.4 cm (page 39)**
8 x Czech charlotte seed beads size 15° (E)
54 x Miyuki seed beads size 15° (F)
1 x Swarovski® pearl 6mm #5810 (Q)

**Peyote ring (page 74)**
32 x Miyuki seed beads size 11° (A)
46 x Miyuki seed beads size 11° (B)
32 x Miyuki seed beads size 15° (C)

**Plain bead ring 2.3cm diameter (page 76)**
40 x Miyuki seed beads size 11° (A)
10 x Miyuki seed beads size 11° (B)

Elements Library

**Short chain sections 3cm (page 25)**
4 x Miyuki seed beads size 11° (A)
4 x Miyuki seed beads size 11° (B)
4 x Miyuki seed beads size 11° (C)
4 x Miyuki seed beads size 11° (D)
2 x Miyuki seed beads size 8° (E)
30 x Miyuki seed beads size 15° (F)

**Small bail link 0.8cm (page 11)**
40 x Miyuki seed beads size 15° (A)

**Small ring 3.4cm (page 105)**
828 x Miyuki seed beads size 15° (A)
13 x Swarovski® pearls #5810 6mm (C)

**Square chaton motif variation (page 53)**
12 x Miyuki seed beads size 11° (A)
96 x Miyuki seed beads size 15° (B)
44 x Miyuki seed beads size 15° (C)
10 x Miyuki seed beads size 8° (D)
22 x Miyuki cube beads 1.8mm (E)
1 x Swarovski® xilion chaton #1088 ss39 8mm (F)

**Three-pane link 3cm (page 49)**
12 x Miyuki seed beads size 11° (A)
40 x Miyuki seed beads size 15° (B)
2 x Miyuki seed beads size 8° (D)
16 x Miyuki cube beads 1.8mm (E)

**Two-pane link 2cm (page 49)**
8 x Miyuki seed beads size 11° (A)
28 x Miyuki seed beads size 15° (B)
2 x Miyuki seed beads size 8° (D)
10 x Miyuki cube beads 1.8mm (E)

**Tudor rose 1.7cm (page 37)**
55 x Miyuki seed beads size 15° (J)
1 x Swarovski® pearl #5810 4mm (K)
15 x Miyuki seed beads size 11° (L)
25 x Miyuki seed beads size 11° (M)
15 x Miyuki seed beads size 8° (N)

Elements Library

## Ropes and braids

**Braid 1 (1 section = 3cm/1¼") (page 107)**
53 x Miyuki seed beads size 15° (A)
2 x Toho or Miyuki seed beads size 15° (B)
1 x Swarovski® pearl #5810 3mm (E)

**Braid 2 (10cm/4" length) (page 108)**
212 x Miyuki seed beads size 15° (A)

**Braid 3 (10cm/4" length) (page 108)**
144 x Miyuki seed beads size 15° (A)
18 x Toho or Miyuki seed beads size 15° (B)

**Flat ribbon link 7.2cm (page 50)**
36 x Miyuki seed beads size 11° (A)
54 x Miyuki seed beads size 15° (B)
54 x Miyuki seed beads size 15° (C)
18 x Miyuki seed beads size 8° (D)

**Honeycomb stitch rope (1 section = 4cm/2") (page 122)**
192 (+9 per end loop) x Miyuki seed beads size 15° (A)
48 (+1 per end loop) x Miyuki seed beads size 11° (B)

*Elements Library*

**Lattice rope (10cm/4" length) (page 60)**
644 x Miyuki seed beads size 15° (A)
112 x Miyuki seed beads size 11° (B)
7 x Swarovski® pearls #5810 6mm (G)

---

**Netted rope (1 section = 4cm/2") (page 74)**
60 x Miyuki seed beads size 11° (A)
120 x Miyuki seed beads size 11° (B)
(Per end loop) 9 x Miyuki seed beads size 15° (C)
(Per end loop) 1 x Miyuki seed beads size 8° (F)
1 x jewellery tube 4mm diameter (length required plus 2.5cm/1")

---

**Peyote stitch rope (1 section = 4cm/2") (page 115)**
24 x Miyuki seed beads size 11° (A)
24 x Miyuki seed beads size 11° (B)
48 (+9 per end loop) x Miyuki seed beads size 15° (C)

---

**Peyote stitch 2-drop spiral rope (1 section = 4cm/2") (page 115)**
12 x Miyuki seed beads size 11° (A)
96 x Miyuki seed beads size 11° (B)
96 x Miyuki seed beads size 15° (C)
96 x Miyuki seed beads size 15° (D)

---

**Right angle weave chain 14cm (page 95)**
48 x Miyuki seed beads size 11° (A)
66 x Miyuki seed beads size 15° (B)
52 x Miyuki seed beads size 15° (C)
2 x Miyuki cube beads 1.8mm (per end loop) (D)

---

**Twisted rope (1 section = 5cm without crystals) (page 12)**
113 x Miyuki seed beads size 15° (A)
88 x Miyuki seed beads size 11° (B)
12 x Swarovski® pearls #5810 3mm (G)
1 x Swarovski® briolette #5040, bicone #5328 or round #5000 6mm (H)
   (Optional for connecting two rope sections together)

Elements Library

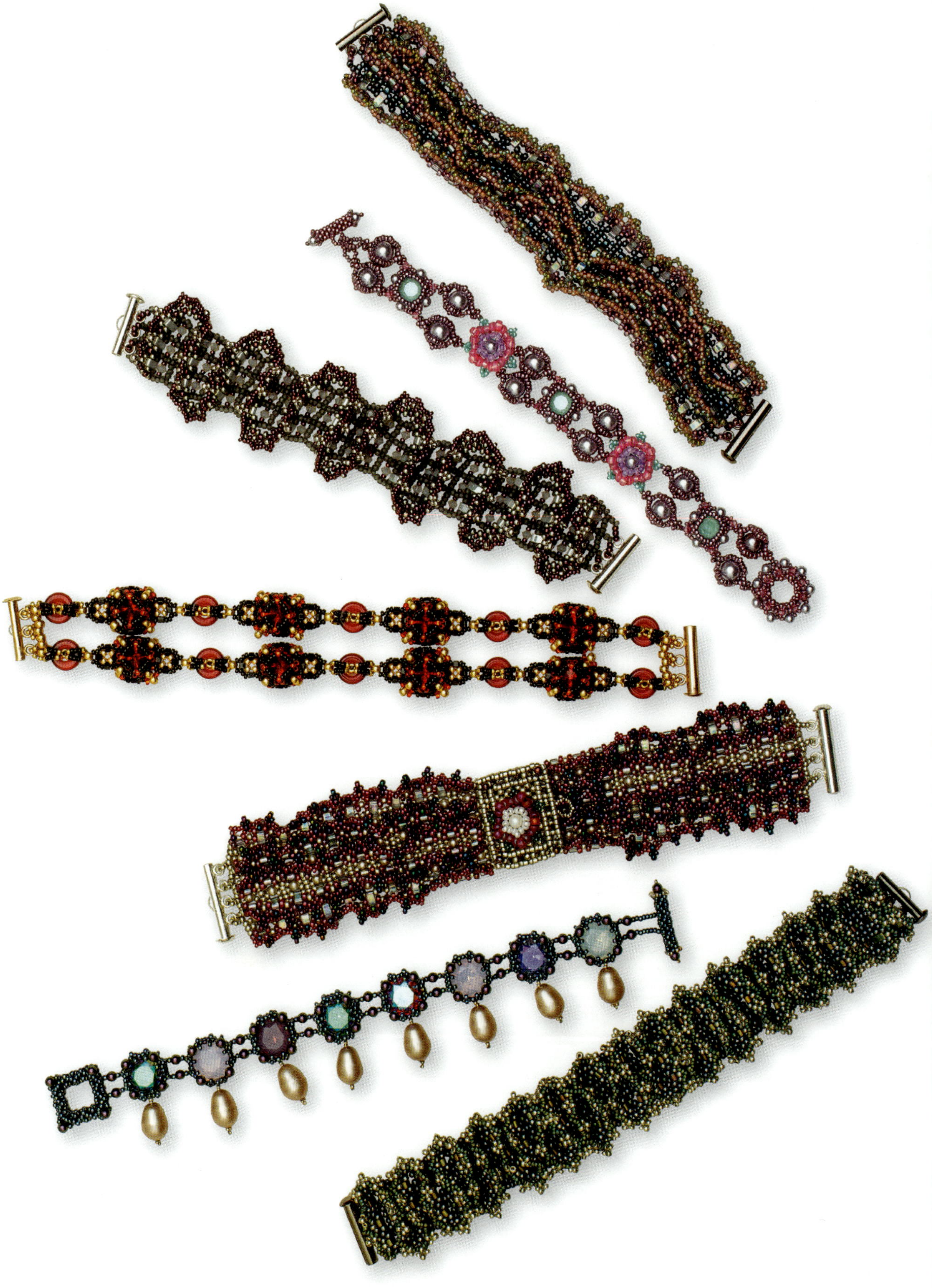

GALLERY

'Oh my gosh, I'm having a blast! Total fun. A thrill and an honor!'

Susan Etkind

'It was exciting being a pattern tester but strange to be beading to a deadline! I'm looking forward so much to seeing the book.'

Susanna Stapleton

'It has been a privilege to be part of Mel's and Heather's journey; I learnt so much and thoroughly enjoyed every minute of it. Thanks, Mel, for putting your trust in me.'

Nitty Chamcheon

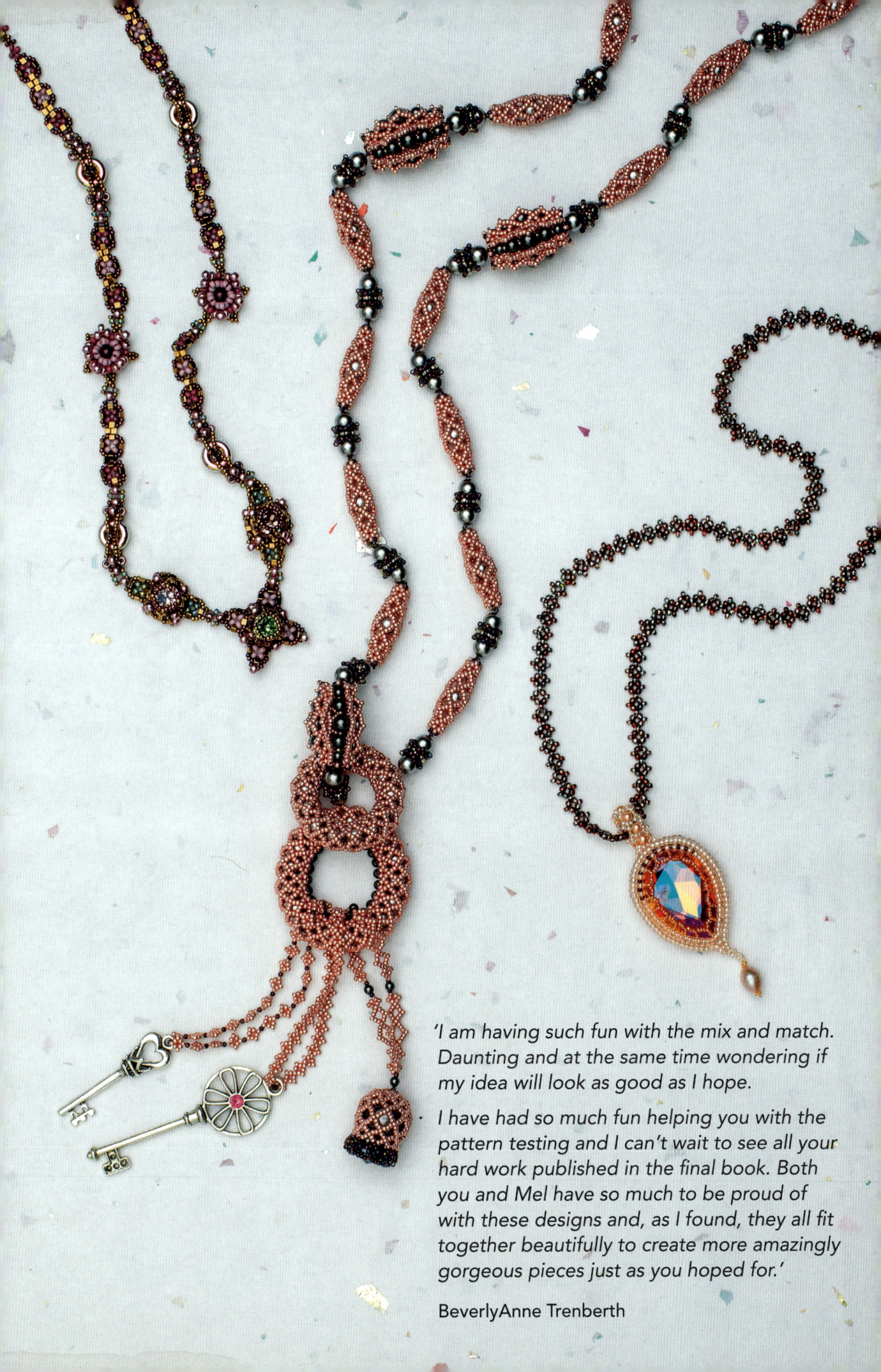

'I am having such fun with the mix and match. Daunting and at the same time wondering if my idea will look as good as I hope.

I have had so much fun helping you with the pattern testing and I can't wait to see all your hard work published in the final book. Both you and Mel have so much to be proud of with these designs and, as I found, they all fit together beautifully to create more amazingly gorgeous pieces just as you hoped for.'

BeverlyAnne Trenberth

'I have so enjoyed participating in this venture. Although at times I did feel out of my depth, I have really enjoyed it. It has been a huge but enjoyable learning curve.

Working with elements has completely changed the way I look at beading and how to put ideas together.'

Caroline Hucklesby

'I enjoyed having the opportunity to be involved in working on pieces for this book. It was both interesting and challenging. Working on a larger piece was absorbing and I found it good to be stretched in techniques and in using colours I would not normally choose. I did find it something of a challenge to then create pieces using elements of the designs and combining the work of two different designers, but enjoyed it once I got into it. It has been such an enjoyable experience and I am looking forward to seeing the end result.'

Louise West

'I really think my beadwork has taken on a different dimension, this project having forced me to think a lot more about design. It's given me so much more confidence in that area and I don't think I'll be able now to just simply reproduce someone else's design without making a few tweaks.'

Janet Bee

'I wanted to represent the richness of the overall designs and the era they are based on. Using elements all the way round worked to balance the focal point of the necklace and give it an extravagant feel. Combining this with the deep autumnal/sunset colours gave that sense of luxury and privilege that's lovely to wear for the day without all the drama that accompanied Renaissance nobility!'

Jessica Hayman

> "By the Quene
>
> Right trustie and wellbiloved, we grete you well. And where as it hath pleased the goodnes of Almightie God, of his infynite marcie and grace, to sende unto us, at this tyme, good spede, in the delyveraunce and bringing furthe of a Princes, to the great joye, rejoyce, and inward comforte of my Lorde, us, and all his good and loving subjects of this his realm; ..."
>
> Letter from Queen Anne Boleyn to Lord Cobham, Anne's Chancellor, informing him of the birth of Elizabeth at Greenwich (7th September, 1533)

---

**Fascinating fact:**

Anne and Henry were so convinced their child would be a boy, the official announcements to be sent throughout the realm and to the European Courts, were prepared with the child listed as a prince. Hastily an 's' was added to the word prince, which was perfectly adequate in the 16th century to signify the word princess.

# ACKNOWLEDGEMENTS

Beadwork is such a joyous and inclusive hobby and many hands have contributed to the completion of this book. Our collective of testers deserve our highest thanks and praise, for their diligence, meticulous beadwork and glorious sense of colour. Their enthusiasm for the projects encouraged us to realise that what we are attempting really does work in the hands of real beaders; we are truly grateful for your many hours of beading, pattern checking and dedication to making such beautiful samples. Thank you:

Janet Bee
Nitty Chamcheon
Susan Etkind
Jessica Hayman
Caroline Hucklesby
Susanna Stapleton
BeverleyAnne Trenberth
Louise West

Our next collective to thank are the team at SRA Books:

Sue Richardson
Kelly Mundt-Czerkawska
Mark Hobin

Kelly for her endless patience and time taken to create the book we held in our imaginations, Mark for his graphics, fonts and colours. Sue Richardson is our third cohort and in many ways curator and mentor of our collaboration. A dear and much loved friend to us both, and with her work hat on, our editor-in-chief and publisher too. Her gentle soothing of creative anxiety moments as our plan metamorphosed beyond our first imaginings, her steadfast belief in our ability to see the project through, despite our often mismatched and crazy work schedules, and her insightful prompts and suggestions have made the whole process a wonderful experience for us both.

We are also deeply appreciative of the beautiful illustrated diagrams for our projects. It was no small task to bring together two very different styles of working and give our work such consistency and clarity. Thank you:

Melissa Grakowsky Shippee

We had great fun creating the images for this book; they are truly lovely thanks to one of the best photographers, who welcomed our beady whirlwind into his calm London studio for several days. Thank you:

Michael Wicks

Our beading world is global, but feels like a village of friendship; one such friend stepped in to proofread our work from a beader's perspective, with amazingly sharp eyes and attention to detail. Thank you:

Claudia Schumann

We have one final thank you, to our great friend and beading artist, for going above and beyond to accommodate a design collision with both grace and elan, and for lending her support and endorsement for what we are hoping to achieve. Thank you:

Marcia DeCoster

# INVITATION TO PARTICIPATE

*Tudor Inspirations* is the beginning of an elemental adventure. We are inviting you to get inspired and come join the party!

First, visit us at www.tudorinspirations.com for news about us and future planned events.

Second, join us on Facebook, via the link on the website, where we'd love you to join us to show and share your own unique creations. We will both be popping onto the page regularly with updates, and can't wait to see how far this adventure can be taken. We want to see you spread your creative wings and fly with us in our fabulous beadwork design adventure.

We look forward to meeting you and sharing the elemental love of creative beading.

**Albion and Hubble Stitch**

If you're new to the techniques of Albion and Hubble stitch, you can find everything you need to know and much more in our books and websites:

Heather: *Albion Stitch I, Albion Stitch II* and *Introducing Albion Stitch.* www.heatherworks.co.uk

Melanie: *Let's Hubble!* and *Hubble Stitch 2.* www.beadschool.co.uk